Demilitarizing
Politics

Demilitarizing Politics

Elections on the Uncertain Road to Peace

Terrence Lyons

LYNNE
RIENNER
PUBLISHERS

BOULDER
LONDON

Published in the United States of America in 2005 by
Lynne Rienner Publishers, Inc.
1800 30th Street, Boulder, Colorado 80301
www.rienner.com

and in the United Kingdom by
Lynne Rienner Publishers, Inc.
3 Henrietta Street, Covent Garden, London WC2E 8LU

Library of Congress Cataloging-in-Publication Data
Lyons, Terrence.
    Demilitarizing politics : elections on the uncertain road to peace / Terrence Lyons.
        p.   cm.
    Includes bibliographical references and index.
    ISBN 1-58826-393-2 (hardcover : alk. paper)
    1. Elections—Case studies.   2. Conflict management—Case studies.
3. Peacebuilding—Case studies.   4. Democracy—Case studies. I. Title.
JF1001.L94 2005
303.6'4—dc22

                                                                    2005018516

British Cataloguing in Publication Data
A Cataloguing in Publication record for this book
is available from the British Library.

Printed and bound in the United States of America

 The paper used in this publication meets the requirements
of the American National Standard for Permanence of
Paper for Printed Library Materials Z39.48-1992.

    5   4   3   2   1

Contents

Acknowledgments

I have benefited from the generosity and support of a wide range of individuals and institutions as this book germinated, transformed, and finally developed into its current form. I would like to thank I. William Zartman, Marina Ottaway, Stephen Stedman, Donald Rothchild, Susan Woodward, Robert I. Rotberg, Gilbert Khadiagala, and Agnieszka Paczynska for their comments along the way on a variety of drafts and portions of the manuscript. Roba Sharamo provided excellent research support. All errors remain my own.

I have also benefited from presenting earlier and partial versions of my argument at conferences organized by the World Peace Foundation, the American Political Science Association, and the African Studies Association and to the students in my seminar on civil wars. The United States Institute of Peace provided a grant in support of this work, and I have received institutional support from the Carter Center; the International Peace Research Institute, Oslo; and the Institute for Conflict Analysis and Resolution, George Mason University. I thank Dan Smith, Sandra Cheldelin, and Sara Cobb for their encouragement.

My family, Agnieszka and Nell, have sustained me as I finished this book. More important, they have filled my life with joy. The book is dedicated to Agnieszka, my love.

1

Demilitarizing Politics
and Building Peace

Creating sustainable peace after a protracted period of brutal civil war is one of the most vexing challenges of our times,[1] reflected in the recent growth of academic attention to the subject.[2] The restoration or creation of a peaceful society is a long-term undertaking—one that must begin during the brief period between the signing of the accord and the installation of the postwar government. It is during these brief interregnums that war-torn societies begin to construct legitimate political institutions, demobilize soldiers and resettle displaced populations, come to terms with past human rights abuses, and initiate the process of moving economies from a cycle of predation and relief to one of development.

Perhaps most critical among the steps taken during the period between the cease-fire and the inauguration of the postwar government are those involving elections. Postconflict elections represent particular opportunities and risks as local leaders and communities assess the relative benefits of working to sustain peace and build democracy in societies still polarized and distorted by war, where demagogues and spoilers can capitalize on people's fears and insecurities. These first steps of the transition from war to peace are crucial because early precedents will shape the paths key actors choose to follow.

What processes encourage transitions that can move war-torn societies toward sustainable peacebuilding? I argue that the answer can be found in recent cases of civil war settlement—Angola (1992), Cambodia (1993), Mozambique (1994), El Salvador (1994), Bosnia-Herzegovina (1996), Liberia (1997), and Tajikistan (1999–2000)—

where elections formed a key, culminating event in the peace implementation process. These cases suggest that elections only sometimes succeed in providing a mechanism for selecting new political leaders and institutions capable of preserving the peace. The elections in El Salvador and Mozambique were successful in this regard. In Cambodia, however, the outcome has been less clear, though the 1993 election resulted in at least a partial opening for a period of time. In Angola the move toward elections precipitated renewed conflict, and in Bosnia-Herzegovina, Liberia, and Tajikistan elections served primarily as a mechanism of war termination, with only a secondary, limited, and perhaps damaging relationship to democratization. Careful analysis of these cases suggests that it is not an election per se that promotes or inhibits transitions to sustainable peacebuilding. Elections are snapshots of power distribution at a given time—they do not create the distribution they reflect.

Postconflict elections to implement civil war peace agreements have been routine international practice in recent years. The 1990s represented the merging of two trends—democratization and negotiated settlements to civil war—leading to the large number of postconflict elections to implement peace agreements. International policy toward conflict resolution in the 1990s was based in part on the liberal internationalist paradigm that posits that peace, both between and within states, is based on market democracy and that constructing democratic political structures is key to conflict resolution. Paris has described such policies as "pacification through political and economic liberalization."[3] As sovereignty was redefined in the post–Cold War era, greater international involvement in postconflict political reconstruction and the development of an international legal norm on behalf of a "democratic entitlement" encouraged the fusing of peace and democratization agendas.[4]

Elections to implement peace agreements have become a core part of what Ottaway called the "democratic reconstruction model."[5] In the post–Cold War era, the terms of a peace agreement had to meet the expectations of the Western leaders who mediated and provided the resources to implement it, and multiparty competition was a key component of these expectations.[6] The agreements routinely featured measures to introduce a process of democratization. The legitimacy of a new, postconflict dispensation through electoral validation was essential.[7] Even in some of the most difficult cases, peace agreements called for elections, as in the 1999 Lusaka peace agreement for the Democratic Republic of Congo and the December 2001 Bonn agreement to rebuild political order in Afghanistan.[8] Iraq is another case in which elections have been regarded as necessary to manage a transitional process and end US occupation. Ottaway is sharply critical of imposing democratization agendas in the unpropitious cases following civil war and state breakdown and Carothers similarly has asked whether it is time to move beyond the "transition paradigm."[9] International practice, however, continues to look to elections as the mechanism to mark the transition and endorse the new postconflict dispensation.

Both protracted civil war and peaceful electoral competition require specific sets of social institutions. Military-dominated regimes and insurgent forces, economies based on humanitarian relief, black-market networks, predation, and social formations and identities shaped by insecurity and fear are all the result of and the necessary institutional basis for protracted civil war. Civilian-oriented political parties; open economies and rule of law; civil society; and diverse, multifarious identities based on security and trust are created by and support sustainable peace and democratization. What is missing from much of the literature and policy debates regarding the relationships between democratization and conflict resolution in general and the role of postconflict elections in particular is the critical role played by institutions in sustaining both war and peace, and hence the critical need to make institutional transformation a central concern for postconflict peacebuilding. How can the institutions that sustained war become institutions capable of sustaining peace? Can the demilitarization of politics make postconflict elections a meaningful step on the path to sustainable peace?

The Demilitarization of Politics

Some postconflict elections have advanced both peace and democratization, thereby promoting peacebuilding and state reconstruction over time. A concept of "demilitarizing politics" best captures the dynamics of these successful transitions. To demilitarize politics entails creating and reinforcing the incentives and opportunities for the institutions of wartime based on violence, insecurity, and fear (such as militias, black markets, and chauvinistic identity groups) to transform themselves into institutions of peacetime based on security

and trust that can sustain peace and democracy (such as political parties, civil society, and open economies). Demilitarization of politics
therefore is a process of institutional transformation that may or may
not take place in the transitional period between cease-fire and postconflict elections. The powerful actors that developed and were sustained during a protracted civil war cannot be wished away. Neither
can the enabling environment for peaceful political competition be
proclaimed into existence through the signing of a peace agreement.

To the extent that politics is demilitarized during the transitional
period, postconflict elections are more likely to empower a new
political order that can sustain peace and democracy. Preparing for
elections provides the context and incentives for institutional transformation, but it is the change within the conflicting parties (as they
become nonviolent political competitors) rather than the voting itself
that promotes peace and democratization. As Call argued in the case
of El Salvador, "the implementation of the accords, especially the
transition of the [insurgent] FMLN to civilian life and into a political
party, took place *in anticipation of* the constitutionally slated elections."[10]

Interim administrative structures created during the implementation period will be critical arenas in which ex-combatants and potential civilian leaders assess whether the postconflict environment will
protect their interests and whether they will make the changes necessary to support peace and democratization. The creation of political
parties and the administration of the electoral process are tasks at the
heart of the preparations for postconflict elections and provide significant opportunities for interim regimes to establish the norms,
precedents, and institutions needed to commence the demilitarization
of politics. In some cases interim regimes have been built around
joint decisionmaking bodies that foster confidence-building and a
new institutional context that can structure competition toward a path
of democracy and peace. This type of transition took place in El
Salvador, Mozambique, and to an extent in Cambodia. In other cases,
interim regimes have failed to promote the demilitarization of politics, leading either to renewed conflict, as in Angola, or electoral ratification and entrenchment of wartime institutions and leaders, as in
Bosnia-Herzegovina, Liberia, and Tajikistan. Such outcomes reinforce the power of hard-liners and stall movement toward more pragmatic policies and leaders, thereby making sustainable peace and
democratization difficult.[11]

The process of demilitarizing politics is a key variable in determining whether transitions from civil war that culminate in elections may serve to promote sustainable peace and democracy: The more demilitarization occurs prior to elections, the greater the chance for a successful transition. Three aspects of demilitarizing politics are particularly important: the construction of effective interim administrations (particularly the creation of credible electoral commissions), the transformation of militarized organizations into effective political parties, and the development of processes of demobilization and security sector reform to construct institutions and norms that can sustain democracy.

Interim governments derive their authority from the extent to which they prepare the country for meaningful elections and turn power over to the winners.[12] In the meantime, however, the country needs to be governed. Critical and contentious policy decisions relating to peace implementation in general and the electoral framework and demobilization in particular must be made and implemented. The process through which such policies are made will shape the expectations of the major actors and may inspire either confidence or fear.

Disputes are inevitable during the transition, as the broad (and often vague if not contradictory) principles listed in the peace agreement must be made operational in a difficult atmosphere characterized by fear and distrust.[13] As suggested by analysts of security dilemmas in civil war termination, a key to successful interim administration is to build institutional frameworks that bind the parties in self-restraint and mutual cooperation without increasing the risk of exploitation from a spoiler who does not comply.[14] Institutions based on joint decisionmaking and consultations provide a framework for continuing cooperation and encourage the development of a constituency that supports such cooperation. Fortna developed similar findings in her examination of the durability of international peace agreements, arguing that such joint commissions provide an important signal of intentions.[15] Parties engaged in such problem-solving institutions may develop a sense of partnership (even if only tentatively and tactically) and perceive a joint interest in managing risk and marginalizing extremists and spoilers (including those within their own parties) who want to derail the peace process. A process of self-interested mutual adjustment of behavior may initiate a self-reinforcing cycle of increased cooperation. In a number of cases, provisions for ongoing negotiations, bargaining, and collaborative problem-solving during the implementation period have helped to build norms of nonviolent governance that foster confidence, legitimize decisions, and thereby reinforce the momentum for successful democratization.[16] Effective interim regimes constructed around sustained dialogue help manage the uncertainty of transitions and thereby encourage democratization.[17]

The second component of a process to demilitarize politics is the transformation of institutions such as insurgencies and military-dominated regimes into political parties able to compete in an electoral environment. It is extremely difficult for insurgents, paramilitary groups, and other militarized institutions that derived their power from the conflict to play the role of competing political parties in a democratic system if they remain organized as they were during the period of armed conflict.[18] In the more successful cases of transition, military organizations were encouraged to transform themselves into political parties capable of operating effectively in a multiparty context. A transformed organization can respond to the different incentives and opportunities of peace and potentially retain or even expand its power and its base of support after the war. In the less successful or failed cases, militias retained the ability to operate as military forces, weakening the capacity of postconflict elections to effect a transition to civilian rule.

Finally, the demobilization of armed forces is a process at the heart of peace implementation. For a successful, sustainable transition from war to peace, the warring parties should create new, accountable security forces. Reducing the number of soldiers under the command of the leaders of the conflicting parties will increase the prospects for effective postconflict elections by reducing the prospects for a return to war. Demobilization has the potential to play an additional role in demilitarizing politics: If demobilization is organized around joint problem-solving and collaborative decision-making, then the process will promote new institutions appropriate for democratization as well as reducing the capacity for armed conflict. In other words, over and above the important part played by reducing the numbers of combatants, demobilization can serve as an opportunity to launch new institutional models, create precedents conducive to sustaining democratization, and establish new norms that support peacebuilding. The process by which demobilization takes place therefore is often as important as the task of demobilization. A top-down or internationally led process of demobilization can meet the goal of reintegrating ex-combatants into civilian life. A process that is based upon consultations and joint decisionmaking will have the additional benefit of building new institutions that demilitarize politics and thereby increase the prospects for sustainable peacebuilding.

Demilitarization of politics has two interlinked components that increase the incentives for organizations to transform themselves so that they can compete effectively in electoral competition rather than on the battlefield. Effective interim administration built around collaborative problem-solving processes that include the parties to the conflict, in particular electoral administration that is perceived as fair by the major parties, helps strengthen the incentives to adopt electoral rather than military strategies to gain and retain power. The conversion of militarized organizations (insurgent groups, militarized governments) into effective political parties is an additional key component. Demilitarization of politics will encourage the institutional transformation from organizations built around the incentives and opportunities of war and violence to structures capable of responding effectively to the incentives and opportunities of democratic electoral competition. Along with processes to make electoral competition more appealing, processes such as demobilization can make military options less available. In addition, if demobilization is achieved through joint commissions and processes that build confidence in the peace process, then the prospects for sustainable peacemaking are enhanced. Successful demilitarization of politics, therefore, will increase the incentives to adopt electoral strategies, decrease the incentives to pursue military options, build confidence in the peace process, and thereby alter both perceptions and behaviors of the formerly warring parties in ways that support peace and democratization.

The Inherent Uncertainty of Transitions

Studies of regime change in general and peace implementation (a specific type of regime change) in particular may be divided roughly into two categories: those that seek structural and those that seek process-driven, contingent explanations.[19] Conflict studies also reflect the classic distinction between the two competing perspectives and approaches of contingency and inherency.[20] A number of scholars of comparative peace processes have focused on how structural conditions shape the opportunities for successful implementation. Downs and Stedman, for example, argued that multiple parties to the conflict, the potential for a party to act as a spoiler, and the availability of "lootable" resources such as diamonds are the variables most often present in cases of failed implementation.[21] Collier and his colleagues have developed a set of arguments relating to how certain types of resources (such as diamonds and remittances from diaspora groups) provide the resource streams necessary for parties to sustain their conflicts.[22] Others have noted the effect of neighbors and the importance of a supportive regional environment for successful peace implementation.[23]

Barbara Walter and others have emphasized the role of the international community in enforcing peace agreements and the deployment of effective international peacekeeping as the key to successful peace implementation. Walter, for example, argued that international "guarantees" and the presence of an appropriate international peace implementation force are the most important variables differentiating the successful from the unsuccessful cases.[24] Third parties are critical to overcome security dilemmas and build confidence in the peace process as well as improving the prospects for implementation through monitoring.[25] Fortna argued that the content of an agreement can shape incentives, reduce uncertainty, and prevent accidental violations, making some agreements more durable than others.[26]

Focusing on the structural conditions, third-party roles, and the content of the agreement and how each factor shapes the prospects for successful implementation can provide insights into the difficult context of peace implementation following civil war. The availability of resources to sustain the conflict in Angola, the multiple parties in Bosnia-Herzegovina, the absence of an appropriate international implementation force in Liberia, the destabilizing region around Tajikistan, and the ambiguities within the Dayton Agreement undoubtedly made peace implementation more challenging in each of these cases. By the same token, the reduction of international patronage to sustain conflict after the Cold War, supportive regional environments, and relatively strong United Nations peace operations all promoted successful implementation in El Salvador, Mozambique, and Cambodia. Structural explanations clearly provide part of the answer as to why some civil war agreements are implemented successfully and initiate sustainable peacebuilding whereas others result in a return to fighting or bring to power authoritarian regimes that resist democratization.

This study explores the related but distinct question of how variation within the transitional process itself provides additional incentives and opportunities for successful implementation. Such a process-oriented approach supplements structural explanations and highlights questions of contingency and choice in the peacebuilding process. Stedman has argued that focusing on implementation "emphasizes the interaction between agency and structure."[27] Regardless of the structures in place at the time of the cease-fire, a transition from war to peace is inherently fraught with uncertainty and risk, and outcomes are in part shaped by the contingency of political choice and the extent to which the implementation process itself creates opportunities and incentives to demilitarize politics and promote peacebuilding.[28] Clearly there are strong continuities with the earlier stages of the conflict, and the legacies of fear will not fade quickly, but the new context following a peace agreement has the potential to create new incentives and opportunities sufficient to alter the calculations and strategies of the parties.[29]

Regime transitions, particularly the transitions following peace agreements, are intrinsically times of great uncertainty and turbulence. The period between the signing of an agreement and an election provides the context for testing and assessing the risks and benefits of cooperation and whether the intentions of former rivals are conciliatory or duplicitous. It is often necessary to leave key issues unsettled in the agreement and to design some kind of contingent process such as an election to determine outcomes.[30] In many cases parties to a conflict adopt the extreme rhetoric of total war during the conflict but shift their language and tactics (if not their goals) during the peace implementation process. During the period between the cease-fire and elections, each party will look for evidence to confirm its fears that its rival is cheating. Noncompliance, however, may be the result of fear or a poorly designed implementation process rather than a lack of commitment to the new rules of the game.[31]

Many analysts doubted that Mozambique National Resistance (Resistência Nacional Moçambicana, Renamo) could make the transition from a fighting organization (some characterized it as a bandit or terrorist organization) to a viable political party able to play a constructive role in a multiparty democracy. At the same time, many anticipated that National Union for the Total Independence of Angola

(União Nacional para a Independência Total de Angola, UNITA) had a solid base of support and could function successfully as a political party.[32] Yet Renamo did transform itself, whereas UNITA remained a military organization. It was only through the process of implementation and the relatively strong incentives to demilitarize politics in Mozambique, in contrast to the weak incentives in Angola, that the capacity of each to contribute to peace and democratization became clear. In El Salvador, the Farabundo Martí Front for National Liberation (Frente Farabundo Martí para la Liberación Nacional, FMLN) launched its largest military offensive in November 1989. As one analyst noted, "at the end of the 1980s El Salvador faced an intensified civil war and was governed by a party that had begun as an anticommunist, antireformist terrorist organization. To most observers, it did not seem to be a situation ripe for political resolution."[33] Yet El Salvador held successful elections in 1994.

It is worth recalling some of the pessimism of observers prior to the 1994 South African transition. In the early 1990s Donald Horowitz described the "long-shot character of the democratic gamble in South Africa."[34] Marina Ottaway spoke of "the gulf that separated the two sides" and concluded that in 1992 "the first phase of the transition process was over; it ended with no progress toward narrowing the gap between the two positions."[35] The difficulty in judging which peace processes are most likely to result in sustainable peace a priori suggests that structural explanations are insufficient and that contingent, process-oriented accounts of the transition process are needed to explain outcomes. It is therefore important to develop a more contingent framework to understand how developments during the interim period between the signing of the peace agreement and elections shape outcomes rather than restricting our focus to the conditions at the time of signing.

Peace processes need to respond to rapidly changing conditions as the initial steps away from violence strengthen some parties, weaken others, and cause strains and sometimes splits in many. Not all of the structures and key actors of the early stages of the peace implementation process are likely to be present in the final stages. In fact, a well-designed peace implementation process should seek to alter the context in which it operates. The polarized and insecure environment at the start of the process needs to be transformed if the outcome is to be sustainable peace. An agreement must be flexible enough to adjust to these changes and "anticipate and devise means to cope with the issues of the future."[36] One of the most important conditions for successful implementation is the ability to renegotiate terms peacefully as conditions change the relative power and interests of the former warring parties.[37] Even a weak peace agreement will provide new opportunities and have the potential to alter the political calculations of parties previously engaged in conflict. As Rothstein argued, peace agreements often do not create peace but rather create "a new set of opportunities that can be [either] grasped or thrown away."[38] Hampson spoke of "nurturing" peace agreements and encouraging them to strengthen and grow from their initial, imperfect state.[39]

Rather than relying on guarantees in the form of provisions in the peace agreement or international promises, actors in a postconflict transition will examine and draw their most determinative conclusions from the patterns, precedents, and institutions developed during the interim period. The ability of these transitional arrangements to build confidence and shape expectations will play a more important part in overcoming the security dilemmas and commitment problems than formal guarantees by external parties or written provisions contained within the formal, signed agreement. Hoddie and Hartzell argued that by implementing the agreement, parties "engage in costly signaling regarding their commitment to the peace, signals that serve to reassure opponents about the prospects for long-term co-existence."[40] The period between the signing of a peace agreement and the culmination of the transition in elections is therefore a critical time of testing and signaling during which each party's expectations of the behavior of the others and the viability of institutions and norms created during the transition will be shaped. Decisions relating to compliance with the electoral process will be based on these expectations. The peace agreement becomes the starting point for another series of negotiations, bargaining, and institution-building rather than a blueprint that must be constructed in an appropriate manner. The interim period represents a fluid time during which parties change; expectations are formed, tested, and re-formed; and the fears and interests that motivated the initial cease-fire agreement are transformed. The outcome of this period of conflict, continued bargaining, and maneuvering for advantage provides the context for postconflict elections more than the structures of the initial agreement or promises from the international community.

Case Narratives: Civil War and Negotiated Peace

In this study I compare seven recent cases of peace implementation to assess whether processes to demilitarize politics were in place during the transitional period prior to elections and whether such processes are linked to outcomes that established sustainable peacebuilding (see Table 1.1). In each of these cases—Angola, Cambodia, El Salvador, Mozambique, Bosnia-Herzegovina, Liberia, and Tajikistan—a negotiated agreement ended a civil war, and each agreement called for multiparty elections as the key, culminating event to mark the end of the implementation process. The brief sketches that follow outline the context and structural conditions at the beginning of the peace implementation period for each of the cases. These short descriptions are designed not to provide a full account of the civil wars or the peace processes—citations will note some of the extensive literature on each case—but to provide enough background to illustrate the difficult challenges and structural constraints and also the contingent nature of each of these transitions. All seven cases represent difficult transitions, but actors in each had opportunities to pursue political rather than military options.

Angola

The civil war in Angola developed out of the multisided liberation struggle against Portuguese colonialism that ended in 1974.[41] The Portuguese brokered the Alvor Agreement, but the agreement broke down and civil war erupted almost immediately after the withdrawal of Portuguese forces in 1975. In a fierce but relatively brief struggle, the Popular Movement for the Liberation of Angola (Movimento Popular de Libertação de Angola, MPLA) defeated its primary rival, the National Front for the Liberation of Angola (Frente Nacional de Libertação de Angola, FNLA), and assumed power in Luanda. The MPLA was not the largest movement but was well organized, was based in the area around the capital, and benefited from military support from Cuba. In the aftermath the FNLA faded away while another group, UNITA, grew into a major insurgency that took up the armed struggle against the MPLA.

The ruling MPLA government, led by José Eduardo dos Santos, and the insurgent UNITA, led by Jonas Savimbi, engaged in a devastating civil war from 1975 to 1992. The MPLA professed a Marxist-Leninist ideology and drew support from urban groups and the

Table 1.1   Major Parties and Peace Agreements

Case and Election	Major Parties to the Conflict	Peace Agreement
Angola, elections held September 1992	• Popular Movement for the Liberation of Angola (MPLA), led by Eduardo dos Santos • National Union for the Total Independence of Angola (UNITA), led by Jonas Savimbi	Bicesse Peace Accords, signed May 31, 1991
Cambodia, elections held May 1993	• Cambodian People's Party (CPP), led by Hun Sen • United National Front for an Independent, Neutral, Peaceful and Cooperative Cambodia (Funcinpec), led by Prince Ranariddh • Khmer Rouge, led by Pol Pot	Paris Peace Agreement, signed October 23, 1991
El Salvador, elections held March 1994	• Farabundo Martí Front for National Liberation (FMLN) • National Republican Alliance (ARENA)	Chapultepec Peace Accord, signed January 16, 1992
Mozambique, elections held October 1994	• Front for the Liberation of Mozambique (Frelimo), led by President Joaquim Chissano • Mozambique National Resistance (Renamo), led by Afonso Dhlakama	General Peace Agreement, signed in Rome, October 1992
Bosnia-Herzegovina, elections held September 1996	• Bosnia Muslims, led by Alija Izetbegović and organized in the Party of Democratic Action (SDA) • Bosnian Croats, led by Croat Democratic Union (HDZ-BiH) • Bosnian Serbs, led by Serb Democratic Party (SDS-BiH) among other parties • Other key actors included allies in Croatia and Serbia	Dayton Agreement, signed December 1995
Liberia, elections held July 1997	• National Patriotic Front for Liberia (NPFL), led by Charles Taylor • United Liberation Movement of Liberia for Democracy (ULIMO), split into two factions: ULIMO-K, led by Al-Haji Kromah, and ULIMO-J, led by Roosevelt Johnson • Liberia Peace Council (LPC), led by Charles Boley	Abuja II Accords, signed August 17, 1996
Tajikistan, elections held December 1999 and March 2000	• People's Democratic Party of Tajikistan, led by Emomali Rakhmonov • United Tajik Opposition (UTO) and the Islamic Renaissance Party (IRP), led by Sayed Abdullo Nuri	General Agreement on the Establishment of Peace and National Accord in Tajikistan, signed in Moscow, June 27, 1997

Mbundu in the north, whereas UNITA drew significant support from the Ovimbundu people in the south. The insurgents controlled a large if sparsely populated zone in the southeast administered from the provisional capital in Jamba and regularly raided other parts, making most of the countryside insecure. The war destroyed the country's economy, with the important exception of the government-controlled oil enclave. External support complicated efforts to end the war, as the Soviet Union and Cuba provided assistance to the MPLA government while the United States and South Africa supported the insurgent UNITA. Both sides believed they could win the war militarily, in part by soliciting more support from their external backers, and resisted efforts to settle their conflict in the late 1970s and 1980s. Battlefield deaths reached an estimated 100,000 to 350,000 with perhaps half of the country's 10 million people displaced.[42]

In the late 1980s the two superpowers were anxious to disengage from proxy war in southern Africa.[43] The U.S.-brokered agreement on Namibia and the United Nations Verification Mission (UNAVEM I) served to confirm Cuban withdrawal from Angola and set the stage for talks on an internal Angolan settlement. Within Angola the MPLA's initial Marxist program had demonstrably failed, and factions within the ruling party pressed for economic and political liberalization, resulting in revisions to the constitution in June 1990 that endorsed a multiparty system.[44] Talks in Gbadolite (1989) sponsored by regional powers were followed by talks in Portugal. After two years of negotiations, and with the United States, the Soviet Union (later Russia), and Portugal acting as facilitators, the MPLA and UNITA signed the Bicesse Accords on May 31, 1991. The Bicesse Accords called for demobilization and the creation of a combined MPLA and UNITA armed force and for elections to be held in September 1992. The schedule for elections was tight, given the extensive damage and distrust prevalent in the war-torn society.[45] Despite the difficult conditions, the cease-fire held and there was a sense of optimism as the Cold War was over, the Namibian transition to independence had gone relatively smoothly, and the African National Congress leader Nelson Mandela had been released and was negotiating a peaceful transition in South Africa.[46] The UN modified the mandate of UNAVEM to promote peace implementation in Angola, but lack of great-power interest as well as the wishes of the two warring parties kept the mission small and mandate unrealistic.

Cambodia

Cambodia suffered the spillover effects of the war in Vietnam, including bombardment by the U.S. military seeking to end sanctuary for the Vietcong. In 1975 the Khmer Rouge guerrillas overthrew the U.S.-backed Lon Nol. From 1975 to 1979, under the destructive reign of the Khmer Rouge and Pol Pot, the country underwent a period of violence during which the cities were emptied and the population subjected to harsh labor that resulted in an estimated 1.5 million deaths. Prince Norodom Sihanouk, who had considerable international and local legitimacy, had been head of state until April 1976, when a new constitution created Democratic Kampuchea. Vietnam invaded in December 1978 and installed a new government in Phnom Penh led by Hun Sen and the Cambodian People's Party (CPP). The Khmer Rouge fled into the western countryside, and Prince Sihanouk fled to China.[47]

The new regime received support from Vietnam and the Soviet Union but faced opposition from three factions: National Union Front for an Independent, Neutral, Peaceful, and Cooperative Cambodia (Font Uni National pour une Cambodge Indépendent, Neutre, Pacifique et Coopératif, Funcinpec) led by Prince Sihanouk's son Prince Ranariddh; the former regime of the Party of Democratic Kampuchea (PDK, also known as the Khmer Rouge), led nominally by Khieu Samphan with former head of state Pol Pot remaining powerful in the background; and the Khmer People's National Liberation Front (KPNLF), a noncommunist republican party. The three opposition movements formed an alliance and operated as a cross-border insurgency with the support of China, the United States, and members of the Association of Southeast Asian Nations (ASEAN). The Khmer Rouge had the greatest military capacity in the alliance. The opposition maintained safe havens within Thailand and small, liberated zones within Cambodia and prevented the CPP regime from receiving international recognition and assistance.[48]

Internationally sponsored talks began in August 1989 and resulted in a cease-fire in May 1991 and the signing of the Paris Peace Accord in October 1991.[49] Altered perceptions and interests by external powers led them to seek disengagement from their proxy conflict in Cambodia and to pressure their clients to settle. The Paris Accord envisioned a transitional period during which a constituent assembly would be elected through a poll organized and certified by the United

Nations. During the interim, the Supreme National Council and the United Nations would administer the state. The implementation of the Cambodian peace agreement called for an expansive United Nations presence to re-create government and thereby shore up the cease-fire agreement reached in Paris.

El Salvador

El Salvador's civil war began in 1980, following a period of failed reform and the development of an alliance between military hard-liners and members of the land-owning elite.[50] The war was caused by a lack of democratic political space or economic opportunity in a country characterized by exclusion and authoritarianism.[51] Repression and violence from these forces of the right led to the creation of the Frente Farabundo Martí para la Liberación Nacional (FMLN), a coalition of Marxist guerrilla groups. Class and ideology—not ethnicity or identity—drove the conflict in El Salvador. Domestic polarization, reinforced by U.S. policy during the Reagan administration in support of the military junta, led to a period of internal conflict marked by human rights abuses and death squads that targeted leftist opponents. An estimated 70,000 people died, 500,000 became refugees, and an additional 500,000 were internally displaced as a result of the conflict.[52]

The junta held elections in 1982 to improve its international image and avoid pressures for a negotiated settlement with the guerrillas. The left boycotted the elections while the economic elite and military leadership formed the National Republican Alliance (Alianza Republicana Nacionalists, ARENA) party and succeeded in having its leader, Robert D'Aubuisson, elected president of the Constituent Assembly (despite his ties to death squads). Such a period of "electoral authoritarianism" demonstrates a country's ability to hold elections without democracy.[53] In 1984 José Napoleón Duarte of the Christian Democratic Party defeated D'Aubuisson in a contest for the presidency. The elections opened a small amount of political space that unions and other civic organizations, some sympathetic to the FMLN, used to campaign for peace and reform. Duarte's attempts to start talks with the guerrillas failed as the armed forces, with the support of the United States, pushed for a military solution.[54]

After a period of military stalemate, Salvadoran politics and prospects for peace brightened under a regional peace plan pushed by Costa Rican president Oscar Arias. Internally, key leaders of the left formed the Convergencia Democrática (CD) party to compete in the 1989 presidential election. The FMLN guerrillas launched a "final offensive" and tried to prevent the 1989 elections. The offensive demonstrated both the FMLN's strength and capacity to operate across the country and its inability to win militarily. ARENA again won the presidency in 1989, but now with the more moderate Alfredo Cristiani rather than D'Aubuisson as its standard-bearer. With both new confidence and a new sense of military stalemate, ARENA was prepared to enter into negotiations. The March 1991 legislative election included leftist candidates organized in the CD, which won a number of seats, providing a sense of confidence that electoral processes could accommodate the previously alienated left. Rubén Zamora, a prominent leftist leader from the CD, became vice president of the chamber. Transitions within the FMLN coalition brought a more pragmatic leadership and a more cohesive organization ready to engage in political talks. These new openings suggested that broad support for the guerrillas could be converted into votes if the FMLN participated in elections. The FMLN "gambled that if military and police impunity could be ended, the judiciary made fair and law-abiding, and a free and fair election organized, then it would win its long-term goals through electoral, democratic means."[55]

International factors, including the decline of the Cold War, the advance toward peace in neighboring Nicaragua, and the transition in Washington from Reagan to Bush, led the United States to endorse talks. As Munck summarized the changes, "there was the opening of left politicians to elections; the reform of ARENA and the strengthening of its position in government; and the global and regional changes that reduced the ideological intensity of the conflict and prepared the way for a shift away from the Reagan administration's uncompromising position."[56] Finally, the United Nations under Secretary-General Javier Pérez de Cuéllar made peacemaking in El Salvador a priority as a way to demonstrate the relevancy of the post–Cold War United Nations.[57]

The government and the FMLN began a complex and lengthy negotiating process under the auspices of the United Nations Secretary-General's Special Representative Alvaro de Soto, starting in September 1989. The first step of the agreement, signed in San José, Costa Rica, called for the establishment of a UN verification mission known as the United Nations Observer Mission in El Salvador (ONUSAL) to monitor human rights. Political talks to end the fighting continued, culminating in a peace agreement signed in the Chapultepec castle in Mexico City on January 16, 1992. This agreement represented not only a cease-fire but also a "negotiated revolution"; it sought to address the underlying causes of the conflict through democratization and human rights.[58]

Mozambique

Mozambique achieved independence in 1974 when Portugal withdrew and the Marxist Front for the Liberation of Mozambique (Frente da Libertação de Moçambique, Frelimo), led by Joaquim Chissano, assumed power in Maputo. During the 1980s Mozambique suffered one of the world's most devastating conflicts. In part fueled by support by rival regional states, particularly South Africa under the apartheid regime, the ruling Frelimo and the insurgent Renamo, led by Afonso Dhlakama, engaged in a brutal conflict that destroyed political, social, and economic life in the country.[59] As a result of the war it was estimated that of Mozambique's 15 million people, 1 million died, 1.5 million became refugees, and 3 million were driven from their villages.[60] One specialist estimated that the war cost $15 billion in a $2 billion per year economy.[61] Many analysts focused on Renamo's ties to white regimes in Rhodesia and then South Africa, but Renamo also drew on popular dissatisfaction with many Frelimo policies.[62] In particular, Frelimo's villagization policies and attacks on traditional authorities generated opposition in the countryside. Cahen characterized Renamo as a "coalition of the marginalized," and Manning argued that it "proved quite successful at identifying local grievances and incorporating them into its own storyline."[63]

By the late 1980s key external powers and neighboring states were pushing for peace. The talks that culminated in the Rome Accords began with a series of exploratory talks with a wide variety of intermediaries.[64] In 1988 the government of Kenya, which had ties to the insurgent leadership, explored the possibility of talks. The following year Mozambican Catholic church leaders met with Renamo representatives in Kenya and began shuttling between the two parties. In 1989 both parties presented rival proposals, and their representatives met in Kenya to discuss options for peace. By 1990 the government had undertaken a variety of reforms, including market-oriented liberalization and a new constitution based on a multiparty system of government. Alden noted that the Mozambican government "in effect unilaterally adopted the opposition's economic and political liberalization . . . in advance of entering into substantive talks."[65]

In 1990 the Community of Sant'Egidio, a Catholic lay organization based in Rome, became involved and facilitated talks over the next two years, with the United States, Italy, and other external powers serving as observers. Representatives of the two parties rarely met face to face except in formal opening and closing meetings. Mediators and observers met negotiators for each party separately and conducted most of the discussions. Pressed by a stalemate created by the urgent need for famine relief after the rains failed in 1992, the two sides signed the Rome Peace Agreements in October 1992.[66]

Bosnia-Herzegovina

The disintegration of Yugoslavia and the subsequent wars in Slovenia and Croatia and then Bosnia-Herzegovina produced the worst violence in Europe since World War II. Early elections in the republics at a statewide level in 1990 polarized the population and rewarded hypernationalist politicians. The question of what constituted a nation and hence who had the right to form a state generated a fierce battle to create demographic "facts" through terror and ethnic cleansing. As Woodward wrote, "There would have been no war in Bosnia and Herzegovina if Yugoslavia had not first collapsed."[67] The international community intervened with a UN Protection Force (UNPROFOR) and a series of efforts to mediate without success. A series of deadly attacks on civilians, human rights abuses, and the humiliation of international peacekeepers increased pressure on the United States and the larger international community to act.

The December 1995 Dayton Agreement represented the use of coercive diplomacy to impose a complex agreement that reflected military facts in the aftermath of the assault and massacres of Muslims in Srebrenica and Žepa by Bosnian Serbs in July 1995, on the one hand, and the capture of the Krajina in Croatia by Croatian forces and advances by Bosnian and Croatian forces in Bihać and in western Bosnia, on the other.[68] After a shell exploded in Sarajevo's main market in August, the North Atlantic Treaty Organization (NATO) bombed Bosnian Serb positions in the surrounding hills.

According to Holbrooke, the United States intended this more aggressive set of policies to force Serbs to engage in serious negotiations on a peace agreement.[69]

In November talks in Dayton began with delegates from the Contact Group (United States, Russia, Britain, France, and Germany) and the presidents of Serbia, Croatia, and Bosnia. The Serbian delegation also included representatives of Republika Srpska (but not indicted war criminals Radovan Karadžić or Ratko Mladic). The Dayton talks lasted for three weeks and were contentious around a number of issues, but the delegates quickly reached agreement on many of the main territorial issues, raising speculation that a deal had existed before the talks began.[70] In the end, a 51-49 percent split divided the territory nearly evenly between the Croatian-Bosniac Federation and the Serbian-dominated Republika Srpska. To provide security during the implementation phase, a large and militarily strong NATO force known as the Implementation Force (IFOR) was deployed. Burg and Shoup characterized the resulting unstable peace as follows: "Thus, for the foreseeable future, the tenuous peace established by the Dayton agreement can be expected to last only as long as the international military force deployed to support it remains in place, and the military strength of the parties remains in approximate balance. Neither of these conditions promises to be long-lasting."[71]

Liberia

The seven-year civil war in Liberia, launched by Charles Taylor and the National Patriotic Front for Liberia (NPFL) in late 1989, devastated the country.[72] The state collapsed; one-tenth of the prewar population of 2.5 million people died, one-third became refugees, and nearly all the rest were displaced at one time or another.[73] In response to the destabilizing threat the conflict represented, a West African peacekeeping force known as the Economic Community of West African States (ECOWAS) Cease-fire Monitoring Group (ECO-MOG) intervened in 1990. During the course of the conflict a plethora of factions, many encouraged and supported by ECOMOG, arose to challenge Taylor and to win a share of the spoils from widespread looting and extortion.

ECOWAS sponsored thirteen different peace conferences, most of which ended with a signed agreement that committed the warring parties to a cease-fire, disarmament, and elections after a quick transition period. Until 1997 none came close to implementation. New militias emerged to engage in looting and to win a place at the table in negotiations to distribute positions in a new government. The United Liberation Movement of Liberia for Democracy (ULIMO), organized with the assistance of Sierra Leone, fought Taylor in the north and west. ULIMO eventually split along ethnic lines between its Mandingo wing, led by Al-Haji Kromah (ULIMO-K), and its Krahn wing, led by Roosevelt Johnson (ULIMO-J). The Liberia Peace Council (LPC), another Krahn faction, controlled areas in the southeast for a time. Taylor's NPFL also split, and the multiple factions and rivalries made reaching a negotiated settlement difficult. Much of the factional fighting was over control of economic assets such as mines and ports or concentrations of humanitarian relief supplies that served to finance and sustain the armed factions.[74]

Efforts by West African leaders to construct a workable interim government went nowhere until a June 1995 meeting between Taylor and the head of Nigeria's military government, General Sani Abacha. Under pressure from an increasingly impatient ECOWAS, a new agreement was signed among the warring factions in Abuja, Nigeria, on August 19, 1995. Under the Abuja Accord, a revamped six-member Council of State was installed on September 1 that included leaders of the ruling factions and three civilians. According to one analyst, "Abuja basically offered the warlords the spoils of office in a desperate attempt to buy peace by giving them a stake in keeping it."[75]

Following the agreement, Taylor and some of his troops entered Monrovia to join the new government. Some diplomats and observers regarded Taylor's embrace of the Abuja Accord as an important sign that this agreement would hold.[76] However, a new round of vicious fighting broke out in Monrovia in April 1996 as two factional leaders, Taylor and Kromah, sought to eliminate one of their rivals, Johnson. After a period of anarchy that left the Liberian capital in ruins, ECOWAS convened another set of peace talks that resulted in the Abuja II Accord.

Abuja II reaffirmed the first Abuja framework but extended the timetable for implementation by nine months and threatened sanctions, including a prohibition against running for elective office, against any leader who violated the agreement. Under Abuja II, a new cease-fire came into effect on August 20, 1996; a new Council of State was created; disarmament was to begin in November 1996; and elections were scheduled for May 1997. According to one Western diplomat, "Sani Abacha wants to get out of Liberia. To do that, he has to find a workable end-game strategy, which will have to involve elections."[77]

Tajikistan

Tajikistan was the creation of the Soviet Union and therefore had a particularly difficult transition to the post-Soviet order.[78] In early 1990 a flurry of opposition movements representing a broad range of viewpoints, but with untested links to constituencies, flowered and engaged in fervent debates about Tajikistan's identity and future.[79] Demonstrations and counterdemonstrations in Dushanbe degenerated into violence. Qahor Makhamov, the Tajik communist leader, was forced to resign in August 1991 because of his support of the failed coup attempt against Gorbachev. Rahman Nabiev, another communist official, won the subsequent elections in November 1991 with 54 percent of the vote. The opposition continued its demonstrations into 1992, and full-scale civil war erupted by May. In November 1992 Imomali Rakhmonov replaced Nabiev as chair of the Supreme Soviet.[80]

Many factors combined to create the Tajikistan civil war, including the collapse of the Soviet Union and the lack of preparedness for independence in Tajikistan; the crucial role played by local, regional, and "clan" ties; ideology (communism, Islam, nationalism); and interference by neighboring states (Russia, Uzbekistan, Afghanistan). Patronage networks based around clan and region became the key to political mobilization, with the Leninabad-Kulyab power bloc ultimately victorious.[81]

Civil war broke out against an opposition, dominated by the United Tajik Opposition (UTO) and the Islamic Revival Party (IRP) led by Sayed Abdullo Nuri, that favored the transformation of the newly independent Tajikistan into an Islamic state. Each side was a loose coalition of often competing regional and clan-based organizations. The UTO included the IRP, but many in the opposition did not support an Islamist agenda. Clan identities mattered more, and many supported the IRP because the IRP leaders were from the Gharmi clan.[82] The conflict escalated, and after a series of government military campaigns most of the opposition had been forced into

Afghanistan by late 1992. Opposition parties were declared illegal in 1993. Imomali Rakhmonov became head of state in November 1993 and subsequently won 52 percent of the vote in November 1994 elections.

Peace talks, with the United Nations, Russia, the Organization for Security and Cooperation in Europe (OSCE), the Organization of the Islamic Conference, and neighboring states all playing various roles, took place in 1994–1997. The September 1994 Tehran Agreement created a preliminary cease-fire and provided a context for further talks. The June 1997 peace agreement legalized opposition parties and established a powersharing formula and a twenty-six-member Commission of National Reconciliation (CNR) that included the opposition and in fact was chaired by UTO leader Sayed Abdullo Nuri. The cease-fire more or less held, and the government's authority extended to greater areas of the state, but the issue of the secular nature of the state and the role of Islam in politics remained unresolved. In addition, several armed groups and powerful leaders, notably former prime minister Abdumalik Abdullajanov, were not included in the agreement, raising the potential for spoilers to derail the process.

Plan of the Book

Violence and election processes are related in a variety of ways, and the literature on democracy and conflict is wide and growing.[83] In this book, I concentrate on a set of elections that were used to implement peace agreements, and on how such elections can serve as opportunities to demilitarize politics and thereby promote sustainable peace. In Chapter 2 I focus on the institutional legacies of civil war, arguing that violent conflicts both generate and are sustained by specific institutions that need to be transformed if postconflict elections are to promote peace. Chapter 3 emphasizes how legacies of fear shape the outcomes of postconflict elections unless processes to demilitarize politics are in place prior to the vote. Chapters 4 and 5 analyze the roles of interim institutions, the transformation of militarized institutions into political parties, and how processes of demobilization and security-sector reform can promote confidence in electoral processes. In Chapter 6 I consider whether short-term demilitarization processes continue to shape political behavior in the

longer term, and in the concluding chapter I elaborate the implications of my findings for both scholarly and policy-oriented analyses
of postconflict peacebuilding.

Notes

1. Mark Malloch Brown, "Democratic Governance: Toward a
Framework for Sustainable Peace," *Global Governance* 9 (2003): 141.
2. Stephen John Stedman, Donald Rothchild, and Elizabeth M.
Cousens, eds., *Ending Civil Wars: The Implementation of Peace Agreements*
(Boulder, Colo.: Lynne Rienner, 2002); Barbara Walter, *Committing to
Peace: The Successful Settlement of Civil Wars* (Princeton, N.J.: Princeton
University Press, 2002); Virginia Page Fortna, *Peace Time: Cease-Fire
Agreements and the Durability of Peace* (Princeton, N.J.: Princeton
University Press, 2004).
3. Roland Paris, "Peacebuilding and the Limits of Liberal
Internationalism," *International Security* 22:2 (Fall 1997): 56. See also
Samuel H. Barnes, "The Contribution of Democracy to Rebuilding
Postconflict Societies," *American Journal of International Law* 95:1
(January 2001): 86–101.
4. Gregory H. Fox, "International Law and the Entitlement to
Democracy After War," *Global Governance* 9:2 (April-June 2003):
179–197; Thomas M. Franck, "The Emerging Right to Democratic
Governance," *American Journal of International Law* 86:1 (1992): 46–91;
Reginald Austin, "Democracy and Democratisation," in William Maley,
Charles Sampford, and Ramesh Thakur, eds., *From Civil Strife to Civil
Society: Civil and Military Responsibilities in Disrupted States* (Tokyo:
United Nations University Press, 2003), pp. 183–186.
5. Marina Ottaway, "Promoting Democracy After Conflict: The
Difficult Choices," *International Studies Perspectives* 4:3 (2003): 314–322.
See also Marina Ottaway, "Rebuilding State Institutions in Collapsed
States," *Development and Change* 33:5 (2002): 1001–1023.
6. Christopher Clapham, "Rwanda: The Perils of Peacemaking,"
Journal of Peace Research 35:2 (1998): 195.
7. Timothy D. Sisk, "Democratization and Peacebuilding: Perils and
Promises," in Chester Crocker, Fen Osler Hampson, and Pamela Aall, eds.,
Turbulent Peace (Washington, D.C.: United States Institute of Peace Press,
2001), p. 785; Ben Reilly, "Democratic Validation," in John Darby and
Roger Mac Ginty, eds., *Contemporary Peacemaking: Conflict, Violence, and
Peace Processes* (Hampshire, UK: Palgrave Macmillan, 2003), pp.
174–183.
8. On the difficult electoral dimensions of the Bonn agreement, see
Jeff Fischer, "Post-Conflict Peace Operations and Governance in
Afghanistan: A Strategy for Peace and Political Intervention," IFES White
Paper, December 20, 2001. On the limits of the democratic reconstruction

model in Afghanistan, see Marina Ottaway and Anatol Lieven, "Peacebuilding in Afghanistan: Fantasy vs. Reality," Carnegie Endowment for International Peace Policy Brief no. 12, January 2002.

9. Ottaway, "Promoting Democracy After Conflict," pp. 314–322; Thomas Carothers, "The End of the Transition Paradigm," *Journal of Democracy* 13:1 (2002): 1–21.

10. Charles T. Call, "Assessing El Salvador's Transition from Civil War to Peace," in Steven John Stedman, Donald Rothchild, and Elizabeth Cousens, eds., *Ending Civil Wars: The Implementation of Peace Agreements* (Boulder, Colo.: Lynne Rienner, 2002), p. 388. Emphasis in original.

11. John Darby and Roger Mac Ginty, "Introduction: What Peace? What Process?" in John Darby and Roger Mac Ginty, eds., *Contemporary Peacemaking: Conflict, Violence, and Peace Processes* (Hampshire, UK: Palgrave Macmillan, 2003), pp. 3–4.

12. Yossi Shain and Juan J. Linz, *Between States: Interim Governments and Democratic Transitions* (Cambridge: Cambridge University Press, 1995), pp. 3–21.

13. Oran R. Young, *The Politics of Force: Bargaining During International Crises* (Princeton, N.J.: Princeton University Press, 1968), pp. 303–306.

14. Barry R. Posen, "The Security Dilemma and Ethnic Conflict," in Michael E. Brown, ed., *Ethnic Conflict and International Security* (Princeton, N.J.: Princeton University Press, 1993), pp. 103–124.

15. Virginia Page Fortna, "Scraps of Paper? Agreements and the Durability of Peace," *International Organization* 57 (Spring 2003): 362.

16. Donald Rothchild, "Bargaining and State Breakdown in Africa," *Nationalism and Ethnic Politics* 1:1 (1995): 54–72. See also Timothy D. Sisk, *Power Sharing and International Mediation in Ethnic Conflict* (Washington, D.C.: United States Institute of Peace, 1996).

17. Adam Przeworski, "Some Problems in the Study of the Transition to Democracy," in Guillermo O'Donnell, Philippe C. Schmitter, and Laurence Whitehead, eds., *Transitions from Authoritarian Rule: Comparative Perspectives* (Baltimore, Md.: Johns Hopkins University Press, 1986), pp. 57, 58. See also Adam Przeworski, "Democracy as a Contingent Outcome of Conflicts," in Jon Elster and Rune Slagstad, eds., *Constitutionalism and Democracy* (Cambridge: Cambridge University Press, 1988), p. 62.

18. Ottaway makes a similar point with relation to national liberation movements. See Marina Ottaway, "Liberation Movements and Transition to Democracy: The Case of the A.N.C.," *Journal of Modern African Studies* 29:1 (March 1991), pp. 61–82. For an update on the evolution of the ANC as an electoral party, see Tom Lodge, "The ANC and the Development of Party Politics in Modern South Africa," *Journal of Modern African Studies* 42:2 (2004): 189–219.

19. Herbert Kitschelt, "Political Regime Change: Structure and Process-Driven Explanations?" *American Political Science Review* 86:4 (December 1992): 1028–1034.

20. Harry Eckstein, "Theoretical Approaches to Explaining Collective Political Violence," in Ted Robert Gurr, ed., *Handbook of Political Conflict: Theory and Research* (New York: Free Press, 1980), develops this distinction. See also Mark I. Lichbach, Christian Davenport, and David A. Armstrong II, "Contingency, Inherency, and the Onset of Civil War," http://www.bsos.umd.edu/gvpt/davenport/cioc.pdf, 2003.

21. George Downs and Stephen John Stedman, "Evaluation Issues in Peace Implementation," in Stephen John Stedman, Donald Rothchild, and Elizabeth M. Cousens, eds., *Ending Civil Wars: The Implementation of Peace Agreements* (Boulder, Colo.: Lynne Rienner, 2002), pp. 54–61.

22. Paul Collier, "Doing Well out of War: An Economic Perspective," in Mats Berdal and David M. Malone, eds., *Greed and Grievance: Economic Agendas in Civil Wars* (Boulder, Colo.: Lynne Rienner for the International Peace Academy, 2000).

23. Francis M. Deng, Sadikiel Kimaro, Terrence Lyons, Donald Rothchild, and I. William Zartman, *Sovereignty as Responsibility: Conflict Management in Africa* (Washington, D.C.: Brookings Institution Press, 1996), pp. 131–167; Michael Pugh and Neil Cooper, eds., *War Economies in a Regional Context: Challenges of Transformation* (Boulder, Colo.: Lynne Rienner, 2004).

24. Walter is categorical on this point: "If an outside state or international organization is not willing or able to provide such guarantees, the warring factions will reject a negotiated settlement and continue their war." Barbara F. Walter, "Designing Transitions from Civil War: Demobilization, Democratization, and Commitments to Peace," *International Security* 24 (Summer 1999): 139.

25. Donald Rothchild, "Third-Party Incentives and the Phases of Conflict Prevention," in Chandra Lekha Sriram and Karin Wermester, eds., *From Promise to Practice: Strengthening UN Capacities for the Prevention of Violent Conflict* (Boulder, Colo.: Lynne Rienner, 2003), pp. 35–66.

26. Fortna, *Peace Time*.

27. Stephen John Stedman, "Introduction," in Steven John Stedman, Donald Rothchild, and Elizabeth Cousens, eds., *Ending Civil Wars: The Implementation of Peace Agreements* (Boulder, Colo.: Lynne Rienner, 2002), p. 20.

28. Matthew Hoddie and Caroline Hartzell, "Civil War Settlements and the Implementation of Military Power-Sharing Arrangements," *Journal of Peace Research* 40:3 (2003): 305.

29. Robert L. Rothstein, "In Fear of Peace: Getting Past Maybe," in Robert L. Rothstein, *After the Peace: Resistance and Reconciliation* (Boulder, Colo.: Lynne Rienner, 1999), pp. 1–2.

30. As Oran Young argued, "A bargain based on contingent devices may be seized upon as a means of terminating a severe crisis. Such a bargain tends to delay the settlement of at least some of the critical issues at stake, thereby permitting a termination of the actual physical confrontation produced by a crisis." Oran R. Young, *The Politics of Force: Bargaining During International Crises* (Princeton, N.J.: Princeton University Press, 1968), p. 285.

31. Stephen John Stedman, "UN Intervention in Civil Wars: Imperatives of Choice and Strategy," in Donald C.F. Daniel and Bradd C. Hayes, eds., *Beyond Traditional Peacekeeping* (New York: St. Martin's Press, 1995), p. 57. See also Rui J.P. de Figueiredo Jr., and Barry R. Weingast, "The Rationality of Fear: Political Opportunism and Ethnic Conflict," in Barbara F. Walter and Jack Snyder, eds., *Civil Wars, Insecurity, and Intervention* (New York: Columbia University Press, 1999), pp. 261–302.

32. See Robert E. Henderson and Edward B. Stewart, *UNITA After the Cease-Fire: The Emergence of a Party* (Washington, D.C.: National Republican Institute for International Affairs, 1991), p. 9.

33. William Stanley, *The Protection Racket State: Elite Politics, Military Extortion, and Civil War in El Salvador* (Philadelphia: Temple University Press, 1996), p. 219. See also Tommie Sue Montgomery, "Getting to Peace in El Salvador: The Roles of the United Nations Secretariat and ONUSAL," *Journal of Interamerican Studies and World Affairs* 37:4 (Winter 1995): 140–141.

34. Donald Horowitz, *A Democratic South Africa? Constitutional Engineering in a Divided Society* (Berkeley: University of California Press, 1991), p. 263.

35. Marina Ottaway, *South Africa: The Struggle for a New Order* (Washington, D.C.: Brookings Institution Press, 1993), p. 2.

36. Kalevi Holsti, *Peace and War: Armed Conflict and International Order* (Cambridge: Cambridge University Press, 1991), p. 353. See also Fen Osler Hampson, *Nurturing Peace: Why Peace Settlements Succeed or Fail* (Washington, D.C.: United States Institute of Peace Press, 1996), p. 3.

37. Suzanne Werner, "The Precarious Nature of Peace: Resolving the Issues, Enforcing the Settlement, and Renegotiating the Terms," *American Journal of Political Science* 43:3 (July 1999): 919.

38. Robert L. Rothstein, "Fragile Peace and Its Aftermath," in Robert L. Rothstein, ed., *After the Peace: Resistance and Reconciliation* (Boulder, Colo.: Lynne Rienner, 1999), p. 224.

39. Hampson, *Nurturing Peace,* p. 3.

40. Hoddie and Hartzell, "Civil War Settlements and the Implementation of Military Power-Sharing Arrangements," p. 304.

41. For background, see Gerald J. Bender, *Angola Under the Portuguese: The Myth and the Reality* (Berkeley: University of California Press, 1978); John Marcum, *The Angolan Revolution* (Cambridge: Massachusetts Institute of Technology Press, 1981); Tony Hodges, *Angola from Afro-Stalinism to Petro-Diamond Capitalism* (Oxford: James Currey, 2001).

42. John A. Marcum, "Angola: War Again," *Current History* (May 1993): 218.

43. Chester Crocker, *High Noon in Southern Africa: Making Peace in a Rough Neighborhood* (New York: W. W. Norton, 1992); I. William Zartman, *Ripe for Resolution: Conflict and Intervention in Africa* (Oxford: Oxford University Press, 1985); Chas. W. Freeman, Jr., "The Angola/Namibia Accords," *Foreign Affairs* 68:3 (Summer 1989): 126–141.

44. Hodges, *Angola from Afro-Stalinism to Petro-Diamond Capitalism,* p. 12.

45. On the peace process, see Alex Vines, *One Hand Tied: Angola and the UN* (London: Catholic Institute for International Relations Briefing Paper, June 1993); Margaret Joan Antsee, *Orphan of the Cold War: The Inside Story of the Collapse of the Angolan Peace Process, 1992–93* (New York: St. Martin's Press, 1996).

46. Keith Somerville, "Angola—Groping Towards Peace or Slipping Back Towards War?" in William Gutteridge and J. E. Spence, eds., *Violence in Southern Africa* (London: Frank Cass, 1997), p. 27.

47. Sorpong Peou, *Conflict Neutralization in the Cambodia War* (Kuala Lumpur: Oxford University Press, 1997); David P. Chandler, *The Tragedy of Cambodian History: Politics, War and Revolution Since 1945* (New Haven, Conn.: Yale University Press, 1991).

48. Frederick Z. Brown, "Cambodia's Rocky Venture in Democracy," in Krishna Kumar, ed., *Postconflict Elections, Democratization, and International Assistance* (Boulder, Colo.: Lynne Rienner, 1998), p. 89; David W. Roberts, *Political Transition in Cambodia, 1991–99: Power, Elitism, and Democracy* (New York: St. Martin's Press, 2001), pp. 1–30.

49. Steven R. Ratner, "The United Nations in Cambodia: A Model for Resolution of Internal Conflicts?" in Lori Fisler Damrosch, ed., *Enforcing Restraint: Collective Intervention in Internal Conflicts* (New York: Council on Foreign Relations, 1993); Mats Berdal and Michael Leifer, "Cambodia," in James Mayall, ed., *The New Interventionism, 1991–1994: United Nations Experience in Cambodia, Former Yugoslavia, and Somalia* (Cambridge: Cambridge University Press, 1996); United Nations, *The United Nations and Cambodia, 1991–1995* (New York: United Nations Department of Public Information, 1995).

50. Tommie Sue Montgomery, *Revolution in El Salvador: From Civil Strife to Civil Peace*, 2nd ed. (Boulder, Colo.: Westview Press, 1995); Hugh Byrne, *El Salvador's Civil War: A Study of Revolution* (Boulder, Colo.: Lynne Rienner, 1996); Patricia Weiss Fagen, "El Salvador: Lessons in Peace Consolidation," in Tom Farer, ed., *Beyond Sovereignty: Collectively Defending Democracy in the Americas* (Baltimore, Md.: Johns Hopkins University Press, 1996); Gerardo L. Munck, "Beyond Electoralism in El Salvador: Conflict Resolution Through Negotiated Compromise," *Third World Quarterly* 14:1 (1993): 76–77.

51. Call, "Assessing El Salvador's Transition from Civil War to Peace," p. 384.

52. Pamela Constable, "At War's End in El Salvador," *Current History* 92:572 (March 1993): 106.

53. Terry Lynn Karl, "Imposing Consent? Electoralism vs. Democratization in El Salvador," in Paul Drake and Eduardo Silva, eds., *Elections and Democratization in Latin American, 1980–85* (San Diego, Calif.: CILAS/Center for U.S.-Mexican Studies, 1986).

54. Byrne, *El Salvador's Civil War.*

55. Michael W. Doyle, "Strategy and Transitional Authority," in Steven John Stedman, Donald Rothchild, and Elizabeth Cousens, eds., *Ending Civil*

Wars: The Implementation of Peace Agreements (Boulder, Colo.: Lynne Rienner, 2002), p. 76.

56. Munck, *Beyond Electoralism in El Salvador,* p. 80.

57. Jack Child, *The Central American Peace Process, 1983–1991: Sheathing Swords, Building Confidence* (Boulder, Colo.: Lynne Rienner, 1992).

58. Montgomery, *Revolution in El Salvador,* p. 226.

59. On the origins of RENAMO, see Tom Young, "The MNR/Renamo: External and Internal Dynamics," *African Affairs* 89:357 (October 1990): 491–509.

60. United Nations, *The Blue Helmets: A Review of United Nations Peace-Keeping* (New York: United Nations, 1996), p. 321.

61. Alex Vines, *Renamo: From Terrorism to Democracy in Mozambique?* (Oxford: James Currey, 1996), p. 1.

62. Christian Geffray, *Les Causes des Armes au Mozambique: Anthropologie d'une Guerre Civile* (Paris: Credu-Karthala, 1990); Stephen Chan and Moises Venancio, *War and Peace in Mozambique* (London: Macmillan, 1998); K. B. Wilson, "Cults of Violence and Counter-Violence in Mozambique," *Journal of Southern African Studies* 18:3 (September 1992): 527–582; Carrie L. Manning, *The Politics of Peace in Mozambique: Post-Conflict Democratization, 1992–2000* (Westport, Conn.: Praeger, 2002); Jessica Schafer, "Guerrillas and Violence in the War in Mozambique: De-Socialization or Re-Socialization?" *African Affairs* 100 (2001): 215–237.

63. Manning, *The Politics of Peace in Mozambique,* p. 41.

64. Cameron Hume, *Ending Mozambique's War* (Washington, D.C.: United States Institute of Peace, 1994); Witney Schneidman, "Conflict Resolution in Mozambique," in David R. Smock, ed., *Making War and Waging Peace: Foreign Intervention in Africa.* (Washington, D.C.: United States Institute of Peace, 1993); Ibrahim Msabaha, "Negotiating an End to Mozambique's Murderous Rebellion," in I. William Zartman, ed., *Elusive Peace: Negotiating an End to Civil Wars* (Washington, D.C.: Brookings Institution Press, 1995).

65. Chris Alden, *Mozambique and the Construction of the New African State: From Negotiations to Nation Building* (New York: Palgrave, 2001), p. 25.

66. Andrea Bartoli, "Mediating Peace in Mozambique: The Role of the Community of Sant'Egidio," in Chester A. Crocker, Fen Osler Hampson, and Pamela Aall, eds., *Herding Cats: Multiparty Mediation in a Complex World* (Washington, D.C.: United States Institute of Peace, 1999).

67. Susan Woodward, "Bosnia and Herzegovina: How Not to End Civil War," in Barbara F. Walter and Jack Snyder, eds., *Civil Wars, Insecurity, and Intervention* (New York: Columbia University Press, 1999), p. 75.

68. Steven L. Burg and Paul S. Shoup, *The War in Bosnia-Herzegovina: Ethnic Conflict and International Intervention* (Armonk, N.Y.: M. E. Sharpe, 1999), pp. 331, 339; Norman Cigar, "Serb War Effort and the Termination of the War," in Branka Magaš and Ivo Žanić, eds., *The War in*

Croatia and Bosnia-Herzegovina, 1991–1995 (London: Frank Cass, 2001), pp. 200–235.

69. Richard Holbrooke, *To End a War* (New York: The Modern Library, 1999), pp. 94–111.

70. Burg and Shoup, *The War in Bosnia-Herzegovina*, p. 363; Anthony Borden and Drago Hedl, "How the Bosnians Were Broken: Twenty-one Days at Dayton," *War Report* 39 (February-March 1996): 26–42.

71. Burg and Shoup, *The War in Bosnia-Herzegovina*, p. 318.

72. Stephen Ellis, *The Mask of Anarchy: The Destruction of Liberia and the Religious Dimension of an African Civil War* (New York: New York University Press, 1999); Terrence Lyons, *Voting for Peace: Postconflict Elections in Liberia* (Washington, D.C.: Brookings Institution Press, 1999); Adekeye Adebajo, *Liberia's Civil War: Nigeria, ECOMOG, and Regional Security in West Africa* (Boulder, Colo.: Lynne Rienner, 2002).

73. Colin Scott, "Liberia: A Nation Displaced," in Roberta Cohen and Francis M. Deng, eds., *The Forsaken People: Case Studies of the Internally Displaced* (Washington, D.C.: Brookings Institution Press, 1998).

74. William Reno, "The Business of War in Liberia," *Current History* 95 (May 1996): 212–213.

75. Adekeye Adebajo, "Dog Days in Monrovia," *West Africa* (April 22–28, 1996): 622–623.

76. Stephen Buckley, "Liberia Tries Peace After 5-Year Civil War," *Washington Post*, September 10, 1995, p. A28.

77. Quoted in Howard W. French, "In Liberia, Life Returns to a Grim Normality," *New York Times*, August 21, 1996, p. A8.

78. For background on the conflict in Tajikistan, see Roald Z. Sagdeev and Susan Eisenhower, eds., *Central Asia: Conflict, Resolution, and Change* (The Center for Political and Strategic Studies, 1995), www.cpss.org/cabook.htm; Kamoludin Abdullaev and Catherine Barnes, eds., *Politics of Compromise: The Tajikistan Peace Process* (London: Conciliation Resources, March 2001); Nasrin Dadmehr, "Tajikistan: Regionalism and Weakness," in Robert I. Rotberg, ed., *State Failure and State Weakness in a Time of Terror* (Washington D.C.: Brookings Institution Press, 2003); Nassim Jawad and Shahrbanou Tadjbakhsh, *Tajikistan: A Forgotten Civil War* (London: Minority Rights Group, 1995); and Bess A. Brown, "The Civil War in Tajikistan, 1992–1993," in Mohammad-Reza Djalili, Frédéric Grare, and Shirin Akiner, eds., *Tajikistan: The Trials of Independence* (New York: St. Martin's Press, 1997), pp. 86–96.

79. Stéphane A. Dudoignon, "Political Parties and Forces in Tajikistan, 1989–1993," in Mohammad-Reza Djalili, Frédéric Grare, and Shirin Akiner, eds., *Tajikistan: The Trials of Independence* (New York: St. Martin's Press, 1997), pp. 52–85.

80. Barnett Rubin, "Russian Hegemony and State Breakdown in the Periphery: Causes and Consequences of the Civil War in Tajikistan," in Jack Snyder and Barnett Rubin, eds., *Post-Soviet Political Order* (London: Routledge, 1998): 128–179.

81. Irina Zviagelskaya, "The Tajik Conflict: Problems of Regulation,"

in Mohammad-Reza Djalili, Frédéric Grare, and Shirin Akiner, eds., *Tajikistan: The Trials of Independence* (New York: St. Martin's Press, 1997); Rubin, "Russian Hegemony and State Breakdown in the Periphery," p. 152.

82. Kathleen Collins, "Tajikistan: Bad Peace Agreements and Prolonged Civil Conflict," in Chandra Lekha Sriram and Karin Wermester, eds., *From Promise to Practice: Strengthening UN Capacities for the Prevention of Violent Conflict* (Boulder, Colo.: Lynne Rienner, 2003) p. 271.

83. Jack Snyder, *From Voting to Violence: Democratization and Nationalist Conflict* (New York: W. W. Norton, 2000).

2

Mobilizing for War

In order to understand the transitional dynamics during peace implementation, it is necessary to analyze the institutional structures that develop during civil war. Peace implementation inevitably will take place in a context shaped and constrained by the institutions of war and by the strategies adopted by parties during the conflict. The context at the time of the cease-fire, generally characterized by powerful military forces, weak civil society, and widespread fear, provides the starting point from which politics must be demilitarized in order to end the war and initiate sustainable peacebuilding. Transforming the institutional legacies of war into a system capable of sustaining security and promoting peacebuilding is exceptionally challenging and takes time. The first steps in such a process must occur during the peace implementation process prior to postaccord elections.

This chapter begins with a discussion of how institutions are necessary to sustain protracted conflict. It then focuses on one specific aspect of institutions—their mobilization strategies—and analyzes the patterns by which militarized organizations use selective and collective incentives in a manner familiar to students of social movements in general and political parties in particular.[1] Finally, this chapter analyzes how the fear and insecurity characteristic of civil war relate to strategies of mobilization used by militarized institutions. When we understand the institutional legacies of civil war, the challenges to the demilitarization of politics become clearer.

The Institutions of Protracted Civil War

Some analysts and much popular reporting have suggested that civil wars are periods of chaos as institutions collapse and violence fills the ensuing void.[2] Rather than operating in an anarchic vacuum, however, actors engaged in sustained warfare create alternative institutions that allow them to accumulate the power and resources necessary both to engage in the conflict and to maintain their organizations. "Engagement in violence is not a regression to atavistic instincts as is so often held in over-convenient analyses. It is rather a narrowing of the available forms of action and at the same time it is a strategic choice."[3] Certain types of violence—communal conflicts, food riots, jacqueries, social banditry, urban riots—may not require a high level of institutionalism and may reflect an unorganized, spontaneous outpouring of frustration or anger.[4] However, the protracted civil wars under consideration here raged for years and resulted in high levels of casualties (Table 2.1). Institutions with highly developed capacities and structures to mobilize supporters and provision armed forces are necessary to sustain such protracted conflicts.

Scholars studying protracted civil wars have noted that such conflicts create vested interests in continuing the struggle and thereby develop a self-reinforcing logic that perpetuates the violence.[5] As conflict expands and escalates, the parties to the conflict become more militarized and polarized, thereby contributing to further escalation. Parties to the conflict evolve and transform themselves in

Table 2.1   Protracted, Large-Scale Civil Wars: Duration and Estimated Casualties

State	Duration of War	Estimated Casualties
Angola	1975–1991	150,000
Cambodia	1978–1991	150,000–1,000,000
El Salvador	1980–1992	30,000–65,000
Mozambique	1975–1992	100,000–400,000
Bosnia-Herzegovina	1992–1995	200,000
Liberia	1989–1996	200,000
Tajikistan	1992–1997	100,000

Source: Casualty figures from Heidelberger Institut für Internationale Konfliktforschung (HIIK); data found at www.hiik.de/de/index_d.htm.

response to the incentives and opportunities created by the conflict, or else they disappear. Such "war systems" can often be robust and endure for many years, creating "war-habituated" systems.[6] Civil society organizations and other social formations of peacetime become distorted under these tremendous pressures. Some collapse, while others adapt and create new forms of social life that are symbiotic with violence.[7]

The institutions that develop within and sustain civil war are based on violence, fear, and predation. War creates specific incentives and opportunities that certain types of institutions can exploit in order to gain power and wealth. Other institutions that are ill adapted to violence fade away or are destroyed. It is characteristic of civil war that the boundaries between military and civilian spheres become blurred. Institutions of war, such as the militarized organizations of the state and the insurgency; black markets and humanitarian relief networks; and chauvinistic, exclusionary identity groups develop and even thrive in the context of conflict. Rather than creating anarchy, war restructures economic, political, and social life in profound and specific ways. Duffield argued that war is "an axis around which social, economic, and political relations are measured and reshaped to establish new forms of agency and legitimacy."[8] War represents, according to Keen, the "creation of an alternative system of profit, power, and protection."[9] In other words, civil conflicts are processes of creative institutional development as well as institutional destruction.

Sustained conflict requires organizations that have overcome the collective action problems that make large social movements difficult. Regardless of how large the grievance or how strong the desire to engage in violence, most people will prefer to have others do the dirty and dangerous work of killing and dying. Institutions are a common means to coordinate action in order to overcome this problem. Civil wars may be initiated by grievance or frustration, but to become protracted and sustained for decades, they require institutions that respond to the incentives and opportunities of violence, successfully mobilize and coordinate large numbers of fighters and supporters, and overcome the collective action problem.[10]

Militarized organizations—whether insurgencies or military-dominated governments—are not above the people. Insurgencies often begin with a small, dedicated group of committed fighters. The Eritrean Peoples Liberation Front started with eleven men, twenty-seven fighters began the National Resistance Movement in Uganda, one hundred the National Patriotic Front for Liberia, and thirty-five the Revolutionary United Front in Sierra Leone.[11] To function for any significant length of time, however, they must elicit or compel cooperation, or at least acquiescence, from a portion of the population. Revenues must be collected and soldiers recruited, trained, and equipped.[12] Of course taxes may be coerced in the form of extortion and recruitment may be through force, depending on whether the state or insurgency is regarded as legitimate. The point here is the organizational capacity such activities require. Successful insurgent groups generally have officials and functionaries who need support and offices that need funding for communications, transportation, and other expenses. "To sustain participation," Lichbach suggested, a movement "needs organization to supply leadership, financing, ideology, communication, strategies, and tactics. In short, enduring dissident action requires dissident organization."[13] Parties to protracted civil war differ on a number of variables—ideology, legitimacy, type of leadership, and so on. In order to remain effective or even viable in the difficult circumstances of civil war, however, each must develop strategies to mobilize supporters and gain access to resources.

Both the insurgent force and the state in cases of civil wars that ended in a negotiated agreement established considerable institutional capacity. By waging sustained war, creating a military stalemate, and participating in peace talks, each party demonstrated that it had found ways to mobilize constituents and resources. Few trials and challenges to organizational capacity and structure are as severe and unforgiving as war. As Clapham suggested, "warfare exposes organizations to the supreme test of prolonged conflict, often accompanied by heavy casualties, and the ultimate indicator of their effectiveness is the way in which they develop or decay over time."[14] Insurgent movements and governments that have the capacity to juggle the contradictory social pressures and the ordeal of a long period of conflict learn flexibility and resilience.[15]

Most insurgencies are put down by the state, often with only brief and low-level violence. In other cases, the state crushes the first signs of opposition organization, but suppression without addressing the underlying source of grievances leads to later eruptions of violence. Insurgencies based on charismatic individual leaders rather than institutions often collapse with the death or capture of the leader, as was the case with the Sendero Luminoso in Peru and the

Kurdistan Worker's Party (PKK) in Turkey. Poorly institutionalized regimes sometimes fall rapidly to insurgents, as was seen in the collapse of Hissen Habre's regime in Chad in 1990, Mohammad Najibullah's government in Afghanistan in the face of the Taliban in 1996, and Mobutu Sese Seko's regime in Zaire in 1997. The fact that both insurgents and the state in cases of negotiated settlements to civil wars managed to fight to stalemate and engage in often lengthy and complex negotiations is evidence of significant institutional capacity.

Civil wars have a powerful tendency to erode the boundaries between civilian and military spheres. As a consequence, governments engaged in protracted civil wars often are organized along military lines and are dominated by the institutions of war and security services. In Mozambique, the ruling Frelimo party developed out of the national liberation movement against Portuguese colonialism. Even after independence the party maintained a military ethos, including its language ("campaigns," "offensives," and "enemies"). Under pressure from the insurgent Renamo, the Frelimo party increasingly relied upon "militarized authoritarianism" to govern.[16] The government in Angola similarly emerged from and retained the legacy of the national liberation struggle. The regime in El Salvador has been analyzed as a "protection racket" state, with clear links to paramilitary death squads.[17] The government in Tajikistan was also based on a coalition of military leaders and black-market dealers deeply involved in the gun and drug trade.

This recognition that specific types of institutions both are created by and help sustain protracted civil wars raises the critical question of how to transform such institutions in the context of short-term peace implementation in ways that support long-term peacebuilding. The literature on democratization and transitions from authoritarian rule argues that economic and political transitions are strongly influenced by the institutional legacies of the preexisting order.[18] A number of scholars on regime transition have developed ideas relating to "path dependency" and "structured contingency" to examine how institutional legacies shape the course of a transition.[19] Thelen and Steinmo, for example, argued, "Institutions shape the goals that political actors pursue and . . . structure power relations among them."[20] Linz and Stepan's study of transitions in southern Europe, South America, and postcommunist Europe as well as Bratton and van de Walle's study of regime transition in Africa base their analyses of transition paths on the characteristics of the previous regime.[21]

For a state entering into a transition following a period of protracted civil war, one of the most important characteristics of the transition will be the distortion or collapse of peacetime political institutions and social structures and the dominance of wartime structures. The legacies of the institutions developed during the war, including insurgent militias, black-market networks, the social formations characteristic of refugee and displaced populations, and an expanded and often unaccountable state security apparatus, will structure the transition process. The nature of the interim regime that manages the implementation process can create the institutional setting that bridges the structures of wartime and the structures needed to support peace and democracy. Transitional arrangements that focus on joint decision-making processes, confidence-building among the former combatants, and the development of new norms can promote the demilitarization of politics and increase the chances that postconflict elections will result in a sustainable transition.

The types and structures of institutions that develop during civil war and that remain powerful at the time of the cease-fire—whether insurgent or state—are critical in shaping peace implementation and the extent to which the transitional process can lead to sustainable peacebuilding. Militarized organizations engaged in civil war must successfully mobilize supporters and gain access to resources to sustain themselves during conflict. Therefore, a key question relating to peace implementation is whether the transition is structured to promote the transformation of war institutions (such as military organizations) into institutions that can sustain peacebuilding and democracy (such as political parties) by capitalizing on such organizational capacities and imperatives.

Mobilization and the Institutions of War

The institutions that develop in response to civil war and help protract such conflicts must mobilize and retain constituencies and gain access to resources in order to sustain themselves. Such imperatives are not unique to institutions of war. Militarized organizations mobilize and sustain themselves in a context of violence, of course, whereas political parties and other social movements more often mobilize and sustain themselves in relatively peaceful contexts.

Their common functions, however, make it useful to apply some of the models and concepts of social movements and political party literature to militarized organizations. Such an analysis highlights the institutional legacies of civil war and how such legacies shape post-conflict transitions.

The close organizational kinship between militarized groups and political parties may be seen in the number of organizations that began as one and then evolved into the other.[22] This is not surprising because, as Michels stated, the "modern party is a fighting organization in the political sense of the term."[23] European fascist parties arose in part from paramilitary organizations, and a number of political parties developed out of World War II resistance movements.[24] The Herut political party in Israel grew out of the armed underground Irgun organization. In Colombia, members of Armed Revolutionary Forces of Colombia (Fuerzas Armadas Revolucionarias de Colombia, FARC) formed the Unión Patriótica party during a period in the 1980s when the guerrilla group was seeking to engage in the political process.[25] The Ethiopian People's Revolutionary Democratic Front, the Ugandan National Revolutionary Army, and the Rwandan Patriotic Front all made the transition from effective insurgencies to dominant political parties able to mobilize voters in electoral competitions. The flip side of this pattern was seen in Lebanon, where certain political parties, such as Kamal Junblat's Druze-based Progressive Socialist Party, proved adept at making the transformation from partisan politics to militia warfare.[26]

In South Africa, Colombia, Turkey, and Georgia, among others, a number of political parties had their own militias or affiliated militant "youth wings."[27] In Rwanda, the ruling National Republican Movement for Development (Mouvement Republicain National pour le Developpement, MRND) party spawned the *interhamwe* and the allied Coalition for the Defense of the Republic (Coalition pour la Défense de la République, CDR) created *impuza-mugambi,* two "Hutu power" paramilitary groups that played key leadership roles in the 1994 genocide.[28] In some conflicts a legal electoral party has close links with an underground paramilitary organization, such as Sinn Fein and the Irish Republican Army and the Herri Batasuna (HB) party and the Basque Homeland and Liberty (Euskadi Ta Askatasuna, ETA) group in Spain.[29]

The close relationships between political and military organizations in the seven cases included in this study further illustrate the common functional requisites of both. In Bosnia-Herzegovina the Croatian Defense Council (HVO) was formed out of the militia attached to the Croatian Democratic Party (HDZ), the paramilitary Croation Defense Forces was a wing of the Croatian Party of Rights (HSP), and Vojislav Šešelj led both the paramilitary White Eagles and the ultranationalist Serb Radical Party.[30] Civilian leftist parties in El Salvador had relationships with the FMLN guerrillas during the civil war, and the ruling ARENA party had links to paramilitary death squads. In Liberia the insurgent National Patriotic Front for Liberia, an effective military organization, turned itself into the National Patriotic Party, an effective vote-winning organization in the 1997 elections. The ruling People's Democratic Party (PDP) in Tajikistan was a coalition of local warlords who controlled certain regions and black-market networks. The ruling parties in several cases were the sole legal party and were closely linked with the state's military. In Mozambique, Angola, and Cambodia, these militarized party-states mobilized supporters, gained access to resources, and generally functioned in many ways like insurgent groups.

Under certain circumstances, therefore, militarized groups may become political parties and political parties may rapidly be transformed into armed factions due to their similar organizational structures. Political parties operating in the context of electoral competition and militarized organizations operating in the context of protracted civil war both need to mobilize and retain large numbers of supporters and gain access to resources to maintain their organizations. From a functional point of view, therefore, the analytical distinction between a militarized faction such as an insurgency or military-dominated regime and a political organization such as a party is a matter of context, as the same institutions can transform themselves from one to the other (and back) as the context and associated incentives and opportunities change. Certain organizations have demonstrated the capacity to operate in response to the incentives of both wartime violence and peacetime competition.

Strategies of Mobilization

Militias, political parties, and general social movements all face the challenge of how to mobilize and retain a base of support and obtain resources both to maintain their organization and to provide rewards to supporters. Students of political parties and social movements have identified two major ways that such mobilization takes place: through selective incentives (such as patronage) and through collective incentives (such as appeals to identity, ideology, or solidarity).[31] These incentives help overcome the collective action problem and facilitate mobilization.

Selective incentives are designed to recruit and retain leaders and activists and may take the form of material (salary, a job) or non-material (prestige, a feeling of efficacy) benefits. Certain individuals are willing to join a political party, social movement, or insurgency because the selective incentives are available only to those who participate. Maintaining the benefits of selective incentives requires establishing a difference between the treatment of one's in-group and the treatment of out-groups. Patronage that is distributed only to supporters of a political party is a common example. Urban political machines in the United States, the post–World War II party system in Italy, and political parties in the newly independent states of Africa all relied heavily on patronage to offer specific rewards to loyal supporters.[32] Political machines use "particularistic, material rewards to maintain and extend [their] control."[33] One key strategy to mobilize supporters, therefore, is to reward loyalty with specific benefits, often derived from access to resources.

In contrast to selective incentives, collective incentives are designed to recruit and retain the large base of the movement, whether dues-payers, demonstrators, voters, or soldiers. Such appeals often include incentives of identity (one participates because one identifies with the organization), solidarity (one participates because one shares the political or social goals of the other participants), and ideology (one participates because one identifies with the cause promoted by the organization). Collective incentives may overcome the collective action problem, but free riders who hope to benefit from the movement without paying the costs of participation remain. Early studies of postindependence political parties, such as Zolberg's account of the Parti Démocratique de Côte d'Ivoire, Apter's of the Convention People's Party in Ghana, or Weiner's of the Indian Congress Party, focused on the role of nationalism, a classic collective incentive for mass mobilization.[34] Most parties use a combination of collective incentives to mobilize broad constituencies and selective incentives to win the support of key activists. The

Convention People's Party, for example, was an effective organization because it was a "Tammany-type machine with a nationalist ideology."[35]

Leaders of movements such as political parties and insurgencies may be seen as "political entrepreneurs" who seek to shape the political "market" of ideas and loyalties to increase the value of collective incentives and thereby build effective organizations.[36] Lichbach saw the imperative to control selective incentives as key: "To assure that they can control the flow of selective incentives to a wary clientele, entrepreneurs design dissident organizations that are able to perform at least three tasks: obtain resources, recruit new members, and retain existing members."[37] According to Panebianco, "the entrepreneur's primary objective is to keep control of his enterprise. Party leaders can pursue this objective only if they secure control over the distribution of organizational incentives."[38] To understand how organizations mobilize, therefore, requires analysis of how leaders act as entrepreneurs to create and control collective and selective incentives that attract supporters.

In addition to the need for resources to reward supporters, organizations require resources to perform other functions of self-maintenance. As Zald and McCarthy put it, "To survive in modern society, [social movement organizations] need financial resources if they are to pursue goals in more than local context. Money is needed for personnel, transportation, office supplies, and the like."[39] Large-scale violence typically requires significant resources to provision fighters and sustain the militarized organization. A party engaged in protracted conflict will need to gain access to resources not only for patronage in order to secure its base of support but also to run the organization. States, of course, need resources to pay bureaucrats and maintain at least some level of critical services, but insurgent organizations also frequently have significant payrolls and need resources to maintain their offices, transportation, and communications systems. Insurgent groups in protracted civil wars often build parallel state structures in areas they control and set up diplomatic offices abroad to advance their goals, making revenue streams as important to insurgents as to states.[40]

Charles Taylor and the NPFL in Liberia and Jonas Savimbi and UNITA in Angola controlled large territories through their respective "capitals" in Gbanga and Jamba. "Greater Liberia" (the area controlled by the NPFL during much of the 1990s) covered the entire country, with the exception of the Monrovia enclave protected by regional peacekeepers. In "Savimbiland," the area around Jamba, UNITA managed an airstrip, a bush hospital, the Voice of the Resistance of the Black Cockerel radio station, and a newspaper.[41] Savimbi had an extensive diplomatic presence in Washington and other capitals and organized high-profile speaking tours.[42] These liberated zones clearly required revenue streams to pay expenses and personnel.

Combatants in a civil war operate in a specific violent context and have many specific characteristics as a result, but they must function as effective organizations in the first place. The institutions that develop and thrive during protracted civil war have successfully developed the means to mobilize supporters and gain control over resources. It is therefore useful to examine how armed parties engaged in civil war overcome the collective action problem, mobilize constituencies through the use of collective and selective incentives, and gain access to resources.

Identity and Collective Incentives

Like political parties and other social movements, militarized organizations make appeals to solidarity or loyalty to a common identity, but they do so in a distinctive context in which identities have been shaped (or distorted) by war and fear. Many students of mass violence and rebellion have analyzed the role of such collective incentives. A number of analysts explain peasant rebellions and revolutions by focusing on the collective incentives of nationalism.[43] Coser recognized that conflict often serves to accentuate and make more salient group identities.[44] Political identities, according to Munck, are "constructed, deconstructed, and reconstructed through struggle."[45] Tarrow similarly suggested that "widespread contention brings about uncertainty and fear; the breakdown of functional transactions that this produces increases the salience of preexisting ties like ethnicity, religion, or other forms of mutual recognition, trust, and cooperation."[46]

In the context of civil war, where no overarching authority can promise security and fear is pervasive, many people caught up in the conflict mobilize on the basis of exclusive, often chauvinistic, identity groups. As insecurity grows, solidarity and appeals to some form of identity often become an increasingly important source of protection and means to obtain resources necessary to survive. The salience of ethnicity, and in particular rigid, polarized identities, rises as a result of conflict and fear. The point of war is often to produce an enemy that will cement the networks that favor extremism and make some leaders powerful while marginalizing others. War is not caused by extremism or ancient ethnic hatreds, but such ideologies are reinforced by war.

In the context of fear and insecurity, identities are not only more salient but also more polarized. Violence facilitates the process of ethnic outbidding or outflanking whereby "competing elites try to position themselves as the best supporters of a group's interests, each accusing the others of being too weak on ethnic nationalist issues."[47] Intraparty dynamics reward those hard-line leaders and factions that push the group's agenda the furthest and frame the conflict in the most categorical, least compromising way. Competition, therefore, is largely within rather than between parties.[48] When fear of violence (if not annihilation) is high, moderate leaders perceived as being soft or accommodating will have great difficulty maintaining their authority and will be vulnerable to charges of treason or betrayal. Mobilization on the basis of solidarity and identity during a time of war is likely to contribute to polarization and rigid distinctions between "us" and "them."

Rather than just responding to rigid identities produced by war, leaders or political entrepreneurs seeking to mobilize people in times of conflict may actively heighten or even generate the perception of threat in order to reinforce and rigidify ethnic differences in ways that reinforce their authority.[49] As Gagnon argued in the context of Yugoslavia, "This political strategy is crucial because, in the case of aggressive nationalism and images of threats to the ethnic nation, it creates a context where ethnicity is all that counts, and where other interests are no longer relevant."[50] Fear creates conditions that reduce multiple, overlapping, and fluid identities and reinforce a single, rigid unity. Often insurgent leaders assert that they are the only legitimate representatives of a given people. Certain elites benefit from such polarization because they can position themselves as the champions and defenders of the threatened group and castigate as traitors rivals with other agendas, including those who favor peaceful accommodation or tolerance. As Fearon and Laitin concluded, "New constructed (or reconstructed) ethnic identities serve to increase support for the elites who provoked the violence while favoring the continuation or escalation of violence."[51]

The creation of distinct, seemingly rigid, identities during times of conflict is common and can sometimes be seen most clearly after a transition when identities become more fluid or break down. For example, in South Africa the multiracial "black" identity that served as an identity of liberation and resistance against the categorizations of apartheid had less salience after multiracial elections.[52] "Southern Sudanese" was a salient identity during conflict with "Northern Sudanese" but became problematic following the Addis Ababa peace agreement that granted the south autonomy and hence encouraged intrasouthern competition in the 1970s.[53]

The character of the brutal fighting within Bosnia-Herzegovina was in part the result of different military organizations seeking to create ethnically "pure" territories to enable more effective mobilization. As the Yugoslavian state weakened and neared collapse, political leaders searched for new bases around which to construct a political movement. Conflict entrepreneurs forced new, exclusive identities on the previously more heterogeneous people of Bosnia-Herzegovina.[54] Rising Serbian and Croatian nationalism engendered the growth of Muslim consciousness in a type of defensive nationalism. Political competition in an uncertain transition led leaders to mobilize groups defined by their identity, and the ensuing conflict strengthened these group identities as vulnerable people sought protection. Burg and Shoup concluded that, rather than causing conflict, "the polarization of Bosnian politics and society along ethnic lines after 1990 was accelerated by, and a reflection of, the disintegration of Yugoslavia."[55]

In Liberia the insurgent NPFL recruited many of its earliest fighters from the Mano and Gio ethnic groups, which had faced collective punishment by the Doe regime for an earlier coup attempt by one of their ethnic brethren. Later ethnic solidarity was particularly important to those military factions based within the Krahn and Mandingo communities that were targeted by the NPFL for their past support of Doe. Given this threat, leaders could readily mobilize the Krahn and the Mandingo to support their factions as a defensive strategy.[56] UNITA won significant support among the Ovimbundu in southern Angola but recruited few from among the *mesticos* and others in the north who mobilized in support of the ruling MPLA. Opposition to the regime in Tajikistan mobilized along "clan" lines (groups that had both identity and patron-client characteristics).[57]

Ethnicity is not the only loyalty or source of collective incentives that can be used to rally support and position one's organization as the leader of a given constituency. In many cases mobilization was not based exclusively or even primarily on identity. In Mozambique, Renamo had a vague "traditionalist" ideology (in contrast with the vague Marxism of Frelimo) and had more support among some ethnic groups (such as the Ndau of central Mozambique) than others. Neither Renamo nor Frelimo, however, were ethnic movements. Renamo succeeded in building what Michel Cahen has called a "coalition of the marginalized" and mobilized rural people on the basis of local grievances.[58] Raul Domingos, the number-two official in Renamo, explained the recruitment process:

> The war was about mobilizing people to get rid of aspects of the regime they found offensive. . . . We used the language of the population, appealing to specific aspects that they experienced. To speak to the population about democracy, liberty, human rights . . . they don't understand. Now if you talk about the pass law, yes sir, this I know, it is very inconvenient. To visit my cousin who is just over there I have to go speak to the president of the Dynamizing Group [local Frelimo officials] to write a pass for me to go there. To get rid of this, this was enough of a motive for someone to go to war. Because he knows that otherwise, if he criticizes this he will go to a reeducation camp. So what is the alternative? He joins Renamo to get rid of this.[59]

Another observer summarized the motives of Mozambicans to join Renamo: "Former guerrilla accounts included a combination of resignation, lack of alternatives, the possibility of gaining access to survival goods, and an element of political conviction which was not insignificant."[60] The ruling Frelimo party was multiethnic, although it had particular support among southerners and residents of the far northern Cabo Delgado province. Some have characterized the Mozambican civil war as in part a conflict between the "haves" and "have-nots" rather than an identity-based conflict.[61]

In El Salvador the FMLN used ideological appeals that emphasized social justice, particularly relating to land, to mobilize marginalized groups in the countryside and to build an "insurgent counterelite."[62] The incumbent ARENA party at first mobilized large landowners with ties to the military, and later more moderate and liberal business leaders with interests in trade and financial services rather than land.[63] The Khmer Rouge and Funcinpec exploited Cambodian hostility to Vietnamese residents in addition to ideological incentives such as Funcinpec's appeals to proroyalist sentiments.[64]

Militarized institutions mobilize constituencies in part by making appeals to solidarity in a manner similar to political parties and other social movements. The use of solidarity as a strategy of mobilization, however, takes on specific characteristics in the context of war. Conflict often functions to increase the salience and polarization of ethnic identity and makes group boundaries more rigid. Fear increases the consequences of identity as insecurity and the breakdown of larger networks lead people to seek protection in narrower family, clan, ethnic, and religious networks. Successful institutions in the context of war will shape their appeals to create and mobilize these newly constructed identities. In some cases leaders will generate or exaggerate threats to polarize communities so that mobilization on the basis of specific cleavages will reinforce their power. Identity is a common basis for solidarity and an often-used collective incentive for mobilization. Cases such as Mozambique and El Salvador, however, indicate that class, or solidarity among the marginalized have-nots, can be an effective basis for mobilization. Militarized organizations engaged in civil war therefore use collective incentives to mobilize support by responding to and creating demand for solidarity, which can provide protection in a context characterized by insecurity.

Patronage

Along with the collective incentives of solidarity, organizations use patronage to construct selective incentives to mobilize key constituencies. Selective incentives are specific rewards available only to those who participate in the conflict, such as payment to soldiers or land or other goods distributed to communities that support one or another side.[65] Insurgents often provide resources to their supporters, such as redistribution of seized land by the Vietminh in Vietnam, the redistribution of goods seized from shopkeepers by Sendero Luminoso in Peru, or the promise of jobs for those who joined Renamo in Mozambique.[66] Governments also use resource incentives to hold on to the support of groups in campaigns to "win the hearts and minds" of segments of the population. A number of insurgent organizations as well as governments use control over basic survival goods (such as food or housing, often provided by international humanitarian organizations) to retain supporters.[67]

To gain patronage, parties to a conflict often position themselves to control access to humanitarian aid or black-market networks critical to obtain key resources. Military organizations often seek to capture high-value commodities (diamonds and other gems, tropical hardwoods, looted goods). Drug trafficking, illegal migration schemes, money laundering and financial fraud, prostitution, gunrunning, kidnapping, and other activities more clearly identified as criminal often serve as a means for parties to accumulate wealth and hence power.[68] In many cases insurgents and governments rely upon patronage and support from neighboring countries, other external powers, and diaspora groups with an interest in the outcome of the struggle in order to gain access to resources that may be used as selective incentives to reward loyal supporters and sustain their organization.[69]

Charles Taylor created the patrimonial NPFL on the basis of resources obtained through commercial alliances.[70] The NPFL operated as a business, and Taylor, ruling 95 percent of Liberia from his capital in Gbarnga, managed his own currency and banking system; ran his own radio network; and engaged in international trade in diamonds, gold, rubber, and timber. He made deals with rubber-plantation owners, sold iron ore to the British firm African Mining Consortium and the French-owned Sollac, and became the third-largest supplier of tropical timber to France.[71] Amos Sawyer, the head of the interim government in Monrovia, complained that for "all practical purposes Mr. Taylor is conducting a clearance sale of Liberia's resources."[72] Other Liberian military factions (as well as the ECOMOG peacekeepers) similarly relied upon looting and black-market commercial arrangements to fund their operations and provide incentives to their supporters. Much of the fighting was motivated by the imperative need to control key economic assets such as diamond mines or transit routes or to control the ports necessary to engage in the lumber trade.

Military groups in Bosnia-Herzegovina similarly constructed complex economic networks to support their movements. Resource flows from international humanitarian organizations and expatriate groups moved to the civilians, municipalities, and "governments" in the region that were linked to paramilitary, militia, and regular armed forces.[73] In some other cases protection rackets were transparent, as when Bosnian Serb leaders in Republika Srpska forced terrorized Muslims to sign documents "willingly" giving up claims to all real property in exchange for exit visas.[74] All three parties to the conflict relied upon criminal networks to smuggle military contraband across international boundaries; smuggling and black marketeering proved to be important sources of revenue. According to Andreas, many fighters were "wooed to Bosnia by the prospect of looting and selling stolen goods on the black market," and the irregular paramilitary units were "substantially composed of common criminals."[75]

In Angola Jonas Savimbi's UNITA insurgency and the ruling MPLA moved from benefiting from Cold War patronage in the 1980s to the exploitation of natural resources in order to sustain the war and support their respective constituencies in the 1990s.[76] Former UNITA chief of staff Arlindo Pena, "Ben Ben," stated, "Diamonds are UNITA's lifeblood. Without them UNITA wouldn't be able to maintain its options."[77] Later, following the collapse of the Bicesse peace process, Savimbi complained about the demands that he surrender his resource base: "The point is UNITA cannot be left without resources. It cannot. You cannot ask for everything: Let us have your army! Here, have it. Let us have your weapons! Here, have them. Let us have your money! Oh come on, get real! Nobody will accept that."[78]

The MPLA government similarly depended on oil revenues for its military mobilization. The Khmer Rouge in Cambodia controlled the gems and hardwood markets while the incumbent government of the Communist Party of Cambodia channeled official aid flows to benefit its constituents. Similarly, in Mozambique the incumbent Frelimo government benefited from high levels of external aid during the war.[79] In Tajikistan multiple parties engaged in drug trafficking and gunrunning, thereby gaining access to considerable resources.

In El Salvador the FMLN delivered highly valued services to the peasants by organizing cooperatives and other development projects.[80] Wood argued that the key to understanding why some Salvadorans participated in high-risk collective action during the civil war, when the collective benefits of redistributed land were available even to those who did not participate, is to recognize that participants valued the selective moral and emotional benefits from their collective action.[81] In particular, Wood saw participation and the pride that campesinos gained through their collective action in terms of the "pleasure of agency," that is, the emotional benefits of taking an active part in participating in the making of one's own history. In the context of extreme poverty, selective incentives need not represent great wealth. In Mozambique "the occasional benefits provided to minor officials, plus the promise of a paying job at the end of the war, would not have been dismissed lightly by most" Renamo recruits.[82]

In order to sustain an organization, in addition to mobilizing and retaining a base of support, a militarized organization—whether an insurgency or the state—needs to develop methods to gain access to resources. These resources can be used both to provide selective incentives to key constituencies and to support needed organizational infrastructure. The literature on the political economy of civil war therefore sheds light on the mobilization strategies that both sustain and are sustained by violence.

The Role of Fear

Although the political party and social movement literature focuses on mobilization through collective incentives such as appeals to solidarity and selective incentives such as patronage, militarized organizations in the context of civil war also mobilize by promising security or threatening violence. The manipulation of fear is not unknown in peacetime political mobilization, as analyses of the "rally 'round the flag" effects and war as domestic diversion have shown.[83] Fear, however, plays a particularly important—even critical—role with regard to mobilization in times of conflict. Militarized institutions differ from institutions such as political parties in large part because they are organized in response to the incentives and opportunities presented by violence. Organizations that can mobilize effectively in a context characterized by fear and pervasive insecurity will become powerful during war.

There are two major variations of mobilization on the basis of fear—either to credibly promise to protect the constituency from a feared rival or to threaten the constituency with violence if support is not forthcoming. These variations are really two sides of the same process. If one does not accept the protection of an insurgency or state that asserts that it is one's legitimate defender, then one is identified as disloyal, traitorous, and a collaborator with the enemy, making one a legitimate target of violence. Militia leaders may threaten a given population and thereby win at least acquiescence to their power as vulnerable groups try to appease the powerful leaders by offering their support. In other cases militarized groups offer to protect frightened groups from dreaded attacks by others. Call and Stanley argued that "public insecurity presents a political opportunity for any group that has sufficient organization and weaponry to present itself as a protector of a given community."[84] Those subject to pervasive insecurity often perceive such leaders, characterized as brutal warlords or war criminals by outside observers, as protectors and heroes.

Violence, rather than being an eruption of frustration and rage, may be understood in instrumental terms, in other words, as a calculated strategy to advance toward a goal. "Violence should be viewed as an instrumental act, aimed at furthering the purposes of the group that uses it when they have some reason to think it will help their cause," according to social protest theorist William A. Gamson.[85] State-sanctioned violence in the form of death squads, for example, can be an instrumental strategy by a weak state to reduce active support for the opposition.[86] Offering protection to a group of supporters is a specific type of selective incentive that will be valued highly in a war-torn society, while credible threats of attack against those reluctant to support one or another side represent powerful selective disincentives. Elwert wrote that the "generation of fear is a particularly cost-effective form of mobilizing."[87]

In some cases support for a militarized organization is directly coerced. Krieger spoke of the use of force in recruiting soldiers to the Zimbabwean national liberation movements. Based on her interviews with peasants, she concluded that the inability of the national liberation movements to offer selective, "utilitarian" appeals such as land compelled the organizations to rely on coercion along with nationalist and cultural appeals.[88] In any event, one critical set of decisions insurgents must make during the period of armed conflict is whether to elicit compliance through coercion, voluntary assent, or a strategy with elements of both.[89]

The use of violence to threaten and coerce support was a major (although not the only) means used by Renamo to establish and retain its base of support in the Mozambican countryside. Renamo's violence against civilians was often horrific and terrifying—in fact, terror was the point of the violence and a critical component of Renamo's strategy to control significant territory. Many analysts noted that "instrumental terror" and the use of violence as one of Renamo's "central operational tools" succeeded in coercing recruits, frightening others into supporting the insurgency, and overall in delegitimating the Mozambican state in the eyes of many who were left vulnerable to the terror.[90] In Angola UNITA had significant support among the southern Ovimbundu people but also used forced conscription and violence to force villagers to retreat with the soldiers into the bush in the late 1970s.[91] UNITA's strategy, like that of many insurgencies, was to prevent the government from establishing administrative control over significant parts of the territory, in part by creating insecurity and economic havoc.

In Bosnia-Herzegovina militants used fear and violence to mobilize communities to engage collectively in ethnic cleansing. Burg and Shoup described the process:

> Local Serbs were not, as a rule, eager to be part of ethnic cleansing. Various stratagems were used by the organizers of cleansing operations to involve the local population in the anti-Muslim campaigns, usually by playing on fears that the Muslims would initiate ethnic cleansing of Serbs if the Serbs did not act first. . . . Once ethnic cleansing had occurred, it appears that local Serbs would usually close ranks against their former Muslim neighbors. . . . Ethnic cleansing thus achieved a two-fold objective: creating largely irreversible facts on the ground, and enlisting the local population in a cover-up of its operation and consequences.[92]

The instigators of the violence were often outsiders, with the local Serbian population mobilized to be complicit and therefore committed to maintain the new ethnic balance. Demonization of the "other" often occurs in times of great violence and insecurity. As fear and hatred spread, mobilizing traumatized groups through threats and protection became easier.

Many in the first wave of recruits to the NPFL were Gios and Manos, groups targeted by Samuel Doe's military for reprisals who fled to areas controlled by the insurgent force for protection. As the war advanced, Krahn and Mandingo fled to areas controlled by ULIMO, Armed Forces of Liberia (AFL), and later the LPC for protection as the NPFL troops singled out these groups associated with the old regime for attack. Ellis put the relationship between violence, protection, and mobilization clearly with relation to the Krahn: "The leaders of both the AFL and the LPC were almost all Krahn, and they were able to capitalize on the fact that the atrocities perpetrated indiscriminately on the Krahns in 1990 had the effect of convincing many of them that they needed the protection of one or the other armed group if they were to survive."[93] In many cases groups feared that they would be targets for repression or violence because they were perceived as favoring one or another side. In El Salvador, for example, many FMLN members joined the movement after attacks by security forces against their families or neighbors.[94]

The parties to the civil wars under examination in this study—Angola, El Salvador, Cambodia, Mozambique, Bosnia-Herzegovina, Liberia, and Tajikistan—all had institutions that mobilized on the basis of solidarity, patronage, and fear. Each organization deployed a combination of these strategies, and the balance varied among them and over time. Each strategy is effective to the extent that it can respond to specific contextual incentives and opportunities. As Chapter 4 shows, some of these militarized organizations were able to maintain their organizations in response to the incentives and opportunities of a peace implementation process, whereas others could not. Those that could not either declined and lost power or defected from the agreement and reverted to violence in an effort to maintain their power.

Notes

1. The question of governance and institutional performance is broader than the focus here.

2. Robert Kaplan, "The Coming Anarchy," *Atlantic Monthly* 273:2 (February 1994): 44–65.

3. Georg Elwert, Stephan Feuchtwant, and Dieter Neubert, "The Dynamics of Collective Violence—An Introduction," in Georg Elwert, Stephan Feuchtwant, and Dieter Neubert, eds., *Dynamics of Collective Violence: Processes of Escalation and De-escalation in Violent Group Conflicts* (Berlin: Duncker and Humblot, 1999), p. 9.

4. Mark Irving Lichbach, *The Rebel's Dilemma* (Ann Arbor: University of Michigan Press, 1998), pp. 218–220; Donald L. Horowitz, *The Deadly Ethnic Riot* (Berkeley: University of California Press, 2001).

5. Edward E. Azar, "The Analysis and Management of Protracted Conflicts," in Vamik D. Volkan, Joseph Montville, and Demetrios A. Julius, eds., *The Psychodynamics of International Relationships* (Lexington, Mass.: Lexington Books, 1991); Louis Kriesberg, "Transforming Conflicts in the Middle East and Central Europe," in Louis Kriesberg, Terrell A. Northrup, and Stuart J. Thorson, eds., *Intractable Conflicts and Their Transformation* (Syracuse, N.Y.: Syracuse University Press, 1989), pp. 109–131.

6. Nazih Richani, "The Political Economy of Violence: The War-System in Colombia," *Journal of Interamerican Studies and World Affairs* 39:2 (1997): 37–81.

7. Trutz von Trotha, "Forms of Martial Power: Total Wars, Wars of

Pacification, and Raid: Some Observations on the Typology of Violence," in Georg Elwert, Stephan Feuchtwant, and Dieter Neubert, eds., *Dynamics of Collective Violence: Processes of Escalation and De-escalation in Violent Group Conflicts* (Berlin: Duncker and Humblot, 1999), p. 39.

8. Mark Duffield, *Global Governance and the New Wars: The Merging of Development and Security* (London and New York: Zed Books, 2001), p. 136. For an earlier argument, see Mark Duffield, "The Political Economy of Internal War: Asset Transfer, Complex Emergencies," in Joanna Macrae and Anthony Zwi, eds., *War and Hunger: Rethinking International Responses to Complex Emergencies* (London: Zed, 1994), pp. 50–69. See also Mary Kaldor, *New and Old Wars: Organized Violence in a Global Era* (Palo Alto, Calif.: Stanford University Press, 1999).

9. David Keen, "Incentives and Disincentives for Violence," in Mats Berdal and David M. Malone, eds., *Greed and Grievance: Economic Agendas in Civil Wars* (Boulder, Colo.: Lynne Rienner, 2000), p. 19. Elwert, Feuchtwang, and Neubert similarly argued that "war is a moment in the creation of a new social totality." Elwert, Feuchtwant, and Neubert, "The Dynamics of Collective Violence—An Introduction," p. 19.

10. The classic account is Mancur Olson Jr., *The Logic of Collective Action: Public Goods and the Theory of Groups* (Cambridge, Mass.: Harvard University Press, 1965). For a systematic review of the literature, see Lichbach, *The Rebel's Dilemma,* 1998; for an application to civil war, see Paul Collier and Anke Hoeffler, "Greed and Grievance in Civil Wars," World Bank Working Paper, October 21, 2001.

11. Jeffrey Herbst, "African Militaries and Rebellion: The Political Economy of Threat and Combat Effectiveness," *Journal of Peace Research* 41:3 (2004): 357–369.

12. Marie-Joëlle Zahar, "Protégés, Clients, Cannon Fodder: Civilians in the Calculus of Militias," *International Peacekeeping* 7:4 (Winter 2000): 107–128.

13. Lichbach, *The Rebel's Dilemma,* p. 261.

14. Christopher Clapham, "Introduction: Analysing African Insurgencies," in Christopher Clapham, ed., *African Guerrillas* (Bloomington: Indiana University Press, 1998), p. 9.

15. On Frelimo, see M. Anne Pitcher, *Transforming Mozambique: The Politics of Privatization, 1975–2000* (Cambridge: Cambridge University Press, 2002), p. 126. On the FMLN, see José Angel Moroni Bracamonte and David E. Spencer, *Strategy and Tactics of the Salvadoran FMLN Guerrillas: Last Battle of the Cold War, Blueprint for Future Conflicts* (Westport, Conn.: Praeger, 1995).

16. Jocelyn Alexander, "The Local State in Post-War Mozambique: Political Practice and Ideas About Authority," *Africa* 67 (Winter 1997): 1–26.

17. William Stanley, *The Protection Racket State: Elite Politics, Military Extortion, and Civil War in El Salvador* (Philadelphia: Temple University Press, 1996); Elisabeth Jean Wood, *Forging Democracy from Below: Insurgent Transitions in South Africa and El Salvador* (Cambridge: Cambridge University Press, 2000).

18. For a classic study, see Guillermo O'Donnell and Philippe Schmitter, *Transitions from Authoritarian Rule: Tentative Conclusions About Uncertain Democracies* (Baltimore, Md.: Johns Hopkins University Press, 1986).

19. Douglass North, *Institutions, Institutional Change, and Economic Performance* (Cambridge: Cambridge University Press, 1990); Terry Lynn Karl, "Dilemmas of Democratization in Latin America," *Comparative Politics* 22 (1990): 1–21.

20. Kathleen Thelen and Sven Steinmo, "Historical Institutionalism in Comparative Politics," in Kathleen Thelen, Sven Steinmo, and Frank Longstreth, eds., *Structuring Politics: Historical Institutionalism in Comparative Analysis* (Cambridge: Cambridge University Press, 1992), pp. 1–32.

21. Juan J. Linz and Alfred Stepan, *Problems of Democratic Transition and Consolidation: Southern Europe, South America, and Post-Communist Europe* (Baltimore, Md.: Johns Hopkins University Press, 1996), p. 55; Michael Bratton and Nicholas van de Walle, *Democratic Experiments in Africa: Regime Transitions in Comparative Perspective* (Cambridge: Cambridge University Press, 1997).

22. Leonard Weinberg and William Lee Eubank, "Political Parties and the Formation of Terrorist Groups," *Terrorism and Political Violence* 2:2 (Summer 1990): 125–144.

23. Robert Michels, *Political Parties: A Sociological Study of the Oligarchical Tendencies of Modern Democracy* (New York: Free Press, 1962), p. 78.

24. James Diehl, *Paramilitary Politics in Weimar Germany* (Bloomington: Indiana University Press, 1977); Maurice Duverger, *Political Parties: Their Organization and Activity in the Modern States* (New York: John Wiley and Sons, 1954), pp. 36–40.

25. Marc W. Chernick, "Negotiated Settlement to Armed Conflict: Lessons from the Colombian Peace Process," *Journal of Interamerican Studies and World Affairs* 30:4 (Winter 1988–1989): 75.

26. Michael C. Hudson, "Power-Sharing in Post–Civil War Lebanon," *International Negotiation* 2:1 (1997): 103–122; Nazih Richani, *Dilemmas of Democracy and Political Parties in Sectarian Societies: The Case of the Progressive Socialist Party of Lebanon, 1949–1996* (New York: St. Martin's Press, 1998), pp. 91–94. See also Oren Barak, "Lebanon: Failure, Collapse and Resuscitation," in Robert I. Rotberg, ed., *State Failure and State Weakness in a Time of Terror* (Washington, D.C.: Brookings Institution/World Peace Foundation, 2003).

27. Weinberg and Eubank, "Political Parties and the Formation of Terrorist Groups," p. 130. On Colombia, see Cynthia Watson, "Guerrilla Groups in Colombia: Reconstituting the Political Process," in Leonard Weinberg, ed., *Political Parties and Terrorist Groups* (London: Frank Cass, 1992), pp. 84–102; Spyros Demetriou, "Rising from the Ashes? The Difficult (Re)Birth of the Georgian State," *Development and Change* 33:4 (2002): 871.

28. African Rights, *Death, Despair, and Defiance* (London: African

Rights, 1994); Gerard Pruniér, *The Rwanda Crisis: History of a Genocide* (New York: Columbia University Press, 1995).

29. On the relationship between Herri Batasuna and ETA, see Richard Gunter, "Spain: The Very Model of the Modern Elite Settlement," in John Higley and Richard Gunter, eds., *Elites and Democratic Consolidation in Latin America and Southern Europe* (Cambridge: Cambridge University Press, 1992), pp. 38–80. On the Sinn Fein–IRA relationship, see Adrian Guelke and Jim Smyth, "The Ballot Bomb: Terrorism and the Electoral Process in Northern Ireland," in Leonard Weinberg, ed., *Political Parties and Terrorist Groups* (London: Frank Cass, 1992), pp. 103–124.

30. Kaldor, *New and Old Wars*, pp. 46–48, 93.

31. Angelo Panebianco, *Political Parties: Organization and Power* (Cambridge: Cambridge University Press, 1988); Mayer N. Zald and John D. McCarthy, eds., *Social Movements in an Organizational Society* (New Brunswick, N.J.: Transaction, 1987), p. 19; Lichbach, *The Rebel's Dilemma*, p. 229.

32. Martin Shefter, "Party and Patronage: Germany, England, and Italy," *Politics and Society* 7:4 (1977): 403–451. On patronage and the institutionalization of Italian parties, see Luciano Bardi and Leonardo Morlino, "Italy: Tracing the Roots of the Great Transformation," in Richard S. Katz and Peter Mair, eds., *How Parties Organize: Change and Adaptation in Party Organizations in Western Democracies* (London: Sage, 1994), pp. 242–277.

33. James C. Scott, "Corruption, Machine Politics, and Political Change," *American Political Science Review* 63:4 (December 1969): 1144.

34. Aristide R. Zolberg, *Creating Political Order: The Party-States of West Africa* (Chicago: Rand McNally, 1966); David Apter, *The Gold Coast in Transition* (Princeton, N.J.: Princeton University Press, 1955); Myron Weiner, *Party Building in a New Nation: The Indian National Congress* (Chicago: University of Chicago Press, 1967); James S. Coleman and Carl G. Rosberg, Jr., *Political Parties and National Integration in Tropical Africa* (Berkeley: University of California Press, 1964).

35. Apter, *The Gold Coast in Transition*, p. 202.

36. See Norman Frohlich, Joe A. Oppenheimer, and Oran R. Young, *Political Leadership and Collective Goods* (Princeton, N.J.: Princeton University Press, 1971); Sidney Tarrow, *Power in Movement: Social Movements and Contentious Politics*, 2nd ed. (Cambridge: Cambridge University Press, 1998), pp. 6, 199.

37. Lichbach, *The Rebel's Dilemma*, p. 229.

38. Panebianco, *Political Parties*, p. 40.

39. Mayer N. Zald and John D. McCarthy, "Social Movement Industries: Competition and Cooperation Among Movement Organizations," *Research in Social Movements: Conflicts and Change* 3 (1980): 4, cited in Lichbach, *The Rebel's Dilemma*, p. 48.

40. Christopher Clapham, *Africa and the International System: The Politics of State Survival* (Cambridge: Cambridge University Press, 1996).

41. William Minter, *Apartheid's Contras: An Inquiry into the Roots of War in Angola and Mozambique* (Atlantic Highlands, N.J.: Zed Books, 1994).

42. Elaine Windrich, *The Cold War Guerrilla: Jonas Savimbi, the U.S. Media, and the Angolan War* (Westport, Conn.: Greenwood Press, 1992).

43. Chalmers Johnson, *Peasant Nationalism and Communist Power: The Emergence of Revolutionary China, 1937–1945* (Palo Alto, Calif.: Stanford University Press, 1962).

44. Lewis Coser, *The Functions of Social Conflict* (Glenco, Ill.: Free Press, 1956).

45. Ronaldo Munck, "Deconstructing Terror: Insurgency, Repression, and Peace," in Ronaldo Munck and Purnaka L. de Silva, eds., *Postmodern Insurgencies: Political Violence, Identity Formation, and Peacemaking in Comparative Perspective* (New York: St. Martin's Press, 2000), p. 5.

46. Tarrow, *Power in Movement*, p. 145.

47. Stephen M. Saideman, "Is Pandora's Box Half Empty or Half Full? The Limited Virulence of Secessionism and the Domestic Sources of Disintegration," in David A. Lake and Donald Rothchild, eds., *The International Spread of Ethnic Conflict: Fear, Diffusion, and Escalation* (Princeton, N.J.: Princeton University Press, 1998), pp. 127–150.

48. Donald Horowitz, *Ethnic Groups in Conflict* (Berkeley: University of California Press, 1985); Robert Hislope, "Intra-Ethnic Conflict in Croatia and Serbia: Flanking and the Consequences for Democracy," *East European Quarterly* 30:4 (Winter 1996): 471.

49. Espen Barth Eide, "'Conflict Entrepreneurship': On the 'Art' of Waging Civil War," in Anthony McDermott, ed., *Humanitarian Force* (Oslo, Norway: PRIO Report 4/97, 1997).

50. V. P. Gagnon Jr., "Ethnic Nationalism and International Conflict: The Case of Serbia," *International Security* 19:3 (Winter 1994–1995): 136–137.

51. James D. Fearon and David D. Laitin, "Violence and the Social Construction of Ethnic Identity," *International Organization* 54:4 (Autumn 2000): 846.

52. Alan Emery and Rupert Taylor, "South Africa: From 'Racial Conflict' to Democratic Settlement," in Ronaldo Munck and Purnaka L. de Silva, eds., *Postmodern Insurgencies: Political Violence, Identity Formation, and Peacemaking in Comparative Perspective* (New York: St. Martin's Press, 2000), pp. 54–70.

53. Francis M. Deng, *War of Visions: Conflict of Identities in the Sudan* (Washington, D.C.: Brookings Institution Press, 1995); Nelson Kasfir, "One Full Revolution: The Politics of Sudanese Military Government, 1969–1985," in John W. Harbeson, ed., *The Military in African Politics* (Westport, Conn.: Praeger, 1987).

54. Eide, "'Conflict Entrepreneurship.'"

55. Steven L. Burg and Paul S. Shoup, *The War in Bosnia-Herzegovina: Ethnic Conflict and International Intervention* (Armonk, N.Y.: M. E. Sharpe, 1999), p. 69.

56. Stephen Ellis, "Liberia, 1989–1994: A Study of Ethnic and Spiritual Violence," *African Affairs* 94 (1995): 178–180.

57. Kathleen Collins, "Clans, Pacts, and Politics in Central Asia," *Journal of Democracy* 13:3 (July 2002): 137–152.

58. Michel Cahen, "Dhlakama e Maninque Nice: An Atypical Former Guerrilla in the Mozambican Presidential Race," *L'Afrique Politique* (1995): 10.

59. Carrie L. Manning, *The Politics of Peace in Mozambique: Post-Conflict Democratization, 1992–2000* (Westport, Conn.: Praeger, 2002), pp. 85–86.

60. Jessica Schafer, "Guerrillas and Violence in the War in Mozambique: De-Socialization or Re-Socialization?" *African Affairs* 100 (2001): 236.

61. Iraê Baptista Lundin, "Partidos Políticos: A Leitura da Vertente Étnico-Regional no Processo Democrático," in Brazão Mazula, ed., *Moçambique: Eleições, Democracia e Desenvolvimento* (Maputo, Mozambique: Inter-Africa Group, 1995); Hans Abrahamsson and Anders Nilsson, *Mozambique: The Troubled Transition, from Socialist Construction to Free Market Capitalism* (London: Zed Books, 1995), cited in Manning, *The Politics of Peace in Mozambique*, p. 90.

62. Wood, *Forging Democracy from Below*, p. 49.

63. Sara Miles and Bob Ostertag, "D'Aubuisson's New Arena," *NACLA Reports on the Americas* 23:2 (1989): 14–38; Carlos Acevedo, "El Salvador's New Clothes: The Electoral Process 1982–1989," in Anjali Sundaram and George Gelber, eds., *A Decade of War: El Salvador Confronts the Future* (New York: Monthly Review Press, 1991).

64. For a discussion of Khmer identity, see Steve Heder and Judy Ledgerwood, "Politics of Violence: An Introduction," in Steve Heder and Judy Ledgerwood, eds., *Propaganda, Politics, and Violence in Cambodia: Democratic Transition Under United Nations Peace-keeping* (Armonk, N.Y.: M. E. Sharpe, 1996), p. 25.

65. For a more formal consideration of selective incentives, see Lichbach, *The Rebel's Dilemma*, pp. 216–241.

66. Samuel L. Popkin, *The Rational Peasant: The Political Economy of Rural Society in Vietnam* (Berkeley: University of California Press, 1979), p. 240; Cynthia McClintock, "Why Peasants Rebel: The Case of Peru's Sendero Luminoso," *World Politics* 37 (October 1987): 81. See also Joel Migdal, *Peasants, Politics, and Revolution: Pressures Toward Political and Social Change in the Third World* (Princeton, N.J.: Princeton University Press, 1974).

67. Joanna Macrae and Anthony Zwi, eds., *War and Hunger: Rethinking International Responses to Complex Emergencies* (London: Zed Books, 1994); Mary B. Anderson, *Do No Harm: How Aid Can Support Peace—or War* (Boulder, Colo.: Lynne Rienner, 1999).

68. R. T. Naylor, *Wages of Crime: Black Markets, Illegal Finance, and the Underworld Economy* (Ithaca, N.Y.: Cornell University Press, 2002).

69. Terrence Lyons, "Diasporas and Homeland Conflict," in Miles

Kahler and Barbara Walter, eds., *Globalization, Territoriality, and Conflict* (New York: Cambridge University Press, 2005); Paul Collier and Anke Hoeffler, "Greed and Grievances in Civil War" (Washington, D.C.: World Bank Policy Research Working Paper 2355, 2000), p. 26.

70. Stephen Ellis, "Liberia's Warlord Insurgency," in Christopher Clapham, ed., *African Guerrillas* (Oxford: James Currey, 1998), p. 161.

71. William Reno, "The Business of War in Liberia," *Current History* 95:601 (May 1996): 212, 213; William Reno, "Reinvention of an African Patrimonial State: Charles Taylor's Liberia," *Third World Quarterly* 16:1 (1995): 109–120; William Reno, "Foreign Firms and the Financing of Charles Taylor's NPFL," *Liberian Studies Journal* 18:2 (1993): 175–878.

72. Quoted in Peter Da Costa, "Liberia: Peace Postponed," *Africa Report* 37:3 (May-June 1992): 52.

73. Vesna Bojičić and Mary Kaldor, "The 'Abnormal' Economy of Bosnia-Herzegovina," in Carl-Ulrik Schierup, ed., *Scramble for the Balkans: Nationalism, Globalism, and the Political Economy of Reconstruction* (New York: St. Martin's Press in association with the Centre for Research in Ethnic Relations, University of Warwick, 1999), p. 98.

74. Laura Silber and Alan Little, *Yugoslavia: Death of a Nation* (New York: Penguin, 1997), p. 246.

75. Peter Andreas, "The Clandestine Political Economy of War and Peace in Bosnia," *International Studies Quarterly* 48:1 (March 2004): 35. See also Kaldor, *New and Old Wars*, p. 53.

76. Philippe Le Billion, "Angola's Political Economy of War: The Role of Oil and Diamonds, 1975–2000," *African Affairs* 100 (2001): 55–80.

77. Human Rights Watch, *Angola Unravels: The Rise and Fall of the Lusaka Peace Process* (September 1999), p. 133.

78. Lisbon Radio Renascenca, June 27, 1996, cited in Paul Hare, *Angola's Last Best Chance for Peace: An Insider's Account of the Peace Process* (Washington D.C.: United States Institute of Peace Press, 1998), p. 126.

79. Mark Chingono, *The State, Violence and Development: The Political Economy of War in Mozambique, 1975–92* (Aldershot, UK: Averbury, 1996).

80. Hugh Byrne, *El Salvador's Civil War: A Study of Revolution* (Boulder, Colo.: Lynne Rienner, 1996), pp. 132–136. See also Cynthia McClintock, *Revolutionary Movements in Latin America: El Salvador's FMLN and Peru's Shining Path* (Washington, D.C.: United States Institute of Peace Press, 1998).

81. According to Wood, the "resolution of the collective action puzzle posed by the Salvadoran insurgency rests principally on selective benefits experienced only by participants but which were emotional and moral rather than material." Elisabeth Jean Wood, "Insurgent Collective Action and Civil War in El Salvador," paper presented at the 2001 annual meeting of the American Political Science Association, San Francisco, August 29–September 2, 2001. See also Elisabeth Jean Wood, *Insurgent Collective*

Action and Civil War in Rural El Salvador (Cambridge: Cambridge University Press, 2002).

82. Manning, *The Politics of Peace in Mozambique*, p. 90. See also Schafer, "Guerrillas and Violence in the War in Mozambique," p. 236.

83. On the question of diversionary foreign policy and domestic politics, see Alastair Smith, "Diversionary Foreign Policy in Democratic Systems," *International Studies Quarterly* 40:1 (March 1996): 133–153; Jack Levy, "The Diversionary Theory of War: A Critique," in Manus I. Midlarsky, ed., *Handbook of War Studies* (New York: Unwin-Hyman, 1989), pp. 259–288. For an assessment of cases that finds no "rally 'round the flag" effect, see Giacomo Chiozza and H. E. Goemans, "Avoiding Diversionary Targets," paper presented at the American Political Science Association meeting, Philadelphia, Penn., August 2003.

84. Charles T. Call and William Stanley, "Civilian Security," in Stephen John Stedman, Donald Rothchild, and Elizabeth M. Cousens, eds., *Ending Civil War: The Implementation of Peace Agreements* (Boulder, Colo.: Lynne Rienner, 2002) pp. 306–307.

85. William A. Gamson, *The Strategy of Social Protest* (Homewood, Ill.: The Dorsey Press, 1975), p. 81. See also Peter K. Eisinger, "The Conditions of Protest Behavior in American Cities," *American Political Science Review* 67:1 (March 1973): 11–28, on instrumental protests that respond to the incentives of political opportunity structures.

86. T. David Mason and Dale A. Krane, "The Political Economy of Death Squads: Toward a Theory of the Impact of State-Sanctioned Terror," *International Studies Quarterly* 33 (1989): 175–198.

87. Georg Elwert, "Markets of Violence," in Georg Elwert, Stephan Feuchtwant, and Dieter Neubert, eds., *Dynamics of Collective Violence: Processes of Escalation and De-Escalation in Violent Group Conflicts* (Berlin: Duncker and Humblot, 1999), p. 90.

88. Norma Krieger, *Zimbabwe's Guerrilla War: Peasant Voices* (Cambridge: Cambridge University Press, 1992), pp. 101–109, 152–157.

89. Nelson Kasfir, "Guerrillas and Civilian Participation: The National Resistance Army in Uganda, 1981–86," *Journal of Modern African Studies* 43 (June 2005): 271–296.

90. Margaret Hall, "The Mozambique National Resistance (Renamo): A Study of the Destruction of an African Country," *Africa* 60:1 (1990): 39–68; K. B. Wilson, "Cults of Violence and Counter-Violence in Mozambique," *Journal of Southern African Studies* 18:3 (September 1992): 531; Schafer, "Guerrillas and Violence in the War in Mozambique."

91. Minter, *Apartheid's Contras*, pp. 176–179, 217–225; Linda M. Heywood, "Unita and Ethnic Nationalism in Angola," *Journal of Modern African Studies* 27:1 (1989): 57–61.

92. Burg and Shoup, *The War in Bosnia-Herzegovina*, p. 174.

93. Ellis, "Liberia's Warlord Insurgency," pp. 155–171.

94. Wood, *Forging Democracy from Below*, p. 47.

3

The Legacy of Fear
and Voting for Peace

F ear, polarization, and power derived from violence will shape the
political context of postconflict elections unless politics is
demilitarized during the transitional period prior to the election.
This legacy of war strongly influences the path of postconflict transitions and creates the context for postconflict elections. Unless an
effective interim regime and processes to demilitarize politics are in
place during the period between cease-fire and elections, the powerful organizations of war are likely to dominate the campaign and
win the election. In a context in which the legacy of fear remains
powerful, postconflict elections are dominated by concerns for security. The outcomes of postconflict transitions ending in elections are
therefore shaped by the institutional legacies of war and whether or
not these institutions are transformed through processes to demilitarize politics.

Voters in postconflict elections often choose to use the limited
power of their franchise either to appease the most powerful faction
in the hope of preventing a return to war or to select the most nationalistic and chauvinistic candidate who credibly pledges to protect the
voter's community.[1] Outside observers often regard these leaders as
warlords or war criminals. By vulnerable voters, however, they are
seen either as powerful protectors capable of defending the voter
from rival military forces or as intimidators to be appeased in order
to preclude a return to the violence that they threaten to unleash if
they lose. Civilian candidates and those who do not have a convincing answer to the issue of postelection security are unlikely to
prevail.

Fear and the legacies of the institutions of war vary across the cases examined in this study. As detailed in Chapter 1, some peace implementation processes took place in a context where the institutions of war remained powerful and entrenched. In such circumstances, unless politics was demilitarized during peace implementation, postconflict elections took place in a context in which the institutions and attitudes of war remained dominant. Candidates sometimes campaigned by threatening to return to war if they lost the election. In Liberia these threats were successful, and many voters cast their ballots to appease the most dangerous candidate, the ex–factional leader Charles Taylor. In Angola UNITA similarly threatened a return to war if it did not win the election, but this strategy backfired, and the majority endorsed the incumbent MPLA government. UNITA demonstrated that its threat was real and subsequently unleashed renewed conflict. In Cambodia the Khmer Rouge also threatened to return to war but lacked the military strength to return the country to the full-scale conflict of the past.[2]

In a second set of cases still distorted by the fears and structures of civil war, parties made appeals to protect their constituencies from other parties. In Bosnia-Herzegovina, parties campaigned in their ethnically defined constituencies by promising to defend that constituency's interests and by heightening the danger of supporting anyone other than a nationalist. Ethnic outbidding led to polarization, and moderate or multiethnic parties did poorly in the first postconflict election. Leaders who have the most violent pasts may make the most convincing claim that a vote for them is a vote for peace.[3] In these cases the best that postconflict elections may be able to do is to reduce the gap between de facto power derived from military strength and de jure power based on votes.[4] Longer-term peacebuilding will be difficult in these circumstances.

In a third set of cases, processes to demilitarize politics during the transitional period created a new institutional context at the time of elections. In El Salvador, Mozambique, and (to a lesser extent) Cambodia politics had been relatively demilitarized prior to elections, and voters therefore had less fear that war would return. Both the ruling ARENA party and the insurgent FMLN in El Salvador transformed themselves into effective political parties prior to the elections and demonstrated a willingness to compete on the basis of electoral politics rather than through violence. In Mozambique relatively effective demobilization, the creation of strong interim institutions based on consultation and joint decisionmaking, and the support given to Renamo to encourage it to make the transition from a military to a political organization reduced the strength of the institutions of war relative to the institutions of democratic governance by election day. Cambodia is an ambiguous case, with some institutions such as Funcinpec making the transition from military to electoral politics more successfully than the ruling Cambodian People's Party or the Khmer Rouge. Interim administration was relatively strong but still insufficient to demilitarize the structures of the incumbent administration or the Khmer Rouge.

This chapter examines the seven cases to determine the extent to which the institutional legacies of war shaped the outcomes of postconflict elections. The outcomes in Angola, Bosnia-Herzegovina, Liberia, and Tajikistan all reflect the powerful and enduring influence of the war on the voting process and the power retained by militarized institutions through the transition. The outcomes in Cambodia, El Salvador, and Mozambique, in contrast, point to the capacity of postconflict elections to promote sustainable peacebuilding if a process of demilitarization of politics has taken place. Chapters 4 and 5 investigate the specific processes of demilitarization of politics and how in some cases they helped to overcome the legacies of war and establish a new institutional framework for political competition prior to elections.

Elections and Threats to Return to War

Angola

The implementation of the Angola peace process was plagued by problems from the start.[5] Despite the destruction of over fifteen years of warfare, both the insurgent UNITA and the incumbent FMLA retained the idea that they could achieve unilateral victory rather than share power with their rival. The Bicesse peace process in part represented a tactical move to win through elections what each had been denied through armed conflict. Neither party delivered troops to the demobilization centers in a timely manner. Continual squabbles broke out over the location and number of the assembly areas. The Joint Cease-Fire Verification and Monitoring Commission included representatives from both parties but failed to function as both UNITA and the MPLA sought unilateral advantage, forcing the weak

United Nations mission to struggle to keep the process on track. In September, on the eve of the election, the new combined armed force had reached less than 20 percent of its approved level, and over half of the separate government and UNITA armies remained mobilized.[6] In effect, Angola reached the date of election with three separate armies.[7] An election-eve deal to name two army chiefs of staff (one from each side) did little to reduce a sense of foreboding.

The peace process called for a very short period between cease-fire and elections at the insistence of UNITA. Despite the risk of moving toward elections without demobilization, delay may have sparked renewed violence. A senior UNITA official told the UN special representative, "UNITA has made clear to the government that our agreement with them under the Bicesse Peace Accords ends on 30 November and that, after that date, if the elections have not been held, then anything could happen."[8] Given the context of a poorly designed and supported peace agreement and the lack of a strategy to manage potential spoilers inclined to defect from the agreement, further delay was unlikely to correct the flawed process.

Many observers expected UNITA to do well in the elections, and the US Embassy expected victory for Savimbi. A preelection report by a US-based nongovernmental organization concluded that "given standard indications for organizational effectiveness—chain of command, responsiveness of policy decisions to local as well as national demands, resilience and regeneration in the face of disruptions, etc.—UNITA ranked favorably against established political parties in Central and South America, the Caribbean, Central Europe, and the Balkans."[9] UNITA had successfully compelled the MPLA to hold elections, had a strong ethnic base among the Ovimbundu people, and was led by the charismatic (if demagogic) Savimbi. The period of the MPLA's rule under José Eduardo dos Santos had been a time of unrelenting conflict, economic hardship, and corruption.

During the campaign, however, Savimbi used threatening language that heightened fears and persuaded many that continuing to live with the MPLA was better than the uncertain and potentially violent future promised by UNITA.[10] Savimbi frightened many voters in the main cities with his antiwhite and antimestizo rhetoric and his threat to purge the civil service of all suspected of supporting the MPLA. Holden Roberto, the leader of the old National Front for the Liberation of Angola, characterized the preelection mood by saying, "People are afraid, very afraid, that this thing won't work."[11] Graffiti on the walls of several towns summed up the choice perceived by many Angolans: "MPLA steals but UNITA kills."[12] Observers noted an atmosphere of "intense distrust" in the lead-up to elections.[13]

Voting on September 29–30, 1992, was peaceful, reportedly because both sides sought international endorsement for the election each believed it would win. In the months preceding the vote, analysts had been divided about who would likely prevail. The election results were quite close, with the MPLA winning a thin majority in the parliament; dos Santos held just below 50 percent in the presidential race (Table 3.1). Both parties carried their core constituencies: UNITA mobilized its Ovimbundu core in the south-central provinces (Huambo, Bié, Benguela, and Cuando Cubango), while the MPLA turned out large numbers of supporters in the urban areas and among the Mbundu people in the north (carrying Luanda, Bengo, Malange, and Kwanza Norte). The MPLA prevailed by outpolling UNITA in the areas outside the parties' respective cores. Some voters balanced their tickets and hedged their bets by voting for Savimbi for president and the MPLA for the legislature.[14]

In a context in which the two parties had fought to a stalemate prior to the peace agreement, Angolan voters split in their perceptions of which party could best deliver peace and security to their communities. The United Nations observers concluded that the election was credible and certified the vote. Savimbi immediately raised charges of fraud and withdrew his forces from the Unified Armed Forces, a violation of the Bicesse agreement. On October 30, UNITA mounted an assault on Luanda, and in the ensuing battle government forces killed a number of high-ranking UNITA officials and large numbers of civilians.[15] The conflict soon escalated into a round of fighting even more destructive than before the peace agreement. In hindsight, at least, it appears as if Savimbi accepted the electoral provisions of the peace agreement because he believed that he would

Table 3.1   Results from the September 1992 Elections in Angola

Party	Presidential Candidate	Percentage of Presidential Vote	Percentage of Parliament Vote
MPLA	José Eduardo dos Santos	49.6	53.7
UNITA	Jonas Savimbi	40.0	34.1

win the elections and seize power through that mechanism. Once it became clear that this stratagem had failed, he fell back on the strategy of war. Rather than furthering democratization or the end of war, the Angolan elections precipitated renewed conflict.

A number of observers have been sharply critical of the United Nations for failing to put an adequate mission in place and for not insisting on demobilization prior to elections.[16] Others have suggested that the lack of resources from the international community in support of the Bicesse Accords "doomed them to failure."[17] Margaret Antsee, the UN special envoy to Angola, recognized the risks and complained that the operation in Angola was "the world's cheapest peacekeeping operation."[18] The United Nations, however, could not play a larger role than the parties to the agreement allowed. Antsee wrote, "Neither the Bicesse nor UNAVEM's mandate, as established by the Security Council, afforded us any means of direct intervention. All we could do, along with the observers, was to try to steer things in the right direction by getting the CCPM [Joint Political and Military Commission] to take action, as long as that body survived, and talk severely in private to whichever side was being more devious at a given moment."[19]

The failure of postconflict elections in Angola to advance either peace or democracy was due less to the clear deficiencies of the UN operation than to the powerful institutions of war that remained in place throughout the period between cease-fire and elections and the failure to demilitarize politics during this interim period. Both UNITA and MPLA continued on a war footing during the implementation process, retaining the capacity to return to war and refusing to transform themselves into institutions suitable for electoral competition. The institutional legacies of civil war retained their strength throughout the transition, preventing elections from contributing to a transition to peace and democratization.

Bosnia-Herzegovina

The 1996 elections in Bosnia-Herzegovina also took place in a context where the attitudes of war remained powerful and wartime organizations and strategies remained largely unreconstructed. Nationalist parties in Bosnia-Herzegovina campaigned in 1996 on the basis of promises of ethnic security, chauvinistic pledges, and dire warnings regarding the consequences of victory for rival nationalist parties. The Croatian Democratic Party (HDZ) issued advertisements warning that the survival of their nation depended on the vote while Republika Srpska television warned that a vote against the Serbian Democratic Party (SDS) would constitute a vote "against the Serb people."[20] The main Bosnian Muslim party made the same sort of appeal: "A vote for the SDA [Party of Democratic Action] is a vote for the survival of the Muslim nation" went the slogan in 1996.[21] As Horowitz and others anticipated, elections in an ethnically polarized context led nationalist leaders to outflank and outbid one another in their ethnic appeals.[22] Fear of nationalist factions still powerful under the Dayton Peace Agreement led voters to rally to the faction that could most credibly promise security for their group. Small, multiethnic parties such as the Joint List that could not guarantee security won few votes.[23]

The role of fear in shaping voting behavior in Yugoslavia predates the breakup of the state and civil war. In 1990 nationalists did well in elections because "a feeling of fear drove persons to vote for the nationalist parties, even when they did not necessarily support these parties' aims."[24] One Yugoslavian journalist concluded that Serbs "simply acted out of fear that even if they withheld their vote from a Karadžić, their Muslim neighbor would still give his vote to an Izetbegović. In the end, they were afraid of weakening their own nation in an hour presaging the ultimate confrontation."[25]

The international community forced Radovan Karadžić to resign from the SDS, but he remained an important presence in the campaign. Although the SDS had a firm hold on political life in Republika Srpska, the HDZ and the Bosniac Party of Democratic Action (SDA) similarly dominated their respective zones in the federation. Media in each territory, in particular influential television broadcasts, fell almost completely into the hands of the three dominant national parties.[26] Much of the competition revolved around these three parties and their efforts to mobilize their ethnic constituencies on the basis of fear. As one commentator noted, "The hopes of the international community that the campaign would boost the fortunes of those opposed to the division of Bosnian society along national lines was not realized."[27] Prior to the elections, one observer noted that "the system of regionally based direct elections makes it extremely likely that the dominant ethnically based parties will remain in power."[28] Sometimes these efforts became violent, as when Haris Silajdžić, the Bosniac competitor to Izetbegović for the

Bosnian presidency and leader of the Party for Bosnia and Herzegovina (SBiH), was badly beaten in June 1996.[29] The Joint List, a multiethnic slate of liberal parties, ran an effective campaign, but its support remained restricted to the exceptional cases of urban Sarajevo and Tuzla.[30] Given the sense of insecurity and uncertainty that prevailed in the context of the recently signed cease-fire, the three ruling parties used the September 1996 elections as an opportunity to consolidate and institutionalize their rule, and consequently to affirm the ethnic divisions and polarization of the war.

Problems relating to free movement of refugees and internally displaced persons distorted the September 1996 electoral process in Bosnia and Herzegovina. Under the Dayton Peace Agreement, voters could register in their home as listed in the 1991 census, in their current place of residence, or in the place where they intended to reside. These criteria led to tactical registration on a large scale to validate through the poll the ethnic cleansing of the war. According to the OSCE, 123,007 Bosnian Serb refugees in Serbia registered to vote in municipalities across Republika Srpska in which they supposedly intended to live, including previously Muslim areas.[31] Croatian and Bosniac authorities pressured displaced persons to register in strategic towns. In response both to calls from Serbian wartime leaders and to pressure from the Bosnian army and Bosniac paramilitary forces, many Serbians left certain (but not all) neighborhoods around Sarajevo. The OSCE electoral authorities postponed municipal elections in part to reduce the impact of such tactical registration and intimidation.[32]

Some observers and analysts argued in September 1996 that elections should be postponed and that the necessary "neutral political environment" was not yet in place.[33] Two observers described the difficult circumstances:

> Indicted war criminals still dominated political life, opposition politician figures had been targets of attack, freedom of media and of movement was minimal, civilians who belonged to minority communities were subject to systematic violence and intimidation by authorities, and brute uncertainty prevailed among Bosnia's residents and its refugees about whether their country could be rebuilt as one or would be split into three. In short, Bosnia's climate was one of such manifest insecurity that the rational vote for people to cast was for the nationalist parties, which most reliably, if narrowly, had always promised to protect their interests.[34]

Two pressures compelled quick elections. First, elections were the necessary first step in getting Bosnia-Herzegovina's new institutions off the ground. Until elections were held, the military organizations that occupied territory would remain in place. Second, and more decisively, the international community insisted on quick elections in order to meet the initial one-year implementation schedule, a precondition for deployment by the United States.[35]

U.S. secretary of state Warren Christopher, for example, stated in June 1996 that "a delay in the elections risks widening the divisions that continue to exist" in Bosnia.[36] International observers and nongovernmental monitoring organizations, most notably the International Crisis Group, called for the postponement of the elections. But, as Woodward has argued, a postponement was unlikely to have made a difference. "The critics who cite inadequacies in current conditions are generally correct. Nonetheless, we gain nothing by delay."[37]

The election itself proceeded calmly. As in other postconflict cases, the parties that expected to win (in this case the nationalist SDS, SDA, and HDZ) had every reason to assure an orderly process and the anticipated international legitimacy that would follow their victory. Although peaceful, the election was a mess administratively. Problems with the registration lists prevented some potential voters from voting. Restrictions on freedom of movement and access by displaced persons to vote in the place where they had lived before the war restricted the poll in many areas.[38]

Problems with the vote count led the International Crisis Group to conclude that turnout was an improbable 104 percent.[39] The OSCE later revised its estimate of registered voters upward. The Coordinator for International Monitoring (CIM) concluded that while "the general climate in which the elections took place was in some cases below the minimum standards of the OSCE Copenhagen Commitments . . . they provide a first and cautious step for the democratic functioning of the governing structures of Bosnia and Herzegovina."[40] In the end, OSCE head of mission Robert Frowick certified the elections as "reasonably free and fair," and the CIM Ed van Thijn characterized the vote as "not free and fair."[41]

Given the recent cease-fire and the continued polarization and legacy of fear at the time of the election, it is not surprising that nationalist candidates did well, and many experts called the results "predictable."[42] In the contest for the three-person, triethnic presidency, Alija Izetbegović easily won the Muslim seat (with 80 percent of the vote), Krešimir Zubak won the Croatian seat (with 89 percent of the vote), and Momćilo Krajišnik won the Serbian seat (67 percent of the vote). Biljana Plavšić ran as the SDS candidate for the Republika Srpska presidency in the place of Radovan Karadžić (who, as an indicated war criminal, could not run) and won 60 percent of the vote, beating out other ultranationalist candidates.[43] The fact that nationalists won the seats was just about inevitable, given that the constitution defined the positions in ethnic terms and encouraged a de facto "tri-national condominium."[44] As one commentator from the region wrote, "Given the war feelings, biased media, and all the other extraordinary conditions, expectations were that all members of an ethnic group would vote for their respective ruling national party, largely out of fear that the others would also."[45]

The 1996 elections elicited a wide range of assessments.[46] Anthony Borden argued that the elections merely consolidated the power of extremist nationalists and reinforced Bosnia's de facto division into ethnic enclaves.[47] Part of the problem was that the elections became the focus for a variety of objectives, some of which were contrary to the Dayton framework or any reasonable expectations regarding what one election could deliver.[48] The *Economist* concluded that the elections "merely entrench ethnic division and legitimize unsavory leadership."[49] Some groups were critical of the elections for failing to create a multiethnic Bosnia, arrest war criminals, create freedom of movement, and achieve a host of other important goals. David Rieff, for example, wrote in a September 1996 editorial that "from any point of view (except that, for now, the guns are silent), the international community has failed as dismally in post-war Bosnia as it did when the fighting was going on."[50] There is much to be said for such criticism of the flawed Dayton Agreement, but many regarded the silencing the guns as the main accomplishment of the agreement.

The lack of demilitarization of politics prior to elections in Bosnia-Herzegovina created a context that reinforced the institutions of war and social division. High Representative Carlos Westendorp concluded in 1997 that there "is a democratic system in the sense that there are democratic elections, but the result of the elections is that they give the advantage to one ethnic group over another. This is only a continuation of the war with other means."[51] The lack of demilitarization of politics meant that the legacies of fear and the inheritance of wartime institutions characterized the context of the vote in September 1996. Hence, it is not surprising that most voters selected militant nationalist parties.

Liberia

In Liberia the Abuja II Peace Agreement was designed to move the country quickly from the violence of April 1996 to elections.[52] The agreement called for very rapid implementation, beginning with a cease-fire in August 1996, disarmament by January 1997, and elections initially scheduled for May and eventually held in July 1997. The interim Council of State lacked the resources and the ability to make decisions necessary to govern at even a rudimentary level during the transition. The country, in desperate need of basic social services, drifted while the West African peacekeeping force (ECOMOG) provided security and international NGOs and UN agencies provided basic humanitarian relief. Although conditions were better than at any time since 1990, new institutions were needed desperately to make the situation sustainable.

The agreement signed in August 1996 called for disarmament to begin in November 1996. Cease-fire violations immediately threatened to derail the peace process. Despite evidence that factions were violating the agreement, ECOWAS decided not to invoke sanctions for fear that parties singled out for punishment would withdraw from the peace process, compelling ECOMOG to return to peace enforcement. Disarmament began slowly but picked up momentum toward the end of January 1997. ECOMOG collected large quantities of weapons, and for the first time in years roadblocks became rare and guns were not visible on the streets except in the hands of peacekeepers. Although many arms were collected, demobilization in terms of breaking the command and control structures over fighters was far less complete. Scarce resources and poor planning reduced demobilization to a twelve-hour process whereby former combatants simply turned in a weapon (or even a handful of bullets), were registered, and then left. Few doubted that the most reliable fighters avoided demobilization while the young and inexperienced went through the process in the hope of obtaining social benefits.[53]

A newly created Independent Electoral Commission (IECOM), consisting of representatives from the three main factions and from civilian parties, women's and youth groups, and unions, struggled to organize the 1997 elections under extremely tight constraints. The IECOM represented a broad cross-section of Liberian society, but lack of time, resources, and independence hampered its work. On May 16, under pressure from nearly every political party and civic organization other than that of Charles Taylor, ECOWAS finally agreed to delay the elections from May 30 until July 19, providing just two more months to organize the poll. Refugees in neighboring states, estimated to number 800,000, could vote only if they returned to Liberia. Given the lack of facilities to receive them, most were effectively disenfranchised.[54]

Several factional leaders who were running for office converted (or at least renamed) their militias into political parties. Charles Taylor turned his NPFL faction into the National Patriotic Party (NPP); Al-Haji Kromah disbanded ULIMO-K and established the All Liberian Coalition Party (ALCOP); and LPC leader George Boley eventually became the standard-bearer for the late President Doe's former party, the National Democratic Party of Liberia (NDPL). Roosevelt Johnson, the ULIMO-J leader at the center of the April 1996 fighting, did not seek office.

A number of previously established political parties also began organizing for the upcoming campaign. These civilian parties founded the Alliance of Political Parties and held a contentious convention in March. The Unity Party left the Alliance and nominated former United Nations official Ellen Johnson Sirleaf as its candidate. Sirleaf and the Unity Party soon appeared to be the leading challenger to Taylor and his NPP. The other civilian parties were small, with only a limited capacity to campaign. Kromah's ALCOP and Boley's NDPL never developed widespread support outside their respective ethnic heartlands.

On election day, July 19, 1997, Liberians turned out in large numbers, with an estimated 85 percent of those registered voting. Approximately 500 international observers watched the election and generally commended the process. The United Nations Observer Mission in Liberia and ECOWAS issued a joint certification that declared the electoral process to have been "free, fair, and credible." Taylor won the presidency in a landslide, with more than 75 percent of the vote, followed by Sirleaf, who took 10 percent (Table 3.2). On August 2, 1997, Taylor was sworn in as president of Liberia.

A number of factors contributed to the NPP's overwhelming victory. Taylor successfully converted his military faction into an effec-

Table 3.2   Results from the July 1997 Elections in Liberia

Party	Presidential Candidate	Percentage of Presidential Vote
National Patriotic Party	Charles Taylor	75.3
Unity Party	Ellen Johnson Sirleaf	9.6
All Liberian Coalition Party	Al-Haji Kromah	4.0
Alliance of Political Parties	Cletus Wortoson	2.6
United People's Party	Gabriel Matthews	2.5
National Democratic Party of Liberia	George Boley	1.3
Seven other parties	—	4.7

tive political patronage machine capable of mobilizing voters. Nearly every town in Liberia had an NPP office, and the country was covered in Taylor signs, bumper stickers, and T-shirts. Taylor's NPFL had operated as the de facto government in much of Liberia for years, and his organization therefore had a nationwide network unmatched by his rivals. Taylor also had far greater resources than his competitors. In a country with few vehicles, Taylor had the money to bring in Land Rovers, buses, motorcycles, and trucks and to lease a helicopter for the campaign. Taylor controlled the formerly state-owned shortwave radio station and thereby dominated the airwaves through which most Liberians outside Monrovia received their news. The NPP distributed rice to prospective voters and engaged extensively in patronage politics. Although the electoral code of conduct placed limits on campaign spending, the lack of enforcement mechanisms allowed Taylor to spend freely. No attempts were made to force the former militia leader to give up resources he had seized during the war.

Taylor campaigned widely, and his rallies matched political speeches with popular entertainment, including music, dance, fashion shows, and games. After so many years of grim warfare, his campaign offered a return to the normal pleasures of the past. Taylor was a master of highly visible generosity and won publicity by paying to fly Liberia's national soccer team to the African Nations Cup, funding the Charles Ghankay Taylor Educational and Humanitarian Relief Foundation, and donating ambulances (with his name prominently displayed on the side of each) to the John F. Kennedy Hospital in Monrovia. In his speeches Taylor promised expansive new programs to address the full range of social needs. His populist message resonated with many of Liberia's poor who regarded Sirleaf as the candidate of the educated, cosmopolitan elite. In some parts of Liberia Taylor was a popular figure who was remembered for defending communities against attacks from rival militias and who had maintained relative order in his zone of military occupation.

Although financial and organizational advantages were critical, they were least important in populous Montserrado County (the area around Monrovia), where easy transportation, FM radio, and a wide range of newspapers were available. Taylor won Montserrado with 55 percent of the vote to Sirleaf's 22 percent, suggesting that far more than the resource imbalance explained the landslide.

Memories of seven years of brutal conflict and the consequent fear of its return clearly shaped how many voters viewed the July 1997 election and the choices available to them. As one observer put it, the voters "were intimidated not by thugs at the polling stations but by the trauma of the last seven years of war."[55] Many Liberians believed—with good reason—that if Taylor lost the election, the country would return to war. Taylor's rivals pointed to his violent past but could not propose credible actions to contain him if he refused to accept the election results.[56] Although a significant number of voters identified with Taylor and his populist message or patronage, many simply seemed cautious and war-weary. Many Liberians made a calculated choice that they hoped would promote peace and stability and used their vote to appease the powerful ex–militia leader. As one Western reporter characterized the choice for Liberia's voters, "Should they support a warrior who has the power to make the result stick? Or should they opt for a civilian, and run the risk that the defeated warlords will go back to the bush and restart the war?"[57] Samuel Kofi Woods, a leading Liberian human rights advocate, explained that "the only thing Liberians wanted was an end to the war."[58] During the campaign young Taylor supporters frightened voters by chanting, "He killed my Pa, he killed my Ma, I'll vote for him."[59] In the end the elections ratified and institutionalized the imbalance of power created by seven years of war. The nature and ending of the war and the lack of a successful process to demilitarize politics—not the election itself—created this result. An organization and leader that had amassed great power during the conflict through violence and intimidation converted that influence into positions of constitutional authority through elections. This result did little to advance democratization and raises considerable concerns regarding long-term stability and peacebuilding and the ability of the electorate to constrain its ruler.

Tajikistan

In Tajikistan elections were held for the president (November 1999) and parliament (February and March 2000) to implement the June 1997 peace agreement. State-controlled media and the candidate registration process favored the ruling People's Democratic Party (PDP) and its candidate President Imomali Rakhmonov.[60] The United Tajik Opposition (UTO), the coalition dominated by the Islamic Revival Party and the cosignatory of the peace agreement, threatened to boycott in response to this imbalance. On the eve of the November 1999 presidential elections, Sayed Abdullo Nuri, the leader of the UTO, and Rakhmonov signed a protocol in which Nuri agreed to call off his boycott of the election and to rejoin the Commission of National Reconciliation in exchange for guarantees of full-scale participation in the March 2000 parliamentary elections.

The presidential elections took place without effective competition (the opposition Islamic Revival Party candidate was registered against his will), allowing the incumbent President Rakhmonov to win with a reported 97 percent of the vote and a truly incredible 98 percent turnout (Table 3.3).[61] International observers and human rights groups criticized the elections and documented wide-scale manipulation to the benefit of the incumbent government.[62] Jmaboi Niyozov, the former chair of the opposition Democratic Party, later said, however, that regardless of the quality of the election Rakhmonov would have won because the opposition failed to unite behind one candidate.[63]

The November 1999 protocol called for an independent elections commission and a revision to the electoral law prior to the February 2000 parliamentary election. The number of seats in both the lower and upper house was controversial, but Rakhmonov and Nuri reached an agreement on December 3. The election law was not passed until December 10, 1999. Elections were scheduled for February 2000. Of the 63 members of the lower house, 41 would be elected in single-mandate constituencies and 22 by party lists. Elections for the upper house were scheduled for March. Of the 33 seats, local assemblies elected 25 and the president appointed 8.[64]

According to the Central Commission on Elections and

Table 3.3   Results from the December 1999 Presidential and February 2000 Parliamentary Elections in Tajikistan

Party	Presidential Candidate	Percentage of Presidential Vote	Number of Parliamentary Seats
People's Democratic Party	Imomali Rakhmonov	97	40
Islamic Revival Party	Davlat Usmonov	2	2
Communist Party	—	—	7
Independents	—	—	9

Referenda, the February 2000 elections for the lower house elicited a 93 percent turnout. The ruling PDP won 40 seats, the Communist Party won 7, independents won 9, and the opposition Islamic Revival Party won just 2.[65] The strong showing by independents reflected the overall weakness of political parties and the strength of multiple, personalized patron-client networks and regional strongmen, often linked to armed factions and black-market networks.

International election observers noted that government control of media, manipulation by local elections officials, and questionable counting procedures resulted in systematic fraud designed to benefit the ruling PDP. The OSCE concluded that the elections "fell short of OSCE election-related commitments" in the areas of transparency, accountability, fairness, and secrecy.[66] The opposition believed that the system of election commissions and courts worked exclusively for the ruling party and its supporters. Regardless of this questionable outcome, the United Nations ended its observer mission in May 2000. The process of elections did little to increase the popular mandate for the regime, and power in Tajikistan remained divided among rival leaders with autonomous militias and fiefdoms.[67] As one report concluded, "The formal structures of the country have proven almost irrelevant to the daily political processes."[68]

In cases such as Angola, Bosnia-Herzegovina, Liberia, and Tajikistan, postconflict elections took place in a context still distorted by fear in which the institutions that had developed as a consequence of the war remained strong. Parties that credibly threatened to return to war and that mobilized constituencies on the basis of fear and promises of protection did well in these elections. In the absence of a process to demilitarize politics, these elections served more to ratify the power of the institutions and leaderships that had arisen in the context of the civil war rather than as an opportunity to transform the legacies of the past into new institutions capable of sustaining peacebuilding.

Demilitarized Politics and Elections

In other cases more successful processes to demilitarize politics allowed elections to advance both peace and democracy. As noted in Chapter 1, El Salvador, Mozambique, and Cambodia (to a lesser degree) signed peace agreements at a time when the main institutions of war were weakening or undergoing reform. The major parties determined that continuing warfare did not serve their interests and so sought to build mechanisms to move their competition from the battlefield to the ballot box. However, the recognition that electoral contests represented a better means to seek power did not by itself translate into effective postconflict elections. As Chapters 4 and 5 show in greater detail, processes to demilitarize politics were necessary to accomplish these transitions. Relatively strong interim regimes, consultative processes to manage the challenges of implementation and electoral administration, successful programs to transform militias into political parties, and processes of demobilization that fostered confidence all contributed to a new institutional context that served to create a bridge from war to peace and democratization.

Cambodia

Cambodia is an ambiguous case in which the demilitarization of politics progressed further in some areas than in others.[69] The Paris Peace Agreement was an effort by the international community to impose peace on a set of local actors who accepted the agreement tactically because each believed, for different reasons, that the process would strengthen its position. The agreement charged the United Nations with creating security and a "politically neutral environment" prior to elections. The large UN Transitional Authority in Cambodia (UNTAC), however, failed to disarm and demobilize the warring factions. The Khmer Rouge resisted UNTAC deployment and defected from the agreement. In addition, although the Supreme National Council consisting of all parties and UNTAC oversaw the administration of the state during the interim, the UN did not remove the ruling Cambodian People's Party from its positions of power and authority, particularly in the countryside.[70] The electoral advantages of incumbency were significant. The CPP maintained campaign offices in most villages (often in state administrative offices), and attendance at party rallies was mandatory for all civil servants.[71]

The Khmer Rouge's refusal to disarm presented UNTAC with a serious dilemma: Should it postpone the elections until the Khmer Rouge agreed to cooperate, or should it follow the original schedule despite the presumption of cooperation behind the Paris agreement? Rather than giving up in the face of this direct challenge, Special Representative Yasushi Akashi shifted the mission's focus to support elections more directly. The necessity (in the eyes of the international community at least) of adhering to the election timetable convinced the UN to revise its plans for military disarmament and demobilization. According to a UNTAC official, "ensuring the security of the electoral process in its entirety is now . . . the principal mission of the military component."[72]

The preelection period was marked by the boycott by the Khmer Rouge; kidnapping of UNTAC officials; harassment of opposition candidates by Hun Sen's ruling Cambodian People's Party (CPP); and widespread violence, particularly against Vietnamese nationals. One observer characterized the atmosphere prior to the vote: "The country was still largely armed; respect for UNTAC had diminished; the neutral political environment was conspicuous in its absence; and one of the major parties had withdrawn, amidst threats of similar retractions by some of the others. Crime was rocketing, violence was the norm, and political intimidation and harassment were unstoppable. . . . The atmosphere was tense and unpredictable, and was aggravated by the Cambodian 'rumor mill' which had the guerrillas just outside the capital city; and by the western press, which was predicting the possibility of a blood bath."[73] In October 1992 the Security Council decided to go ahead with the election despite the dangerous conditions, and UNTAC proceeded to organize the poll in those areas where it had control.[74]

Twenty-two parties registered, but not the Khmer Rouge.

Political organizations within Cambodia were structured in part on patron-client networks, making it difficult for an individual voter to shift from one to another.[75] Funcinpec's electoral strength surprised many observers who failed to detect its "subterranean" mobilization of old patron-client networks.[76] Both Funcinpec and the KPNLF opened provincial offices across the country.[77]

Many voters regarded Funcinpec as the party best positioned to come to a settlement with the Khmer Rouge and rejected the brutal and violent behavior and militant rhetoric of the ruling CPP during the election campaign. According to one anecdote, a Cambodian farmer spoke of harassment by CPP state officials who had told him that "if I didn't vote for them, they would kill me. Because of this, I voted for Funcinpec."[78] The CPP campaign suggested that Funcinpec was in league with the Khmer Rouge, and since many Cambodians believed that a deal with the Khmer Rouge was necessary for peace, they voted for Funcinpec.[79] The deputy leader of Funcinpec took advantage of the desire for peace by highlighting his party's links to the Khmer Rouge: "Some parties [e.g., the CPP] promise that if they win they won't let the Khmer Rouge come back. But will they make war in order that the Khmer Rouge don't return? We have had four-teen years of war already, and Khmer killing Khmer. . . . We are sick of war which we have had since 1970. We won't take your children to go to war. . . . Do you want war, or peace? If FUNCINPEC wins, we will make an invitation to the Khmer Rouge. . . . So vote for FUNCINPEC so it can solve the problems of Cambodia."[80] Many voters believed that a vote for Funcinpec would lead to an accommo-dation with the Khmer Rouge and an end to the armed conflict, thereby making a vote for Funcinpec a vote for peace.

Despite this inauspicious environment and growing threats to disrupt the election violently, the actual voting proceeded relatively peacefully.[81] From May 23 to 28, 4.2 million voters, representing approximately 90 percent of those registered, voted. Funcinpec won 45 percent of the vote, the CPP won 38 percent, and the Buddhist Liberal Democratic Party (an offshoot of the Khmer People's National Liberation Front) won 4 percent. William Shawcross inter-preted the vote: "Despite intimidation by Hun Sen's local security forces only 38 percent voted for his party, which they associated with Vietnam, with communism and with unending war against the Khmer Rouge. Forty-five percent voted for FUNCINPEC, which was seen as devoted to Sihanouk and the traditional ruling family, and whose leader Prince Ranariddh pledged 'reconciliation,' including with the Khmer Rouge."[82]

Akashi declared that the results "fairly and accurately reflect the will of the Cambodian people and must be respected."[83] Many observers were surprised by the outcome. As one put it, "For the first time in Cambodian history millions of Khmer had voted freely and fairly, and a majority had opposed an armed incumbent regime."[84]

The relative success of peace implementation and postconflict elections in Cambodia derived from the ability of external and regional actors to convince their clients to seek their best deal through UN-organized elections. The Khmer Rouge miscalculated in thinking it could use UNTAC to weaken its rivals, the government of Cambodia miscalculated in thinking it could use threats to transform its administrative dominance into votes, and Funcinpec correctly perceived that it could win through the ballot by promising peace. Some analysts concluded critically that the peace process did not resolve the underlying conflict but "merely changed the vehicle for communicating hostility and confrontation from war to elections."[85] The management of conflict through electoral procedures, however, represented a critical shift from the civil war of the 1980s and early 1990s. A shift from violent conflict to electoral competition opened up a vast new array of options to address underlying grievances.

Immediately following the 1993 elections, the ruling CPP claimed that fraud and malpractice had distorted the results. CPP members resigned from the Constituent Assembly, and some threatened to organize the secession of several provinces they controlled. In this tense context in which a return to war seemed imminent, Prince Sihanouk negotiated a powersharing pact that institutionalized a fifty-fifty division of power between Funcinpec and the CPP. Sihanouk stated, "We have to share power equally otherwise the violence cannot end."[86] Ultimately, Funcinpec lacked the ability to govern or to challenge the CPP's hold on the levers of power.

El Salvador

At the time of the signing of the peace accord in El Salvador in January 1992, the institutions of war were fading in a context of military stalemate, changes within the ruling ARENA and insurgent FMLN that led the leaders of both to perceive opportunities to do well in electoral politics, and a change in the interests of regional powers and the United States that led them to wish to disengage from the protracted civil war. Moving from the lingering fear and militarized institutions at the time of the cease-fire through the transition to electoral politics was not automatic and entailed a complex and ultimately successful process of peace implementation and demilitarization of politics.

The period between cease-fire and elections was beset by a number of controversies. Delays in land reform and transfer, problems in reintegration programs for ex-combatants, difficulties in establishing a new police force, and revelations that the FMLN had secret arms caches in Nicaragua created significant tensions but ultimately did not derail the elections. The election date was set by the 1983 constitution, not by the peace agreement, and was regarded as nonnegotiable.[87] Several acts of violence, including the murder of senior political leaders of both the insurgent FMLN and the governing ARENA party, threatened the prospects for a peaceful election. The United Nations Observer Mission in El Salvador (ONUSAL) worked to keep all the parties talking and working together through the contentious issues of the transition. As the election neared, the FMLN focused its resources on creating a national network of party activists and building alliances with other parties on the left. In the end the FMLN supported Rubén Zamora of the Democratic Convergence Party for president and concentrated on Assembly and mayoral elections.[88]

The ONUSAL Electoral Division, headed by Rafael López Pintor, was not fully operational until October 1993, providing little time for electoral organization prior to the March 1994 poll.[89] The Supreme Electoral Tribunal (TSE) proved to be both highly politicized (members were appointed based on votes garnered in past elections, thereby excluding the FMLN) and incapable of managing the complex system for registering voters.[90] Montgomery called the TSE a "cauldron of incompetence and partisanship."[91] The legacy of fraudulent elections and what Karl called "electoralism" with little real choice or participation from the left made many skeptical.[92] A UN study revealed that 27 percent of eligible voters were not registered in August 1993.[93] Lack of registration cards, logistical difficulties, and a cumbersome process threatened to distort the register and delegitimate the election by disenfranchising significant numbers of the poor and those in FMLN-dominated regions.[94] Given the chaos, the UN became more active in supporting the registration process.

The 1993 elections served to select the president, Assembly deputies, and mayors at the same time, something that happens only every fifteen years given the different lengths of terms for office-holders in El Salvador. Six parties and one coalition competed for the presidential election. The largest were the incumbent Nationalist Republican Alliance (ARENA) led by Armando Calderón Sol; the coalition composed of the Democratic Convergence (CD), the National Revolutionary Movement, and the FMLN led by the CD's Rubén Zamora; and the Christian Democratic Party (PDC) led by Fidel Chávez Mena. The coalition supported a common presidential candidate but competing legislative candidates. The FMLN worked to transform itself into a political party in time for the elections, developing new political skills, selecting and training candidates, registering supporters, and negotiating an alliance with other parties. In the end, "the FMLN succeeded remarkably in transforming itself from a clandestine organization to an open, well-organized party."[95] The campaign was sometimes violent, including assassinations of political leaders, and political rhetoric was often hostile. ARENA's huge financial advantages allowed it to dominate the media.[96] Although a return to war seemed unlikely by the time elections were held, the ARENA campaign still suggested that a vote for the FMLN would be a vote for chaos and violence.[97]

The two principal parties manipulated their compliance to the peace agreement in ways to maximize their ability to hold on to their core electoral constituencies and to appeal to uncommitted voters. This process created tensions and worried assessments from ONUSAL from time to time but served the purpose of encouraging the transition from organizations devoted to engaging in war to political parties engaging in voter mobilization. The FMLN, for example, pushed harder on the issue of land distribution and support for its demobilized soldiers than on reform of the military in order to hold on to its rural supporters who had joined the movement in support of the fight for social justice. This focus on land led the FMLN to endorse land occupations in contradiction to the provisions of the peace agreement. By the same token, ARENA delayed and obstructed provisions relating to security sector reform in order to avoid alienating its support within the armed forces. As part of this political process (as distinct from the formal peace implementation process), Holiday and Stanley suggested, "some groups within the FMLN pushed for delays in the purge of high-level military officers and accepted the transfer of certain military units into the civilian police in exchange for economic considerations in the form of land and improved reinsertion programs."[98] In other words, demilitarization of politics and the electoral strategies adopted by the major organizations sometimes clashed with the formal provisions of the peace agreements.

Elections were held on March 20, 1994, and were monitored by nearly 900 UN observers. ONUSAL chief of mission Augusto Ramìrez Ocampo declared that the election had generally been carried out under adequate conditions of liberty, competitiveness, and security, although concerns regarding organization and transparency were noted.[99] Turnout was less than expected (1.5 million), in part because of the chaotic registration process. The official results for the presidential election showed ARENA winning 49 percent, Coalition Convergencia Democratica–FMLN–Movimento Nacional Revolucionaria 25 percent, and Partido Democrata Cristiano 18 percent, with a number of smaller parties making up the remainder. The FMLN coalition had won the second-largest number of seats, attracting more votes than the long-established Christian Democratic Party. In the legislature, ARENA won 39 seats, FMLN won 21, PDC won 18, and three other parties split the remaining 6. ARENA won 206 of 262 mayoralties, with only 16 going to the FMLN. The runoff for the presidential race (since no one had won a majority) was held on April 24, and Calderon Sol, the ARENA party candidate, won. Salvadoran voters made their selection on the basis of policy preferences with less concern that the outcome would reignite conflict, although some voters reportedly voted against the FMLN because of its involvement in the war.[100]

The election was not the centerpiece of the peace process but represented a reform of an existing electoral process. The confusion over registration and other problems with the administration of the poll did little to increase public confidence.[101] The election represented a mechanism that promoted the incorporation of groups from the left into the political system. The FMLN made a strong showing despite its lack of political experience and resources, creating a sense that it could play an important part in national policy through participation in elections.

Mozambique

The October 1992 Rome Peace Agreement called for Mozambique to undergo a thorough transformation prior to elections. The United

Nations Operation in Mozambique (ONUMOZ) served as the focal point for the international community's efforts to assist in implementation by monitoring the cease-fire, demobilizing both Frelimo and Renamo armed forces, creating a unified national army and police force, removing mines, rebuilding basic infrastructure, resettling refugees and internally displaced persons, and supporting elections. The agreement, however, envisioned a timetable that, according to US observer Cameron Hume, the parties "could not possibly keep to, even in the first weeks after a cease-fire."[102] In addition, ONUMOZ faced delays in deploying its forces.

As a result, both Frelimo and Renamo missed deadlines for the encampment of their troops and put off election preparations. The Frelimo army in particular was slow to demobilize, and Renamo boycotted meetings to buy time and to pressure international donors to provide support. Despite the delays, the cease-fire held with little supervision, indicating that neither party had incentives to return to war. A larger problem for the demobilization program was mutinies by soldiers anxious to leave both armed forces.[103] Some suggested that the poverty of Mozambique, in contrast to Angola, forced an end to the fighting once outside support had ended. In order to force the pace and compel the Mozambicans to set an election date, the UN set a timetable for withdrawal of ONUMOZ. The Secretary-General's Special Representative Aldo Ajello insisted on significant demobilization prior to elections and received significant amounts of money from the international community to accomplish the task. Referring to the Angolan debacle, Ajello stated, "Lesson number one: no elections without demobilization. I am adamant on that and the parties are committed as well."[104]

Holding elections acceptable to both parties was essential to implementation and the consolidation of the gains achieved in the Rome Peace Accord. Multiparty elections had been a key Renamo demand, and Frelimo wanted to end questions about its legitimacy by winning the vote. After a series of delays, the Mozambicans set an election date of October 27–28, 1994. Renamo, with the support of ONUMOZ, donors, and South Africa, tried to get an agreement on power-sharing prior to the voting, but Frelimo refused, preferring a winner-takes-all formula.[105]

Both parties campaigned on similar programs. Joaquim Chissano and the ruling Frelimo party had a decided advantage in organizational capacity and financing, and the state-owned media unambiguously favored Frelimo. Renamo leader Afonso Dhlakama proved to be a spirited campaigner; he tried to tap into popular resentment against Frelimo-dominated urban areas and held well-attended rallies, even in northern areas believed to be strongholds of Frelimo. Renamo campaigned on its record of bringing democracy to Mozambique (by forcing Frelimo to negotiate) and criticized Frelimo for corruption and incompetence.[106] Chissano developed a sophisticated media campaign, drawing on the incumbents' financial advantages and working with Brazilian consultants, and mobilized his urban base effectively.[107] With few exceptions, the campaign was free of violence.

Perhaps the most dangerous moment in the transition occurred on the first day of voting. Dhlakama announced the withdrawal of his party, citing fraud and throwing the entire exercise into chaos.[108] Observers, however, noted that many areas outside Maputo did not hear Dhlakama's call for a boycott, and voting continued even in some pro-Renamo areas.[109] Under enormous pressure from diplomats and neighboring leaders, Dhlakama changed his mind and urged his supporters to vote on the second and third days. (A third day was added to make up for some of the confusion.)[110]

Despite the initial call for a boycott and immense logistical difficulties, turnout was high, with nearly 88 percent of the 6.1 million registered voters casting ballots.[111] Chissano won 53.3 percent and Dhlakama won 33.7 percent in the presidential voting, while Frelimo won 129 (52 percent) and Renamo 112 (45 percent) of the 250 seats in parliament in an election that Ajello declared free and fair. Each party won five of the country's ten provinces. Renamo's support was concentrated in the central and northern parts of the country, including the second-largest city, Beira, and the key agricultural province of Nampula. Frelimo carried vote-rich Maputo and the southern provinces of Maputo and Gaza. There was evidence of tactical voting by many Mozambicans who sought to reinforce the peace process by splitting their vote between Chissano for president and Renamo for the legislature.[112] Dhlakama accepted the results.

Conclusion

This analysis of postconflict elections in the seven cases in the 1990s where the peace agreement designated elections as the final stage of peace implementation indicates the importance of the legacies of war in shaping outcomes. In Angola, Bosnia-Herzegovina, Liberia, and Tajikistan the pervasive fear and insecurity still present at the time of the poll led many voters to select candidates who either promised to protect them or threatened to return the country to war. In Cambodia, El Salvador, and Mozambique the legacies of civil war were not as powerful, and voters had greater scope of choice. The latter cases suggest that processes during the peace implementation period helped demilitarize politics prior to elections, allowing postconflict elections to better serve the purposes of long-term peacebuilding and democratization. The next section of this study will investigate these processes to demilitarize politics.

Notes

1. Leonard Wantchekon, "On the Nature of First Democratic Elections," *Journal of Conflict Resolution* 43:2 (April 1999): 245–258.

2. A similar pattern was evident in the 2002 elections in Sierra Leone, where the parties most associated with the war (the Revolutionary United Front Party and the Peace and Liberation Party) fared poorly while the incumbent Sierra Leone People's Party won in a landslide because voters perceived it as having delivered on its promises to end the war. See Jimmy D. Kandeh, "Sierra Leone's Post-Conflict Elections of 2002," *Journal of Modern African Studies* 41:2 (2003): 189–216.

3. David Keen, *The Economic Functions of Violence in Civil Wars* (London: International Institute for Strategic Studies, Adelphi Paper 320, 1998), p. 31.

4. Marina Ottaway, "Rebuilding State Institutions in Collapsed States," *Development and Change* 33:5 (2002): 1001–1023.

5. For background, see Margaret Joan Antsee, *Orphan of the Cold War: The Inside Story of the Collapse of the Angolan Peace Process, 1992–93* (New York: St. Martin's Press, 1996); Alex Vines, *One Hand Tied: Angola and the UN* (London: Catholic Institute for International Relations Briefing Paper, June 1993); and Marina Ottaway, "Angola's Failed Elections," in Krishna Kumar, ed., *Postconflict Elections, Democratization, and International Assistance* (Boulder, Colo.: Lynne Rienner, 1998).

6. Antsee, *Orphan of the Cold War,* p. 67.

7. Dennis C. Jett, *Why Peacekeeping Fails* (New York: Palgrave, 2001), pp. 104–108.

8. Antsee, *Orphan of the Cold War,* p. 88, citing UNITA foreign secretary Abel Chivukuvuku.

9. Robert E. Henderson and Edward B. Stewart, *UNITA After the Cease-Fire: The Emergence of a Party* (Washington, D.C.: National Republican Institute for International Affairs, June 17, 1991), p. 9.

10. Revelations in January 1992 that UNITA leaders Tito Chingunji and Wilson dos Santos and their families had been executed a few months earlier increased perceptions of UNITA as a violent organization based around a cult of personality surrounding Savimbi. See "Politics of Vengeance and Victory for UNITA," *Africa Confidential* 33:13 (July 3, 1992), p. 2.

11. Kenneth B. Noble, "Election Makes Skeptics of Angolans," *New York Times,* June 28, 1992, p. A8.

12. Vines, *One Hand Tied,* p. 6. One analyst wrote, "On the one hand, the MPLA is seen as corrupt, bureaucratic, incompetent, and largely played out. On the other, UNITA is regarded as brutal, uncouth, tribalist and, perversely, more totalitarian that the *soi-disant* socialist MPLA ever managed to be." "Angola: Two Elephants Fight," *Africa Confidential* 33:13 (July 3, 1992): 1.

13. John A. Marcum, "Angola: War Again," *Current History* (May 1993): 219.

14. Ibid., p. 220. See also Anthony W. Pereira, "The Neglected Tragedy: The Return to War in Angola," *Journal of Modern African Studies* 32:1 (March 1994): 1–28.

15. "Angola: Luanda Shoot Out," *Africa Confidential* 33:22 (November 6, 1992): 8.

16. Virginia Page Fortna, "Success and Failure in Southern Africa: Peacekeeping in Namibia and Angola," in Donald C.F. Daniel and Bradd C. Hayes, eds., *Beyond Traditional Peacekeeping* (New York: St. Martin's Press, 1995), p. 293. Ottaway details the damage done by the elections: "Far from constituting a valuable first experience with democracy, the 1992 elections traumatized the country. They taught the population that elections can lead to greater violence; that they are a less effective source of power than weapons; and that the people's choice is ultimately meaningless because leaders do not respect it." Ottaway, "Angola's Failed Elections," p. 150.

17. Fen Osler Hampson, *Nurturing Peace: Why Peace Settlements Succeed or Fail* (Washington, D.C.: United States Institute of Peace Press, 1996), p. 88.

18. Quoted in Noble, "Election Makes Skeptics of Angolans," p. A8. See also Antsee, *Orphan of the Cold War,* p. 223.

19. Antsee, *Orphan of the Cold War,* p. 529.

20. International Crisis Group, *Elections in Bosnia and Herzegovina,* September 22, 1996, www.intl-crisis-group.org/projects/bosnia/reports/bh16rep1.htm.

21. Cited in Susan L. Woodward, "Bosnia and Herzegovina: How Not to End Civil War," in Barbara F. Walter and Jack Snyder, eds., *Civil Wars, Insecurity, and Intervention* (New York: Columbia University Press, 1999), p. 96.

22. Donald Horowitz, *Ethnic Groups in Conflict* (Berkeley: University of California Press, 1985), p. 340.

23. The Joint List won less than 5 percent in the September 1996 elections for the Bosnian State Parliament. See David Chandler, *Bosnia: Faking Democracy After Dayton,* 2nd ed. (London: Pluto Press, 2000), p. 70. The Joint List did better in the local elections of September 1997. In Tuzla,

Bosnia's second-largest city, where multiethnic institutions protected minorities during the war, Mayor Selim Beslagic of the Joint List defeated the nationalist SDA candidate. See Bill Egbert, "A Noble Act of Harmony in the Balkans," *Christian Science Monitor,* October 9, 1997.

24. Steven L. Burg and Paul S. Shoup, *The War in Bosnia-Herzegovina: Ethnic Conflict and International Intervention* (Armonk, N.Y.: M. E. Sharpe, 1999), p. 57. See also Elizabeth M. Cousens and Charles K. Cater, *Toward Peace in Bosnia: Implementing the Dayton Accords* (Boulder, Colo.: Lynne Rienner for the International Peace Academy, 2001), p. 18.

25. Ljiljana Smajlović, "From the Heart of the Heart of the Former Yugoslavia," *Wilson Quarterly* 19:3 (Summer 1995):100–113. See also Woodward, "Bosnia and Herzegovina," p. 77.

26. Radivoje Budalic and Mark Wheeler, "Press War by Other Means," *War Report* 42 (June 1996).

27. Paul Shoup, "The Elections in Bosnia and Herzegovina: The End of an Illusion," *Problems of Postcommunism* (January-February 1997): 9.

28. Lenard J. Cohen, "Bosnia and Herzegovina: Fragile Peace in a Segmented State," *Current History* (March 1996): 112.

29. International Crisis Group, *Elections in Bosnia and Herzegovina.*

30. Shoup, "The Elections in Bosnia and Herzegovina," p. 9. On non-nationalist voting in the 1997 municipal elections, see Michael Pugh and Margaret Cobble, "Non-Nationalist Voting in Bosnian Municipal Elections: Implications for Democracy and Peacebuilding," *Journal of Peace Research* 38:1 (2001): 27–47.

31. Cited in International Crisis Group, *Elections in Bosnia and Herzegovina,* p. 23. See also Ian Fisher, "Abuse of Bosnia Election Rules Is Alleged," *New York Times,* August 24, 1996, p. A6.

32. See, for example, *Report from the Observation of the Elections in Bosnia and Herzegovina, 14 September 1996* (Oslo: The Norwegian Helsinki Committee, October 1996), pp. 3, 10, www.sol.no/dnh/bosnia.htm.

33. International Crisis Group, *Elections in Bosnia and Herzegovina.*

34. Cousens and Cater, *Toward Peace in Bosnia,* p. 115.

35. Elizabeth M. Cousens, "Building Peace in Bosnia," in Elizabeth M. Cousens and Chetan Kumar, with Karin Wermester, eds., *Peacebuilding as Politics: Cultivating Peace in Fragile Societies* (Boulder, Colo.: Lynne Rienner for the International Peace Academy, 2001), p. 132.

36. Steven Erlanger, "Bosnian Elections to Go Ahead in '96, Christoper Says," *New York Times,* June 3, 1996, p. A1.

37. Susan L. Woodward, statement to the House Committee on International Relations Hearing on the Prospects for Free and Fair Elections in Bosnia, June 11, 1996.

38. "The Elections in Bosnia and Herzegovina, 14 September 1996: Preliminary Statement of the Co-ordinator for International Monitoring (CIM)," OSCE press release, September 14, 1996.

39. International Crisis Group, *Elections in Bosnia and Herzegovina.* See also Anna Husarska, "Bosnian Elections: The 103.9% Solution," *Wall Street Journal,* October 3, 1996, p. 14; Chris Bennett, "Voting Early, Voting

Often," Institute for War and Peace Reporting, October 1996, www.iwpr.net/index.pl?archive/war/war_46_199610_02.txt.

40. "The Elections in Bosnia and Herzegovina, 14 September 1996: Preliminary Statement of the Co-ordinator for International Monitoring (CIM)," OSCE press release, September 14, 1996. Cited in International Crisis Group, *Elections in Bosnia and Herzegovina.*

41. Shoup, "The Elections in Bosnia and Herzegovina," p. 10.

42. See Susan L. Woodward, "Bosnia After Dayton: Year Two," Current History 96:608 (March 1997): 97.

43. Burg and Shoup, *The War in Bosnia-Herzegovina,* p. 385.

44. Susan L. Woodward, "Implementing Peace in Bosnia and Herzegovina: A Post-Dayton Primer and Memorandum of Warning," (Washington, D.C.: Brookings Institution Press, May 1996), p. 55.

45. Senad Advic, "The Limits of the Landslide," Institute for War and Peace Reporting, October 1996, www.iwpr.net/index.pl?archive/war/war_46_199610_01.txt.

46. Chandler, *Bosnia,* pp. 154–180.

47. Anthony Borden, Slavenka Drakulic, and George Kenny, "Bosnia's Democratic Charade," *Nation* 263:8 (September 23, 1996): 14.

48. James A. Schear, "Bosnia's Post-Dayton Traumas," *Foreign Policy* 104 (Fall 1996): 96.

49. "Bosnia: Market Shimmer," *Economist,* September 7–13, 1996, p. 48.

50. David Rieff, "The Case Against the Serb War Criminals," *Washington Post,* September 8, 1996, p. C1.

51. Cited in Chandler, *Bosnia,* pp. 111–112.

52. This section draws from Terrence Lyons, *Voting for Peace: Postconflict Elections in Liberia* (Washington, D.C.: Brookings Institution Press, 1999). See also Adekeye Adebajo, *Liberia's Civil War: Nigeria, ECO- MOG, and Regional Security in West Africa* (Boulder, Colo.: Lynne Rienner, 2002).

53. Friends of Liberia, "Liberia: Opportunities and Obstacles for Peace," unpublished report, December 1996. See also Victor Tanner, "Liberia: Railroading Peace," *Review of African Political Economy* 25 (March 1998): 133–147.

54. The decision to disallow refugee voting was popular not only in neighboring states anxious to repatriate refugees but among most Liberians, who feared fraud in the camps. See Denis Gallagher and Anna Schowengerdt, "Refugees and Elections: A Separate Peace" (Washington, D.C.: Refugee Policy Group, 1997).

55. Tanner, "Liberia," p. 140.

56. For example, anti-Taylor posters with pictures of the brutalities of the war and the caption "Chuck [Charles Taylor] Did It" served to increase the levels of fear and raise anew concerns that the civilian candidates would not be able to prevent him from doing it again. "Chuck Did It" was a slogan that appeared on NPFL T-shirts during the war. See Bill Berkeley, *The Graves Are Not Yet Full: Race, Tribe, and Power in the Heart of Africa* (New York: Basic Books, 2001), p. 52.

57. "Liberia: Wooing Warriors," *Economist*, July 12, 1997, p. 40. See also Tina Susman, "Liberia Race Between Woman, Warlord," Associated Press, July 18, 1997.

58. "Interview with Samuel Kofi Woods of Liberia," *African Affairs* 99 (2000): 107.

59. Stephen Ellis, *The Mask of Anarchy: The Destruction of Liberia and the Religious Dimensions of an African Civil War* (New York: New York University Press, 1999), p. 109. Such characterizations were featured in a number of press reports on the election. A Liberian was quoted as saying, "He [Taylor] killed my father but I'll vote for him. He started all this and he's going to fix it." John Chiahemen, "Liberians Vote in Peace Against War," Reuters, July 19, 1997. Another voter is quoted as saying, "Charles Taylor spoiled this country, so he's the best man to fix it." Donald G. McNeil Jr., "Under Scrutiny, Postwar Liberia Goes to Polls," *New York Times*, July 20, 1997.

60. Organization for Security and Cooperation in Europe (OSCE), Office for Democratic Institutions and Human Rights (ODIHR), *The Republic of Tajikistan Elections to the Parliament, 27 February 2000: Final Report* (Warsaw, May 17, 2000).

61. Human Rights Watch, *Human Rights Watch Press Backgrounder on Tajikistan*, October 5, 2001, www.hrw.org/backgrounder/eca/tajikbkg1005.htm. Rafis Abazov, "Battling in Peace," Tajikistan Annual Report 1999, http://archive/tol.ca/countries/tajar99.html. The IRP leader Davlat Usmonov, who was put on the ballot against his wishes, claimed that the results had been falsified in the "Soviet tradition." See BBC, "Tajik Election Victory Is Challenged," November 7, 1999; Nasrin Dadmehr, "Tajikistan: Regionalism and Weakness," in Robert I. Rotberg, ed., *State Failure and State Weakness in a Time of Terror* (Washington D.C.: Brookings Institution Press for the World Peace Foundation, 2003).

62. OSCE/ODIHR, *The Republic of Tajikistan*, pp. 1, 22. See also OSCE/ODIHR, "Joint Statement Issued on Tajikistan Parliamentary Elections," press release, February 28, 2000. The United Nations concluded that the election "did not meet minimum standards." *Interim Report of the Secretary-General on the Situation in Tajikistan*, S/2000/214, March 14, 2000, para. 10.

63. Quoted in International Crisis Group, *Tajikistan: An Uncertain Peace* (ICG Asia Report no. 30, December 24, 2001), p. 3.

64. United Nations, *Interim Report of the Secretary-General on the Situation in Tajikistan*.

65. Ibid.

66. OSCE/ODIHR, *The Republic of Tajikistan*, pp. 1, 22. See also OSCE/ODIHR, "Joint Statement Issued on Tajikistan Parliamentary Elections." The United Nations concluded that the election "did not meet minimum standards." *Interim Report of the Secretary-General on the Situation in Tajikistan*, para. 10.

67. An international aid worker claimed in 1998 that "the problem is that the country is run by a government of six men and one figurehead, who have no control over the troops, the militias, and the various mafias." Cited

in Lucian Kim, "Bringing Peace to Tajikistan's Mountain Fiefdoms," *Christian Science Monitor,* September 15, 1998, www.csmonitor.com/durable/1998/09/15/p6s1.htm.

68. International Crisis Group, *Central Asia: Crisis Conditions in Three States* (ICG Asia Report no. 7, August 7, 2000).

69. For background on the postconflict elections in Cambodia, see Frederick Z. Brown, "Cambodia's Rocky Venture in Democracy," in Krishna Kumar, ed., *Postconflict Elections, Democratization, and International Assistance* (Boulder, Colo.: Lynne Rienner, 1998); David W. Roberts, *Political Transition in Cambodia, 1991–99: Power, Elitism, and Democracy* (New York: St. Martin's Press, 2001); Steve Heder and Judy Ledgerwood, eds., *Propaganda, Politics, and Violence in Cambodia: Democratic Transition Under United Nations Peace-Keeping* (Armonk, N.Y.: M. E. Sharpe, 1996); Pierre P. Lizée, *Peace, Power, and Resistance in Cambodia: Global Governance and the Failure of International Conflict Resolution* (New York: Palgrave Macmillan, 2000).

70. Steven R. Ratner, "The United Nations in Cambodia: A Model for Resolution of Internal Conflicts?" in Lori Fisler Damrosch, ed., *Enforcing Restraint: Collective Intervention in Internal Conflicts* (New York: Council on Foreign Relations, 1993), p. 248.

71. Brown, "Cambodia's Rocky Venture in Democracy," p. 92.

72. John M. Sanderson, "UNTAC: The Military Component View," in *Conference Papers,* IPS/UNITAR International Conference on the United Nations Transitional Authority in Cambodia: Debriefing and Lessons, Singapore, August 2–4, 1994 (Geneva: UNITAR, December 1994), p. 80, cited in Jianwei Wang, *Managing Arms in Peace Processes: Cambodia* (Geneva: United Nations Institute for Disarmament Research, 1996), p. 67.

73. Roberts, *Political Transition in Cambodia, 1991–99,* pp. 77–78. Findlay wrote that the election campaign was "marred by numerous violent incidents, murders, intimidation and undemocratic practices . . . mostly perpetuated by . . . government personnel." Trevor Findlay, *Cambodia: The Legacy and Lessons of UNTAC,* SIPRI Research Report No. 9 (Oxford: Oxford University Press, 1995), p. 75.

74. See S/RES/783 (1992) in UN Bluebook; Jianwei Wang, *Managing Arms in Peace Processes: Cambodia* (Geneva: United Nations Institute for Disarmament Research, 1996), p. 23.

75. Heder and Ledgerwood, "The Politics of Violence: An Introduction," in Steve Heder and Judy Ledgerwood, eds., *Propaganda, Politics, and Violence in Cambodia: Democratic Transition Under United Nations Peace-Keeping* (Armonk, N.Y.: M. E. Sharpe, 1996), p. 26.

76. Kate Frieson, "The Politics of Getting the Vote in Cambodia," in Steve Heder and Judy Ledgerwood, eds., *Propaganda, Politics, and Violence in Cambodia: Democratic Transition Under United Nations Peacekeeping* (Armonk, N.Y.: M. E. Sharpe, 1996), p. 184.

77. Sorpong Peou, *Conflict Neutralization in the Cambodia War* (Kuala Lumpur: Oxford University Press, 1997), p. 69.

78. B. A. Brown, "Cambodia's Shaky Step," *Freedom Review* 24:4

(July-August 1993), cited in Roberts, *Political Transition in Cambodia, 1991–99*, p. 73–74. Um also concluded that the use of violence by the CPP and Khmer Rouge "served to reinforce the need for a third alternative" and hence support for Funcinpec. Khatharya Um, "Cambodia in 1993: Year Zero Plus One," *Asian Survey* 34:1 (January 1994): 75.

79. Judy Ledgerwood, "Patterns of CPP Political Repression and Violence During the UNTAC Period," in Steve Heder and Judy Ledgerwood, eds., *Propaganda, Politics, and Violence in Cambodia: Democratic Transition Under United Nations Peace-Keeping* (Armonk, N.Y.: M. E. Sharpe, 1996), pp. 117, 130.

80. Cited in Frieson, "The Politics of Getting the Vote in Cambodia," p. 200. Lizée argued that many Cambodians voted on the basis of a logic that "a FUNCINPEC victory would mean that Prince Sihanouk would return to power and that he would then bring peace to Cambodia by initiating a rapprochement between the four Cambodian factions." Lizée, *Peace, Power, and Resistance in Cambodia*, p. 125.

81. Heininger wrote, "It was a good thing the Phnom Penh administration expected to win. If it had not, it could have derailed the electoral process by stepping up its campaign of harassment and intimidation against opposition candidates. It might also have refused to cooperate with UNTAC, which could have caused the collapse of the peace process." Janet E. Heininger, *Peacekeeping in Transition: The United Nations in Cambodia* (New York: The Twentieth Century Fund Press, 1994), p. 113.

82. William Shawcross, "Tragedy in Cambodia," *New York Review of Books,* November 14, 1996.

83. United Nations, Report of the Secretary-General on the Conduct and Results of the Elections in Cambodia, UN document S/25913, June 10, 1993.

84. Roberts, *Political Transition in Cambodia, 1991–99*, p. 79.

85. Ibid., p. 32.

86. Cited in ibid., p. 112.

87. Charles T. Call, "Assessing El Salvador's Transition from Civil War to Peace," in Stephen John Stedman, Donald Rothchild, and Elizabeth M. Cousens, eds. *Ending Civil Wars: The Implementation of Peace Agreements* (Boulder, Colo.: Lynne Rienner, 2002), p. 408.

88. Tommie Sue Montgomery, *Revolution in El Salvador: From Civil Strife to Civil Peace,* 2nd ed. (Boulder, Colo.: Westview Press, 1995), p. 253.

89. Tommie Sue Montgomery, "Getting to Peace in El Salvador: The Roles of the United Nations Secretariat and ONUSAL," *Journal of Interamerican Studies and World Affairs* 37:4 (Winter 1995): 153; Tommie Sue Montgomery with Ruth Reitan, "The Good, the Bad, and the Ugly: Observing Elections in El Salvador," in Tommie Sue Montgomery, ed., *Peacemaking and Democratization in the Western Hemisphere* (Miami, Fla.: University of Miami North-South Center Press, 2000), pp. 139–163.

90. Richard Stahler-Sholk, "El Salvador's Negotiated Transition: From Low-Intensity Conflict to Low-Intensity Democracy," *Journal of Interamerican Studies and World Affairs* 36:4 (1994): 24.

91. Montgomery and Reitan, "The Good, the Bad, and the Ugly," p. 142.

92. Terry Lynne Karl, "Imposing Consent? Electoralism vs. Democratization in El Salvador," in Paul Drake and Eduardo Silva, eds., *Elections and Democratization in Latin America, 1980–85* (San Diego, Calif.: CLAS/Center for U.S.-Mexican Studies, 1986).

93. Report of the Secretary-General on the United Nations Observer Mission in El Salvador, UN document S/26606, October 20, 1993, para 10.

94. Stahler-Sholk, "El Salvador's Negotiated Transition," p. 25.

95. Montgomery, *Revolution in El Salvador,* p. 253.

96. Ian Johnstone, *Rights and Reconciliation: UN Strategies in El Salvador* (Boulder, Colo.: Lynne Rienner for the International Peace Academy, 1995), pp. 52–53.

97. Stahler-Sholk, "El Salvador's Negotiated Transition," p. 30; Elisabeth Jean Wood, *Forging Democracy from Below: Insurgent Transitions in South Africa and El Salvador* (Cambridge: Cambridge University Press, 2000), p. 105.

98. David Holiday and William Stanley, "Under the Best of Circumstances: ONUSAL and the Challenges of Verification and Institution Building in El Salvador," in Tommie Sue Montgomery, ed., *Peacemaking and Democratization in the Western Hemisphere* (Miami, Fla.: University of Miami North-South Center Press, 2000), p. 43.

99. Montgomery, "Getting to Peace in El Salvador," p. 155.

100. Montgomery, *Revolution in El Salvador,* p. 266.

101. Jack Spence, David Dye, and George Vickers, *El Salvador: Elections of the Century* (Cambridge, Mass.: Hemisphere Initiatives, July 1994).

102. Cameron Hume, *Ending Mozambique's War* (Washington, D.C.: United States Institute of Peace, 1994), p. 138.

103. Martinho Chachiua and Mark Malan, "Anomalies and Acquiescence: The Mozambican Peace Process Revisited," *African Security Review* 7:4 (1998): 24.

104. Quoted in Jim Wurst, "Mozambique: Peace and More," *World Policy Journal* 11:3 (Fall 1994): 80. Secretary-General Boutros Boutros-Ghali stated that "in light of the recent experiences in Angola, I believe it to be of critical importance that the elections should not take place until the military aspects of the agreement have been fully implemented." Cited in "Mozambique Accords Aid Relief Effort," *Africa Recovery* (December 1992–February 1993): 25.

105. "Mozambique: The Freelance Warriors," *Africa Confidential* 33:19 (September 23, 1994): 3. Dennis C. Jett, *Why Peacekeeping Fails* (New York: Palgrave, 2001), pp. 103–104; Chris Alden, *Mozambique and the Construction of the New African State: From Negotiations to Nation Building* (New York: Palgrave, 2001).

106. Carrie Manning, *The Politics of Peace in Mozambique: Post-Conflict Democratization, 1992–2000.* (Westport, Conn.: Praeger, 2002), pp. 141–142; "Mozambique: The People for Peace," *Africa Confidential* 35:22 (November 4, 1994): 1; "Skeptical and Confused, Mozambicans Prepare to

Vote," *New York Times*, September 27, 1994, p. A15; Keith B. Richburg, "Mozambique Vote Turnout Could Signal New Stability: High Participation Defies Predictions of Apathy," *Washington Post*, October 31, 1994, p. A19.

107. Alden, *Mozambique and the Construction of the New African State*, p. 64. Geoffrey Wood and Richard Haines, "Tentative Steps Towards Multi-Partyism in Mozambique," *Party Politics* 4:1 (1998): 107–118.

108. Bill Keller, "Mozambican Elections Thrown in Doubt," *New York Times*, October 28, 1994, p. A6; Keith B. Richburg, "Ex-Rebel Group's Withdrawal Mars Mozambique's 1st Multi-Party Vote: Pullout on Eve of Election Stirs Fears of Renewed Civil War," *Washington Post*, October 28, 1994, p. A33.

109. Robert D. Lloyd, "Mozambique: The Terror of War, the Tensions of Peace," *Current History* 94:591 (April 1995): 154; Dan Isaacs, "Mozambique: Fulfilling a Dream," *Africa Report* 40:1 (January 1995): 13–21; Carolyn Nordstrom, *A Different Kind of War Story* (Philadelphia: University of Pennsylvania Press, 1997), pp. 226–227.

110. Keith B. Richburg, "Mozambique Ex-Rebel Joins Vote: Chief U.N. Envoy Promises Full Investigation of 'Irregularities,'" *Washington Post*, October 29, 1994, p. A25.

111. Lloyd, "Mozambique," p. 155.

112. Alex Vines, *Renamo: From Terrorism to Democracy in Mozambique?* (London: James Currey, 1996), p. 159. As noted, Renamo won 45 percent of the parliament seats while Dhlakama won only 34 percent of the vote for the presidency.

4

Building New
Political Institutions

Postconflict elections without prior processes to demilitarize politics take place in environments still distorted by the legacies of fear and in which the institutions of war remain strong. Such elections therefore often fail to encourage transitions to lasting peace and democratization and instead result in either consolidation of an authoritarian order or resurgence of deadly conflict. Some scholars have advocated that postconflict elections should be held much later in the transitional process, that powersharing pacts should be negotiated prior to elections to manage the uncertainty of the transition, or that electoral rules should be drafted to encourage inclusive regimes. Pacts, powersharing, and electoral rules, however, require a degree of confidence in the process that often is lacking in these cases, and international guarantees are often not credible to parties emerging from protracted conflict. If politics has not been demilitarized, additional time, pacts, and electoral systems are unlikely to be sufficient to overcome the legacies of fear.

Institutions to Shape Postconflict Electoral Behavior

The timing of postconflict elections shapes their capacity to promote the dual goals of war termination and democratization. In some cases the pace of implementation may be different for these two distinct challenges. Democratization requires time and will be encouraged by a slower pace of change that places elections at the end of a sequence of events such as demobilizing and reintegrating combatants, repatriating refugees and displaced people, and rebuilding the basis of a functioning state.[1] War termination may require a more rapid tempo to obtain the consent of the warring parties, build momentum from a cease-fire, and assure sufficient participation by international peace-keepers and donors. Rothstein noted this tension and stated that "measures such as phased implementation, close supervision of terms (or high initial standards), starting with small pilot projects, and clear and powerful sanctions for violations are perfectly sensible and may succeed in diminishing the risk of catastrophic, worst-case outcomes; but they may also delay the achievement of the kind of rapid, substantive benefits that are necessary to build support for an agreement and to avoid a rapid descent into disillusionment and bitterness."[2] Waiting too long may lead to the collapse of the peace process and a return to war rather than to better elections. Policies relating to demobilization, repatriation, human rights, and reconstruction—and indeed, democratization—may need to wait until after some minimal agreement has been implemented and the fighting ended. To insist that postconflict elections be delayed until the enabling environment of democratization is in place risks missing opportunities to assist war termination, a necessary first step for democratization.

In several cases it seems unlikely that additional time would have improved prospects for a more democratic outcome and quite possibly might have derailed the peace process. In Angola a longer transition that did not change the fundamental flaws of the peace process or construct a strategy to contain Savimbi's threat as a spoiler probably would not have changed the outcome. The shortcomings of the Bosnian election were tied fundamentally to the Dayton Accords and international policy and also would not have been changed substantially by delay.[3] In Liberia the dysfunctional nature of the interim institutions and the unwillingness of the regional peacekeepers or the broader international community to support a longer transition made holding elections quickly after the cease-fire imperative. Although some analysts suggested that the quick elections favored Taylor, his superior resources gave him the ability to hold his political organization together over a longer period of time than his rivals, suggesting that he would have won a postponed election as well.[4] It is at least highly uncertain that later elections in these difficult postconflict cases would have made a democratic outcome more likely unless politics had been demilitarized during the additional time.

Some of the literature on political transitions suggests that the best way to manage conflicts in the context of breakthrough elections is to negotiate powersharing arrangements or political pacts to construct the broadest possible coalition in government. Political pacts are a set of negotiated compromises among competing elites prior to elections that distribute power and thereby reduce uncertainty.[5] A number of transitions in Latin America, the Round Table talks in Poland, and the Convention for a Democratic South Africa process were organized around implicit or explicit agreements designed to provide powerful actors with sufficient guarantees that they would accept the change.

Pacts, however, ultimately rely upon other mechanisms for enforcement and do not by themselves end uncertainty or resolve the difficulty in making credible commitments.[6] Pacts are more likely among elites with relatively clear and loyal constituencies, such as traditional political parties, labor unions, or other institutions in a corporatist setting. In the aftermath of a protracted civil war, such political and social organizations generally are absent and the ability of military leaders to deliver the compliance of even their own fighters is often questionable. In addition, the polarization and extreme distrust arising from the conflict will make such pacts more difficult if not impossible to negotiate. Finally, the ability to assess the political power of a military faction is difficult, and the identity of the critical constituencies to include in a pact is unclear immediately following a conflict. Even if the military balance among factions is relatively clear (as indicated by a stalemate on the battlefield), the relative political power of these factions and the extent to which they are capable of representing significant civilian constituencies in peacetime may be unknown.[7] Unless there is demilitarization of politics, a pact will be difficult to negotiate and unlikely to hold or may even serve to entrench the militarized institutions made powerful by the war.

The ability to assess the relative strengths of parties and thereby create a formula for a powersharing pact is inherently difficult in the context of postconflict elections. Many observers expected UNITA to win the Angola elections, and many others were surprised by the ability of the National Patriotic Party in Liberia, Renamo in Mozambique, Funcinpec in Cambodia, and the FMLN in El Salvador to win significant votes. It is notable that the best examples of powersharing pacts took place *after* postconflict elections, when the relative political power of the parties was clearer. In Nicaragua the Sandinistas negotiated control over the military, and in Cambodia the CPP forced a powersharing arrangement following the elections when relative political power was more apparent.

In addition, putting pressure on parties to negotiate a powersharing pact prior to elections may put the peace agreement and cease-fire at risk. Parties often accept a cease-fire and agree to hold elections in the expectation that they will win the vote and gain power. Such parties will resist additional constraints imposed after the peace agreement, preferring to compete in a winner-take-all election. The Carter Center tried to engage Charles Taylor in discussions of post-election powersharing in Liberia, but Taylor refused, perceiving (correctly) that such an agreement would limit his power after he won. In Angola and Mozambique as well, the international community pressed the parties to agree to powersharing in a government of national unity, but the parties refused.[8] Even when a powerful international implementation force compelled powersharing in Bosnia-Herzegovina, parties to that conflict simply refused to cooperate in the establishment of the new multiethnic and interentity institutions.[9] In the difficult circumstances following protracted civil war, a powersharing pact, while desirable, is likely to be impossible without placing the entire peace process at risk.

A substantial body of literature analyzes the relationship of electoral system choice to the potential for conflict.[10] Sisk and Reynolds concluded that "electoral systems—the rules and procedures under which votes are translated into seats in parliament or the selection of executives—are a critical variable in determining whether elections can simultaneously serve the purposes of democratization and conflict management."[11] The electoral rules of the game will shape the strategic decisionmaking of key leaders, convincing some that accepting democratic competition is the best way to assure at least a voice in policymaking. Proportional representation systems are generally regarded as more suitable for societies that are divided because they more often create broad, inclusive governments. Other schemes designed to overcome social cleavages involve various types of vote pooling and federalism.[12] Some advocate consociational systems that emphasize accommodation by ethnic group leaders at the political center combined with guarantees of group autonomy and minority rights (as in Belgium, Lebanon, and Bosnia).[13] Others promote integrative powersharing arrangements that are designed to encourage cross-ethnic alliances (as in South Africa).[14] Like powersharing pacts, however, electoral systems generally fail to overcome the security dilemmas and fears that drive postconflict transitions.

It is difficult to imagine what type of electoral system would increase the attractiveness of a postconflict election to competing parties in the immediate aftermath of civil war. Stedman has argued that "Savimbi and UNITA received more from the Angolan settlement than any of the losing parties in El Salvador, Mozambique, Nicaragua, and Zimbabwe received in theirs."[15] Yet Savimbi defected from the agreement after losing the election. The political and economic structures of many postconflict states are such that even an offer of local or regional leadership positions is unlikely to be sufficient to a party that lost the election for national leadership. Most resources, and international aid in particular, flow through the capital and are under the control of the national executive, making the position of regional governor or mayor a weak power base. Renamo decided not to compete in 1998 local elections in Mozambique in part because it perceived that such posts were unimportant and subject to budget allocations under the control of its rival in Maputo.[16] Seats in a parliament or even cabinet positions meant little to the opposition in Liberia, given the strong presidential system enshrined in the Liberian constitution.

Incentives, Opportunities, and the Demilitarization of Politics

The organizations (insurgents, militarized governments) that enter into a peace process respond to incentives and rationally assess options with regard to which best promise to assure their organizational survival.[17] As Shugart has argued, "decisions by regime and rebel leaders alike to seek a democratic 'exit' from a conflict are based upon rational calculations of the possibilities and limitations inherent in playing the competitive electoral game versus continuing the armed conflict."[18] Nancy Bermeo pointed out that "elites in emerging, post-war democracies face a double challenge. On the one hand, they must raise the costs of violent competition. On the other hand, they must lower the costs of electoral competition. The probability of stable democracy is a function of both these processes and the many variables that drive them."[19] This challenge is true both for

leaders and for organizations. If perceptible progress on demilitarizing politics takes place during the transitional peace implementation
period leading to elections, then key decision-makers will alter their
strategies and pursue electoral rather than military opportunities.

The manner by which interim institutions and new norms are
established to manage the peace implementation period will create
precedents, expectations, and patterns of behavior that will shape
how politics function after the election. In some cases institutions
built around collaborative decisionmaking, transparency, and confidence-building managed the implementation process.[20] In
Mozambique, for example, the two formerly warring sides engaged
in joint decision-making processes on issues such as the electoral
system and worked together to monitor the cease-fire and demobilization.[21] Similar institutions operated in El Salvador and to a
degree in Cambodia. In Angola, in contrast, the two parties rarely
met during the interim, and the transition was marked by suspicion
and bad faith during the failed demobilization process. The interim
administration during the implementation phase in Liberia similarly
was stalemated due to the division of power among the warring factions. The manner in which interim institutions operate will influence
whether postconflict elections move a war-torn state toward peace
and democratization.

Demilitarizing of politics has two interlinked aspects. The
process entails building institutions capable of supporting democratization, such as effective, credible interim regimes (particularly electoral authorities), and transforming or replacing militarized organizations by building strong political parties and joint decision-making
bodies to manage the demobilization and security sector reform
process. These processes increase and make more credible the
rewards for participating in and accepting outcomes of electoral
competition. In addition, demilitarization of politics entails restruc-
turing of the security apparatus through demobilization and the construction of new, accountable armed forces and police. If done well,
these processes decrease both the incentives and the capacity to
return to war. These two aspects are interlinked, and progress on one
encourages progress in the other. For example, building effective
political parties increases the prospects for demobilization as groups
perceive that they can protect their interests through a political rather
than a military means. Processes to demilitarize politics both
increase the incentives to play by the rules of nonviolent electoral

competition and decrease the incentives to seek power by engaging in violence.

Interim Institutions

Interim institutions are critical arenas in which ex-combatant and potential civilian leaders assess whether the postconflict environment can protect their interests and whether the democratization process warrants their support. The administration of the electoral process includes tasks at the heart of the peace implementation process and provides critical opportunities for interim regimes to establish the norms, precedents, and institutions needed to start the demilitarization of politics. In some cases, interim regimes have been built around joint decisionmaking bodies that foster confidence-building and a new institutional context that can move competition toward a path of democracy and peace. This type of transition took place in El Salvador and Mozambique and to some extent in Cambodia. In other cases interim regimes have failed to promote the demilitarization of politics, leading either to renewed conflict, as in Angola, or electoral ratification of wartime institutions and leaders, as in Bosnia-Herzegovina, Liberia, and Tajikistan.

Interim governments derive their legitimacy and authority from the extent to which they prepare the country for meaningful elections and turn power over to the winners.[22] In the meantime, the country needs to be governed. In the period between the signing of the cease-fire and the swearing in of a duly elected postconflict government, critical and contentious policy decisions relating to peace implementation in general and the electoral framework and demobilization in particular must be made. The process through which such policies are made will shape the expectations of the major actors and may either inspire confidence or ignite fears.

In many peace processes, such as the one in El Salvador, ad hoc temporary institutions have been established to oversee aspects of implementation, particularly of contentious issues such as electoral, security, and human rights issues, while the incumbent regime remained in place to administer day-to-day policies. In Angola, Mozambique, and Tajikistan the peace agreements envisioned the incumbent regimes expanding their administration to include areas previously under the control of the insurgents, although resistance from the insurgents and lack of governmental capacity often left implementation incomplete.

In other cases the international community played a larger administrative role during the transitional period or an entirely new interim regime assumed at least nominal authority. In Cambodia the United Nations assumed a large role in the administration of the state, although the incumbent CPP regime maintained its authority over many issues, in part due to the lack of UN capacity to manage day-to-day affairs. The large international presence in Bosnia-Herzegovina played a decisive role in managing key areas of administration, although the Dayton Accords left other areas under the authority of local, ethnically based institutions. In Liberia the peace process established an interim Council of State with representatives of the major warring factions charged with administering the country. The council was weak and polarized, leaving the United Nations and international nongovernmental organizations to manage the minimal functions of the state.

Interim administration may be extensive or limited and may have a greater or lesser involvement by the international community. The key question with regard to the process of demilitarization of politics is the roles these transitional mechanisms play in creating the incentives and opportunities for the transformation of wartime institutions into institutions that can support long-term peacebuilding. In some cases, such as Angola, Bosnia-Herzegovina, Liberia, and Tajikistan, the interim administration left the power of militarized organizations in place and largely unreconstructed, thereby reducing the incentives for such institutions to transform themselves into political organizations. In other cases, such as Mozambique, El Salvador, and Cambodia, the interim administration promoted institutional transformation by creating new opportunities and shifting incentives.

Interim Regimes That Reinforce the Institutions of War

In some cases the interim administration failed to promote the demilitarization of politics as a means to overcome the divisions and fears of the war and thus did little to encourage the institutional transformation of organizations made powerful by war. Angola, Liberia, Bosnia-Herzegovina, and Tajikistan demonstrate how weak implementation may create transitional arrangements that fail to build the confidence or provide the incentives that are associated with a transition to sustainable peacebuilding. In these cases the institutions and fears that arose in the context of war remained powerful throughout the transition, thereby limiting the ability of postconflict elections to initiate democratization. Weak and factionalized interim institutions encouraged actors to retain their military options and evade the demilitarization of politics.

Angola. Under the 1991 Angolan settlement, the Joint Political and Military Commission (CCPM) was charged with monitoring the demobilization of both the MPLA and UNITA and overseeing the creation of a unified armed force. The CCPM consisted of representatives of both parties, with representatives of the main states involved in negotiating the treaty (the so-called troika of Portugal, the United States, and the Soviet Union, later Russia) as observers. The small and underfunded United Nations Verification Mission (UNAVEM II) had a mandate to "verify the arrangements agreed by the two Angolan parties."[23] In effect, the peace agreement called on the parties to demobilize and prepare for elections, established the CCPM assisted by the troika as observers to monitor implementation, and charged the United Nations with the task of monitoring the monitors. Neither the Angolan parties nor the major international parties wanted a more robust role for the United Nations.[24]

The CCPM struggled to manage the transition and overcome the distrust between the two warring parties that composed it. Pro forma meetings did not change behavior or encourage institutional transformation and instead may have fostered a false sense of confidence in the parties' commitment to the agreement. UNITA walked out of the CCPM from time to time to draw attention to its charges of cheating by the MPLA, particularly with regard to demobilization and election preparations.[25] UNITA refused to participate in meetings to form an electoral commission or to attend a forum of all political parties to discuss voting preparations.[26] Savimbi remained in the bush with his soldiers and continually postponed his arrival in Luanda. In December 1991, nine months before the September 1992 elections, President dos Santos said that the CCPM was not capable "of resolving the problems the country is facing today within the framework of pacification and national democratization."[27]

Both UNITA and the MPLA maneuvered to gain or strengthen their hold on strategic towns and economic assets during the transitional period leading up to elections. UNITA probably had a stronger military posture on the eve of the election than it had when the peace agreement was signed.[28] Armed clashes were frequent. Demobilization failed, the military structures remained in place at the time of the elections, and war resumed immediately after the vote. The CCPM failed to demilitarize politics, and the main parties continued to follow the incentives of military competition.

Liberia. Under the Yamoussoukro, Cotonou, and Abuja Agreements in Liberia, interim administration was parceled out to each of the many factions with a weak and generally stalemated Council of State assigned the impossible job of coordination. The interim Liberian Council of State established by the final Abuja II Agreement consisted of representatives of the major warring factions along with representatives of civilian organizations without clear mandates. The transitional regime had a wide array of representatives but was deadlocked. The rival parties rarely engaged in multilateral talks regarding the administration of the interim period or to build a sense of confidence in the peace process. All rather sought to place loyalists in key locations within the bureaucracy, where they could tap into resources and patronage. The West African regional organization ECOWAS led efforts to assist peace implementation but was regarded with suspicion by many in Liberia and acted with little transparency. The United Nations Observer Mission in Liberia (UNOMIL) had a weak mandate and deferred to ECOWAS. The Liberian peace process therefore represented a minimal framework to end the fighting with little attention to building interim institutions capable of longer-term peacebuilding and democratization.[29] As in Angola, the transitional administration did little to demilitarize politics and instead reinforced the power of the militarized factions.

Bosnia-Herzegovina. Under the Dayton Accords in Bosnia-Herzegovina, a Joint Interim Commission that included the prime ministers of Bosnia-Herzegovina, the Bosniac-Croat Federation, and the Serb Republika Srpska met regularly, with the high representative of the international community as the chair. Under the agreement, however, state-level institutions such as the Joint Interim Commission were institutionally weaker than canton- and substate-level institutions that generally were ethnically homogeneous. The commission discussed a broad range of issues, but each entity responded to autonomous and often contradictory sets of political dynamics based in its own institutions, making cooperation difficult. Croatian institutions, for example, continued to be dominated by nationalist Croats from southwestern Bosnia who looked toward Zagreb rather than Sarajevo and who were committed to the "parastate" of Herzeg-Bosna they had established during the war. By the same token, Republika Srpska remained under the control of those determined to leave Bosnia-Herzegovina and unite with Serbia. The political agendas of the major actors were set within the three distinct entities rather than in the context of Bosnia-Herzegovina.[30] Bosnian leaders often delayed and obstructed the functioning of various offices. Even the Federation of Bosnia-Herzegovina formed by Bosniac Muslim leaders and Croatian leaders that predated the Dayton Agreement never functioned as envisioned. Incentives to retain militant nationalist strategies and pursue independent goals were more powerful than incentives to pursue political strategies based on accommodation within a multiethnic Bosnia-Herzegovina. Politicians who championed the respective nationalist causes of the three entities had more success than those who advocated multinational cooperation or supranational identity.

As the existing civil authorities failed to operate effectively, the international community increased its role, leading some to regard the international community in its various incarnations as operating a de facto protectorate. Each party continued to pursue unilateral advantage, thereby preventing effective forms of joint decisionmaking and leading the United Nations to act unilaterally and without the consent of local leaders on a number of contentious topics. Chandler argued that the unilateralism of the international community weakened local decisionmakers as the "cut and thrust of democratic consensus building, at the level of the tripartite Presidency, Council of Ministers and Parliamentary Assembly, was often seen as an unnecessary delay to vital policy implementation."[31] Encouraging interim institutions that operated on the basis of problem-solving and debate conflicted with key international goals regarding outcome.

Tajikistan. The June 1997 peace agreement in Tajikistan legalized opposition parties and established an interim powersharing formula between incumbent president Imomali Rakhmonov and his People's Democratic Party (PDP), the United Tajik Opposition (UTO) led by Sayed Abdullo Nuri, and the Islamic Renewal Party (IRP). The settlement established a Commission of National Reconciliation (CNR) that included both the government and the opposition and was chaired by Nuri. The CNR, however, failed to operate effectively and did little to demilitarize politics.

The first meeting of the CNR took place in Moscow, reflecting the fact that many opposition leaders were in exile. Subsequent meetings in Dushanbe and the return of exiled politicians represented a potential political opening. The CNR had four subcommissions on refugees, military, political, and legal issues, with two chaired by government representatives and two by opposition members.[32] The CNR was inclusive but operated in a nontransparent manner, thereby contributing to what Zoir and Newton called the "democratic deficit" of the transition.[33]

The implementation period was contentious, with a number of opposition parties banned, opposition members nominated to ministerial posts denied confirmation by the PDP-dominated parliament, and assassinations of leading opposition figures. Demobilization was delayed, the original timetable proved wildly unrealistic, and local warlords and criminal organizations retained significant military capacity.[34] The UTO periodically walked out of the CNR and regularly threatened to boycott elections. This chaotic interim period did little to promote the demilitarization of politics or to create incentives for the UTO or PDP to transform themselves into political organizations.

Summary. The cases of Angola, Liberia, Bosnia-Herzegovina, and Tajikistan demonstrate that weak interim administration that retains and reinforces the divisions created during the war generally fails to demilitarize politics or establish the conditions to encourage institutional transformation. Angola demonstrates that a peace implementation process may serve as the framework for rearming and strengthening the institutions of war as readily as an opportunity to demilitarize politics. As in earlier failed peace agreements in Liberia and cease-fires in numerous cases, the parties accepted a pause in the fighting for tactical reasons and in the belief that they would be better able to pursue their ends through unilateral military moves at a later date. In Liberia the dysfunctional interim government reinforced factionalism and failed to create opportunities for new institutions to develop. In Bosnia-Herzegovina each party to the conflict remained driven by the separate dynamics within their divided communities, with few institutions capable of bridging these divisions.

The Tajik peace process failed to provide a context for some of the warring parties to participate effectively in the interim administration, leaving them largely outside the governing process. In each of these cases, the interim administration did not alter the incentive structures sufficiently to transform the militarized organizations into political organizations.

Interim Administration to Demilitarize Politics

In contrast to Angola, Bosnia-Herzegovina, Liberia, and Tajikistan, the transitions in Cambodia, El Salvador, and Mozambique illustrate how interim institutions based on joint decisionmaking can demilitarize politics and thereby encourage transitions that advance both conflict resolution and democratization. Effective interim administration will create opportunities for collaboration and joint problem-solving, thereby promoting the bridging of wartime divisions and helping to overcome fears. Regular, ongoing discussions, often facilitated by a strong and respected third party, can build confidence in the peace process and create new norms and expectations of cooperation. As Doyle wrote, transitional authority must be constructed through "painstaking negotiation" and "endorsed through negotiated schemes of powersharing."[35]

Cambodia. In Cambodia the 1991 Paris Peace Accords established an elaborate set of overlapping institutions to administer the country during the peace implementation period. The complexity of these transitional structures reflected the fact that the question of who would govern during the interim was one of the most contentious issues during the negotiations. The Cambodian parties formed the Supreme National Council (SNC), which was designed to work with both an expansive United Nations Transitional Authority in Cambodia (UNTAC) and the incumbent, CPP-dominated bureaucracy.[36] The SNC consisted of twelve members: six from the CPP and two from each of the three insurgent functions (Funcinpec, the Khmer Rouge, and the Khmer People's National Liberation Front) and was chaired by Prince Norodom Sihanouk.[37] When the SNC could not reach an agreement by consensus, Prince Sihanouk had the authority to give advice to UNTAC, and UNTAC had the authority to act unilaterally. The SNC was something of a legal fiction, but because of the widespread authority and legitimacy possessed by

Sihanouk, it played an important role.[38] Prince Sihanouk, who had the charisma and traditional authority to call the Cambodian parties together and mediate disputes, undertook some of the most important consultations. The SNC continued to function even after the Khmer Rouge withdrew. Alongside the SNC, the international community had a number of roles in the interim administration. The United Nations special representative of the Secretary-General, Yasushi Akashi, acted as the final arbiter regarding whether SNC decisions adhered to the Paris Agreement. Representatives of the permanent members of the UN Security Council and other interested states and donors also had authority and pressed for collaborative decisionmaking.

This set of institutions contained a number of checks and balances, incentives for collaboration, and opportunities for a wide range of opinions to be heard. Doyle described this arrangement as an "ad hoc, semisovereign artificial body." Decisionmaking was cumbersome and slow, but regular consultations among this "circle of authority" helped manage unilateral actions that might have threatened any party.[39] These interim institutions, however, did not fully succeed in creating the neutral political atmosphere called for in the Paris Accord. The Khmer Rouge withdrew from the agreement, and the ruling CPP retained significant advantages of incumbency, enjoying "intrusive management of all aspects of state activity," from the army to local civil authorities in the provinces.[40]

El Salvador. In El Salvador the 1991 peace accords set up the National Commission for the Consolidation of Peace (Comisión Nacional para la Consolidación de la Paz, COPAZ), a body with representation evenly split between the government and its allies and the opposition, including the FMLN insurgents, with observer status for the United Nations and the Catholic Church. COPAZ was conceived as the major forum for verifying compliance and resolving disputes during the implementation of the peace agreements and was an important guarantee to the FMLN (since the insurgents did not have representation in the parliament at the time).[41] COPAZ debated and passed implementing legislation under the peace agreement, ranging from a new electoral law to constitutional amendments that redefined the role of the armed forces. Because the commission was evenly split between the government and the opposition, "hammering out compromises became a political necessity—and a newly acquired skill for many politicians."[42] When problems arose over the electoral system, over delays in reforming the police, or over the discovery of an FMLN arms cache after the deadline for disarmament, COPAZ was able to keep the parties talking and to keep the process moving toward elections.[43] The parties came to recognize that while the transition was uncertain, at least interim institutions in which they had an effective voice were managing their fears of losing everything. Wood captured the character of peace implementation in El Salvador: "The course of the implementation of the accords was determined by a process of political bargaining [whereby] . . . political actors hammered out agreements and concessions on the various issues that reflected the evolving balance of power among the contending interests."[44]

Mozambique. The implementation of the Rome Accord in Mozambique required more negotiation to finalize a wide range of critical operational issues. Hume suggested that because of the "defects in the agreements, the process of implementation would have to be constantly preceded or accompanied by a process of renegotiation."[45] Joint decisionmaking and monitoring bodies such as the Supervisory and Monitoring Commission (CSC) and the Cease-Fire Commission (CCF) brought together the major political actors with the major donors in a consultative process chaired by a resourceful special representative of the UN Secretary-General, Aldo Ajello. Other specialized joint commissions dealt with reintegration of ex-combatants, reform of the Mozambican defense forces, and preparations for the election.[46] These interim administrative organs privileged consensus and equality between Renamo and Frelimo based on their status as ex-combatants and signatories to the peace agreement. As a result, the CSC and other joint commissions became the arenas for political contestation between the two formerly warring parties between the time of the cease-fire and the postconflict election.[47]

The institutions did not function at the beginning of the interim period and developed their authority and effectiveness only as the implementation process unfolded. In March 1993 the work of the CSC and CCF stalled as Renamo's representatives left Maputo for consultations at their organization's headquarters in Marinque. Renamo constantly complained that it could not function in Maputo without logistical support in the form of offices; housing; and additional resources for transportation, communications, and other needs.

Frelimo similarly dragged its feet and resisted cooperation with either the UN peacekeeping mission or the joint commissions. In April 1993 a multiparty conference to discuss the new electoral law collapsed amid accusations. Finally the United Nations threatened to withdraw its peacekeeping operations and to end its support for the transition in Mozambique. The Mozambican parties, recognizing that working with the international community represented their best option, began to cooperate in the joint interim institutions. The new electoral law, for example, was passed in December 1993, and the new National Election Commission began to function in early 1994.[48] Thereafter, these interim institutions created the context for overcoming some of the legacies of the civil war, promoted the process of demilitarizing politics, and supported the dual transitions to peace and democracy.

Summary. Interim institutions responsible for administration during the period between a cease-fire agreement and elections to implement a peace accord have the opportunity to begin the process of demilitarizing politics. In El Salvador, Mozambique, and Cambodia such interim administration helped create the context for successful elections while in Angola, Liberia, Bosnia-Herzegovina, and Tajikistan weak interim governments left the structures of war in place and failed to alleviate the legacies of fear prior to elections. To the extent that transitional regimes operate on the basis of joint decisionmaking and collaborative problem-solving and create norms that protect the interests of key constituencies, they can build confidence in the peace process and provide an institutional context that encourages the demilitarization of politics and successful elections. Effective interim regimes will be better positioned to promote demilitarization of politics, particularly with regard to the development of democratic institutions such as political parties and electoral administrations.

Electoral Commissions

One of the key tasks of interim administrations leading up to postconflict elections is to organize the polls that will close the transition. Electoral commissions are therefore particularly critical institutions with the potential to promote the demilitarization of politics and encourage sustainable peace and democratization. In some cases election commissions have failed to build confidence in the process, often because they could not overcome the mistrust of one or more of the parties or were perceived as favoring one side over another. In Mozambique and El Salvador, however, electoral authorities based on the participation and monitoring of all parties succeeded in organizing credible elections and thereby encouraging the transformation of militarized institutions. This section discusses the roles of electoral administration with particular emphasis on postaccord commissions and will use cases to suggest how certain processes of administering elections can promote the demilitarization of politics and sustainable peacebuilding.[49]

The Roles of Electoral Commissions

With so much at stake, decisions on electoral plans and processes inevitably are highly contentious, and electoral institutions become the focus of partisan struggles. Ex-combatants and new political parties recognize that the rules and procedures that shape how an election will be run have implications for their political aspirations. In a context of high mistrust, parties fear that their opponents will capture the electoral commission and tilt the rules to their disadvantage. Electoral administration that does not address the fears and mistrust of key parties, particularly recently warring and incompletely demobilized parties, may reignite conflict. If, however, collaborative institutions can be developed to manage the electoral process during the transition, greater confidence in the peace process can be nurtured during the implementation period and enhance the prospects for an election that promotes both peace and democracy. Electoral commissions therefore are particularly critical institutions with the potential to promote the demilitarization of politics and the initiation of a period of peace and democratization.

Elections are simultaneously the supreme political act and a complicated and often contentious set of administrative activities.[50] The primary purpose of any electoral administrative body is to deliver credible election services to candidates and voters. Issues relating to impartiality and independence, efficiency, professionalism, and transparency are particularly important in the context of suspicion and mistrust that characterize postconflict elections. Furthermore, the precedents established in a postconflict election—as in any "breakthrough" or "founding" election in a process of democratization—are likely to shape popular perceptions for years to come.[51] The memories of earlier electoral fraud can pose yet another challenge to postconflict electoral authorities, as in El Salvador, Liberia, and Tajikistan. In cases where a stolen election was a cause of the conflict, the character of the postconflict election will be scrutinized and regarded with great suspicion.

There is no single best model for electoral commissions, and international practice is diverse. An electoral management body may be temporary or permanent; partisan, partially partisan, or nonpartisan; centralized or decentralized; a specialized judicial body or government ministry; or a mixture of several of these types. In a number of European countries and in many former French colonies, a government ministry administers elections. In other cases, an independent electoral commission manages the process. In still other cases, political parties designate representatives for the electoral commission in order to assure that major political actors have representation and the ability to monitor the commission's activities.[52]

In a number of postconflict cases, an international organization has played an important role in electoral administration as a means to increase public confidence in the process. The United Nations played a major role in Cambodia and Mozambique; a smaller but critical role in El Salvador; and a lesser role in Angola, Liberia, and Tajikistan. The Organization for Security and Cooperation in Europe both ran and monitored elections in Bosnia-Herzegovina and monitored elections in Tajikistan. The Economic Community of West African States had oversight along with the UN in Liberia. International organizations such as the United Nations Development Program, international NGOs such as the International Foundation for Electoral Systems, and regional organizations such as the Center for Electoral Assistance and Promotion (a Central American institution) often provided expertise, training, and resources to assist local electoral authorities. All of these postconflict elections had observers from international organizations and nongovernmental organizations as well as domestic observers.[53] Ottaway and Chung have raised concerns that the extensive international involvement in these elections created an unsustainable set of institutions.[54] Although issues of sustainability are important, the multiple roles of postconflict elections and their potential to serve war termination goals suggest that they are special events that require extraordinary resources.

Electoral administration is a challenging task under any circumstances, involving a series of events that are technically and logistically challenging and that require significant capacity and human capital. An electoral commission must design an electoral system; train large numbers of temporary workers; conduct civic and voter education; establish liaisons with political parties, the government, media, and civil society; register voters and political parties; establish rules for observers; manage the secure movement of ballots and other sensitive material; verify voters' identities and guard against fraud on election day; count and transmit the results from a large number of often remote locations quickly, accurately, and securely; verify and announce results; and investigate and adjudicate complaints.[55]

Elklit and Reynolds have argued that "the quality of electoral administration has a direct impact on the way in which elections in the developing world and their outcomes are regarded" and hence how legitimate the outcome is perceived to be, both by international actors and most importantly by domestic actors.[56] The inherent tensions between administrative efficiency, political neutrality, and public accountability make electoral governance contentious. An electoral commission must create procedural certainty and reliability in order to create substantive uncertainty of outcomes and hence legitimacy.[57] Partisan actors, however, often press for electoral procedures that will provide them with a competitive edge.

In a postconflict situation the prevailing sense of mistrust and fear will make each step subject to suspicious, even paranoid, interpretations. Inevitable technical, administrative, and logistical problems are liable to become political problems and threaten not only the election but also the peace process. If the election commission is perceived by any party as under the control of or dominated by its rivals, minor mistakes will be interpreted as fraud, diminish the election's acceptability, and raise the potential for renewed war. Postconflict elections are in a sense an accident waiting to happen as political suspicion and administrative incapacity collide.[58]

There is a growing literature from specialists proposing what types of electoral systems and administration are best in specific contexts.[59] Decisions on electoral matters, however, are likely to be a product of the peace implementation process in which recently warring parties compete for advantage and the international community has a significant role through its peacekeeping operations and funding. The opportunities for "engineering" an ideal system are likely to be limited, and decisions will be based on what the competing parties and international donors will support under the constraints of shortage of time and resources. As one scholar noted, "Electoral systems are rarely designed, they are born kicking and screaming into the world out of a messy, incremental compromise between contending factions battling for survival, determined by power politics."[60] The electoral system, like other components of the peace process, often represents a very imperfect compromise driven by fear and distrust.

Models of Postconflict Electoral Administration

Models of electoral administration in postconflict cases are diverse and vary in the extent to which they help encourage the demilitarization of politics prior to the vote. As with other aspects of interim administration, institutions based on broad participation, transparency, and collaborative problem-solving are critical for electoral commissions. Given the inevitable suspicions and distrust, all major parties need a role in either overseeing or actively engaging in decisions relating to elections or else the credibility of the poll will be suspect. Such inclusive oversight and control should extend beyond the actual casting of votes and include questions of electoral design, access to the media, the hiring of workers, registration of voters, the counting of votes, and adjudication of disputes. An election process that fails to incorporate all of the main actors in the electoral administration process may reinforce mistrust.

Postconflict electoral administration often fails to promote the demilitarization of politics by missing opportunities to include opposition groups effectively in decisionmaking. Often the interim electoral commission at least formally includes representatives of all parties, but these commissions lack the capacity or authority to actually manage the process. Multiparty commissions or oversight boards existed, on paper at least, in Angola, Bosnia-Herzegovina, Liberia, and Tajikistan. But in each case either key decisions were managed by external powers (the UN in Cambodia, the OSCE in Bosnia-Herzegovina, and ECOWAS in Liberia) or the incumbent government (in Angola and Tajikistan) organized the election with only perfunctory reference to the multiparty commissions. In El Salvador and Mozambique, in contrast, more effective and inclusive electoral commissions that had meaningful roles and authority helped both to build confidence in the process and to alleviate concerns that the incumbent party would manipulate the election to hold on to power. Inclusive commissions built around bargaining, joint decisionmaking, and collaborative problem-solving support the demilitarization of politics and postconflict elections capable of promoting both war termination and democratization.

Angola. In Angola, postconflict elections contributed to neither war termination nor democratization. The Bicesse Peace Agreement gave the task of organizing elections to the incumbent MPLA government.[61] A new National Election Council (CNE) was established that included representatives from all major political parties, including the opposition UNITA, along with government officials, judges, and "experts." The CNE was very large and could not serve as a decisionmaking body or as a meaningful institution for collaboration.[62] Ottaway wrote that the "councils were relatively weak, and did not become arenas where the grievances of political parties and candidates could be discussed and negotiated, and consensus about democracy consolidated."[63]

Even when the MPLA administration organized discussions on electoral matters, UNITA refused to attend, further limiting opportunities for joint deliberation and confidence-building. The government, for example, organized a multiparty meeting in January 1992 to discuss electoral law and preparations for the poll. UNITA argued that the Bicesse Agreement granted it equal standing with the MPLA and that the CCPM (composed of the two parties to the peace agreement) was the appropriate setting for policy decisions. UNITA therefore refused to participate in consultations that included other small parties, many of which were offshoots of the MPLA. The rules and regulations for the election subsequently were adopted by the Angolan parliament in April 1992 with minimal consultation with UNITA.[64]

Election preparations proceeded very slowly, particularly given the short period of eighteen months provided for the transition in the peace agreement.[65] UNITA raised regular complaints about the implementation of the electoral procedures and charged, for example, that the government-dominated electoral authorities were not registering its supporters. The lack of interim electoral institutions that could serve as a mechanism for consultations and joint decisionmaking in Angola reinforced UNITA's suspicions of the process at the time of the elections. Adding to the distrust of the electoral administration, the broader peace implementation process lacked effective interim institutions, failed to transform the former warring parties into political parties, and was unsuccessful in demobilizing the two armed forces. Consequently, although the September 1992 elections were peaceful and the United Nations certified that the MPLA had won a majority of the vote, Savimbi refused to accept this outcome and returned to war, leading Angola into an even more brutal and destructive period of conflict.[66]

Bosnia-Herzegovina. The Dayton Agreement mandated that the OSCE "supervise" but not "conduct" postconflict elections in Bosnia-Herzegovina.[67] The OSCE established the Provisional Election Commission (PEC) to establish the rules for registration, observation, and campaigning. The PEC included representatives of the Bosnian government, the Muslim-Croat Federation, the Bosnian Serb Republic, other individuals selected by the OSCE, and a representative of High Representative Carl Bildt and was chaired by the OSCE.[68] The international chairman had the authority to make decisions unilaterally in the absence of a consensus, and the chair's decisions were final. Local election commissions remained in the hands of local authorities with OSCE supervision. Concerns regarding conflict of interest between the OSCE's mandate to supervise the elections and its mandate to monitor the process led to the establishment of the Coordinator for International Monitoring, headed by former Dutch minister of the interior Ed van Thijm. By election day 1,200 OSCE election supervisors were helping to coordinate the election, and an autonomous OSCE monitoring effort added 850 short-term international observers to the 25 long-term observers.[69]

Despite the PEC's multiethnic character and the presence of a number of local representatives, international concerns dominated its decisions, particularly US emphasis on quick elections as part of its exit strategy. Bildt, for example, told of his surprise that OSCE head of mission and US diplomat Robert Frowick pressed for quick decisions on electoral rules in February 1996 despite the fact that Bildt and others believed a more consultative process would be more effective in the longer term: "The more we could now build up a consensus between the local parties themselves, preferably based on their common pre-war experiences, and the less we had to rely on international decisions from above, the easier it would be to gradually hand over the entire process to the authorities of the country themselves. I did not want to establish a protectorate."[70]

Rather than serve as an instrument of joint decisionmaking or consensus-building, the PEC reaffirmed the divisions within Bosnia-Herzegovina and the dominant role of the international community in setting the terms for postconflict governance and administration. The electoral administration therefore failed to promote the demilitarization of politics necessary for long-term peacebuilding. Reinforcing the lack of collaborative electoral institutions, the peace implementation process in Bosnia-Herzegovina lacked effective, inclusive interim administration and failed to transform nationalist organizations based on fear into effective political parties capable of competing effectively in a pluralistic, democratic context. In the end the three major nationalist parties dominated their respective zones of control, leading the election to affirm the trinational division of power created by the war and institutionalized in the Dayton Agreement.[71]

Liberia. In Liberia the Abuja II Peace Agreement called for a new commission to manage the electoral process. The Independent Elections Commission (IECOM) consisted of three members nominated by the three main factions (NPFL, ULIMO-K, and LPC) and one each selected by women, youths, unions, and civilian political parties. G. Henry Andrews, a former journalist nominated by the civilian parties, served as chair.[72] In addition, ECOWAS, the Organization of African Unity, and the United Nations each named a nonvoting international commissioner. IECOM made its decisions by consensus, giving the nonvoting ECOWAS commissioner who represented the regional peacekeepers de facto veto power. The commission represented as broad a range of Liberian political interests as any organization in the country at the time, but lack of time and resources combined with inexperience hindered its work. Furthermore, IECOM had difficulty establishing its autonomy from ECOWAS and lacked the mandate under Abuja II to make decisions on crucial matters such as the electoral timetable.[73]

The process of debating and drafting the special elections law took place largely behind closed doors between the IECOM and ECOWAS and did not involve Liberian political parties or civic organizations in a serious or systematic manner. Although the broad components of the electoral system to be used in the special election had been announced, critical details were lacking in the months and weeks leading up to the scheduled vote. Political parties did not know the rules relating to deadlines for party registration, the criteria for party candidate lists, and many other legal requirements that affected their campaigns. An increasing number of Liberian civic and political groups began to speak out on the need for credible elections, and many urged a postponement.[74]

ECOWAS special envoy and Nigerian foreign minister Chief Tom Ikimi, however, stated that all decisions related to the elections rested with ECOWAS, not with Liberian political parties, the Liberian IECOM, or Liberian voters. "Only the ECOWAS heads of state can take a decision" regarding postponing the election, Ikimi said.[75] Charles Taylor's National Patriotic Party, an organization that had developed out of his NPFL militia, also kept up pressure for adhering to the May 30 deadline stipulated in the Abuja Accord. Taylor warned that he would not feel bound by any of the Abuja provisions—including the cease-fire—if the election date were changed. Several ECOMOG troop-contributing states, notably Ghana, threatened to withdraw their forces immediately if the elections were postponed. These powerful pressures on the IECOM made planning and thoughtful consideration of the requirements of a credible electoral process difficult. In the end electoral decisions were made largely by Nigeria and others within ECOWAS rather than through a process of deliberation and joint problem-solving among the Liberian parties. The IECOM's inability to manage the election, combined with the weak interim regime, minimal demobilization, and lack of effort to transform militias into effective political parties, led the Liberian elections to reaffirm and legitimize the power of the dominant military organization rather than initiating a process of demilitarizing politics.

Tajikistan. Under the June 1997 peace agreement in Tajikistan, opposition UTO representatives were to be included in the Central Commission on Elections and Referenda (CCER) and local electoral commissions. Despite these inclusive structures, electoral preparations were contentious, and the UTO regularly threatened to boycott elections. A new constitution was drafted and endorsed by a referendum, but little public discussion took place.[76] Opposition candidates claimed that government officials prevented them from gathering the signatures necessary to win a place on the ballot.[77] On the eve of the November 1999 presidential elections, UTO leader Nuri and the PDP leader, President Rakhmonov, signed a protocol in which Nuri agreed to call off his boycott of the election and to rejoin the Commission of National Reconciliation in exchange for guarantees of full-scale participation in the March 2000 parliamentary elections. The presidential elections took place without effective competition (the IRP candidate was registered against his will), allowing the incumbent Rakhmonov to win with a reported 97 percent of the vote and a truly incredible 98 percent turnout.[78] The OSCE refused to observe the election.

The CCER was composed of fifteen members nominated by the president but with four members guaranteed to the UTO in the November 1999 protocol. Little consultation took place, however, and the incumbent government managed the electoral process unilaterally and to its advantage. The election law was not passed until December 10, 1999, and received little debate. A number of violent incidents, including the death of one candidate in a car bombing, marred the electoral campaign. The IRP argued that the ruling party had not fulfilled its commitments relating to 20 percent representation by the opposition on local election commissions. International observers and human rights groups criticized the elections and documented wide-scale manipulation to the benefit of the incumbent government.[79] In the end the UTO won only two seats and subsequently faded as a major party in Tajikistan. The failure of effective and inclusive electoral administration, along with weak interim institutions and the failure to transform militias into political parties, resulted in a postconflict election that at best marked the end of a phase of the conflict but with negative implications for democratization. Full-scale civil war has not returned to Tajikistan, but the state remains dominated by rival militias, and prospects for democratization are dim. As one report concluded, "The formal structures of the country have proven almost irrelevant to the daily political processes."[80]

Cambodia. In Cambodia the Paris Peace Agreement established a complicated set of overlapping institutions to administer the country during the peace implementation period. Representatives from the major parties formed the Supreme National Council (SNC), which was designed to work with both an expansive United Nations Transitional Authority in Cambodia (UNTAC) and the incumbent bureaucracy.[81] The elections were administered largely by the United Nations. Doyle argued that it was "absolutely vital" that the UN had the authority to run the election because "an election run by one of the factions and only monitored by the UN (as in El Salvador) would have been prone to severe exploitation and manipulation."[82] Relations remained tense and violent between the incumbent regime and its Cambodian People's Party (CPP), the royalist National Union Front for an Independent, Neutral, Peaceful, and Cooperative Cambodia (Funcinpec), and the Khmer Rouge throughout the electoral campaign.

In the days leading up to the election, the Khmer Rouge threatened to attack the process and prevent the vote. Many Cambodians and several UN officials were killed in preelection violence. In this tense atmosphere UNTAC put in place several special procedures to reassure voters concerned that they would face retaliation for their votes. The ballots listed political parties rather than candidates, allowing the parties to keep their leaders in greater safety. Prior to counting ballots, returns from a number of districts were mixed together so that no one could determine how a specific commune had voted (and hence threaten retaliation). To overcome the problem of voter ID cards being seized to prevent voting, UNTAC devised a type of tendered ballot procedure that enabled registered voters to cast ballots without their identification cards.[83]

In the end Funcinpec won, but the CPP forced its way into a coalition government. Inclusive electoral administration did not play a significant role in building confidence in the peace process in Cambodia, but a relatively strong interim regime and the successful development of Funcinpec into a political party supported a process of demilitarization of politics and an election that promoted war termination and at least tentative steps toward democratization.

Summary. In these five cases—Angola, Cambodia, Bosnia-Herzegovina, Liberia, and Tajikistan—electoral administration did not provide meaningful opportunities for formerly warring parties to begin a process of consultation and confidence-building. Instead, either external organizations drove the process, as in Cambodia, Bosnia-Herzegovina, and Liberia, or the incumbent government ran the elections, as in Angola and Tajikistan. Whether the elections were relatively well run, as in Angola, Cambodia, and Liberia, or poorly run, as in Bosnia-Herzegovina and Tajikistan, the results reflected the strength of institutions made powerful by the war.

Mozambique and El Salvador provide examples of more suc-

cessful peace implementation based in the processes of demilitarization of politics, which resulted in postconflict elections that promoted both war termination and democratization. In contrast to the five
cases sketched earlier, these two demonstrate the potential to use
electoral commissions as an arena for collaborative problem-solving
and joint decisionmaking, thereby encouraging confidence in the
peace process and reducing fear by election day. Although other
processes such as relatively effective demobilization, well-designed
and -supported UN peacekeeping operations, and generally more stable regional environments also shaped the outcomes in Mozambique
and El Salvador, interim administration and electoral authorities
were necessary components of successful transitions in these two
cases.

Mozambique. In Mozambique a series of controversies between
Renamo and Frelimo threatened to derail the peace process and
forced the postponement of the election. The government's mode of
managing the electoral process at first was to present a Frelimo-
drafted electoral law to a multiparty conference for discussion.
Renamo and other opposition parties objected to this system, and
Renamo in particular used the threat of boycott and the intense attention such threats received from the international community as leverage for a larger role in managing the electoral process. For example,
Frelimo initially proposed a commission of "independent and balanced citizens" appointed by President Chissano (the Frelimo party
leader). Renamo balked and demanded equal representation, arguing
that its status as a signatory to the peace agreement justified equality.
Conflict over electoral plans held up progress on other peace implementation tasks as Frelimo tried to construct "neutral" rules and
institutions while Renamo insisted on a "balanced" system.

After extended talks and with the active involvement of Ajello
and the United Nations, the parties reached an agreement that allocated 10 seats to Frelimo, 7 to Renamo, and 3 to other political parties. The process of bargaining over the electoral commission established a number of critical precedents and norms that would shape
subsequent negotiations and decisionmaking processes. To a significant degree, Renamo successfully used its ability to threaten to
defect from the peace process to get the international community to
pressure Frelimo to accept balanced interim institutions based on
equality between the two signatories to the peace accord. The con-

tentious process demonstrated "the importance and difficulty of involving all relevant actors in the construction of new institutions [and] the inherently political nature of the institution building process."[84]

The partisan balance made efficient decisionmaking difficult but increased the confidence of each party in the process. Over time and under the leadership of Professor Brazão Mazula, its independent chair, the CNE developed a reputation for nonpartisan decisionmaking.[85] Unlike the Cease-Fire Commission and other commissions that included international actors along with representatives of the parties, the CNE was an independent and wholly Mozambican organization. The Technical Secretariat for Election Administration was similarly balanced among political parties (with two vice presidents, one each from Renamo and Frelimo). The presence of UN technical advisers working within the secretariat provided the parties with additional confidence in the process.[86]

El Salvador. The peace agreement in El Salvador also created a new electoral commission, the Supreme Electoral Tribunal (TSE), composed of representatives from five political parties, including the leftist Democratic Convergence (CD). Although the tribunal was broad-based, partisanship, "institutionalized distrust," and incompetence created gridlock, a crisis over voter registration, and chaos on election day.[87] A multiparty Board of Vigilance that had oversight over the TSE alleviated some of the suspicion toward the electoral authority.[88] However, the Byzantine voter registration system collapsed in the face of untrained workers and an illiterate and uninformed population.[89] The United Nations Mission in El Salvador (ONUSAL) stepped in with the resources needed to enable the elections to take place.[90] According to Montgomery, ONUSAL "had to flatter, cajole, and bully the Supreme Electoral Tribunal (TSE) to do the job it was created to do."[91]

El Salvador demonstrates that a consultative interim administration and other components that demilitarize politics can counterbalance the distrust created by a weak electoral administration and successfully promote the demilitarization of politics. Due to the relatively strong and consultative interim administration, effective demobilization, and the transformation of military organizations into political parties, politics was demilitarized prior to the election. The March 1994 elections resulted in a victory by the incumbent ARENA party, but the insurgent FMLN made a strong showing despite its lack of political experience and resources, creating a sense that it could play an important part in national policy through participation in elections. Despite a weak electoral commission, postconflict elections in El Salvador promoted both peace and democratization.

Transforming Militias into Political Parties

It is extremely difficult for insurgents, paramilitaries, military governments, and other militarized institutions that derived their power from the conflict to play the role of competing political parties in a democratic system if they remain unreconstructed and organized as they were during the period of armed conflict. In the more successful cases of transition, particularly in El Salvador and Mozambique, processes to demilitarize politics encouraged military organizations to transform themselves into political parties able to operate effectively in an electoral context. In the less successful or failed cases, particularly Angola, Liberia, and Tajikistan, insurgents and military regimes retained the ability to operate as military forces at the time of elections, thereby weakening the capacity of postconflict elections to mark a transition to civilian rule. These comparative cases suggest that if the powerful military organizations in place at the time of the cease-fire can be transformed into effective political parties by the time of postconflict elections, then the prospects for sustainable peace and democratization are greater. Transforming militarized parties into political parties is a crucial component of successful processes to demilitarize politics and makes sustainable peace and democratization more likely.

The Roles of Political Parties

In a democratic system parties play a number of critical roles and are expected to represent the interests of their constituencies.[92] Parties are crucial institutions to aggregate individual interests into broader collective interests and to channel demands into the political process rather than to violence. Huntington saw parties as critical intermediaries between newly mobilized social groups and the state: "Parties provide the basis for stability and orderly change rather than for instability."[93] Given the importance of political parties, partybuilding must be a key component of promoting democratization as a means to resolve conflicts and implement peace agreements. Relatively little, however, has been written on the roles of parties in political transitions in the 1990s and almost nothing on the role of parties in sustaining peace through postconflict elections.[94]

The militarized organizations (insurgents and militarized governments) that sign peace agreements will almost inevitably remain the most powerful organizations in the immediate aftermath of civil war. The signatories will determine the structure of the transition to elections and generally will insist on a transitional process that they believe will favor their claims to power. As noted in Chapter 2, power tends to gravitate toward militarized and militant organizations during protracted conflict and the resulting context of insecurity and distrust. During the initial transitional period, ex-military organizations will retain a degree of structure and coherence that generally serves the purposes of a political campaign. Organizations active in the armed struggle are likely to have a presence in rural areas, whereas parties created after the cease-fire are often urban-oriented and draw their support from the thin ranks (often depleted by war) of civil society leaders, intellectuals, and professionals. Mass-mobilizing parties from before the war often lose their networks of cadres and supporters during the fighting and have insufficient resources to re-create their presence in the countryside. Many militarized organizations have at least putative constituencies, often an ethnic group or class, but it is difficult to assess the extent to which these constituencies will continue to support the military leaders in the context of peace. Finally, in the immediate aftermath of a civil war militarized organizations will have a direct answer to the question of security that will most dominate voters' minds. Parties that cannot provide a credible answer to how they will enforce peace and contain potential spoilers are unlikely to win significant support in a postconflict election in which voters are still worried about their security. A political party of civil society leaders will have difficulty making credible promises to provide protection.

If the peace agreement holds, however, more diverse interests likely will rise in salience, and the overwhelming polarization of the conflict will recede. Fear, of course, does not disappear overnight, and building a sense of security is a long-term process. If security is maintained, however, the general population will over time have less and less need to rally behind militant leaders whose main attraction is their promise to protect. In a secure context individuals will gradually join and create new, more diverse social networks organized around the agendas of peacetime rather than the polarization and security agendas of wartime. The parties that dominated during the fighting will have to transform themselves in order to be relevant and retain power during peacetime.

Institutions endure and thrive in part through their capacity to adjust to changing contexts.[95] A change from violence to security will compel a transformation if the organization is to remain vital. Students of social movements, political parties, and other organizations have argued that each seeks self-preservation in the first instance through strategies to meet its maintenance needs. As Zald and McCarthy argued, "Organizations exist in a changing environment to which they must adapt. Adaptation to the environment may itself require changes in goals and in the internal arrangement of the organization."[96] This adaptation to a changing environment will be particularly challenging when the context moves from one set of incentives and opportunities, such as war, to another, such as electoral competition. The means by which organizations manage this challenge will be critical to demilitarizing politics and to the outcome of postconflict elections.

The Transformation of Militias into Political Parties

One of the most important aspects of successful cases of demilitarized politics is the institutional transformation of that most characteristic institution of civil war, the insurgency or military government, into that distinctive organization of electoral competition, the civilian political party. In Mozambique and El Salvador, the main insurgent movements succeeded in changing their character, organizational structure, and even to a degree leadership over the course of the transition. At the same time, particularly in El Salvador, the incumbent military government reformed itself to improve its chances of retaining political power through the ballot box, making participation in elections a less risky choice. In Mozambique and El Salvador, the institutions that competed in postconflict elections were significantly different from the organizations that had engaged in the earlier armed struggle. These two cases therefore suggest that the transformation of the militarized institutions of the war into political institutions capable of competing effectively in electoral processes is a key component of the process of demilitarizing politics and an important part of creating the conditions for sustainable peace and democratization.

Mozambique. A critical element in the successful Mozambique peace process was the extent to which Renamo transformed itself with external assistance from an armed insurgency into a viable civilian political party able to play a constructive role in a multiparty democracy. Renamo had its earliest origins within the Rhodesian Central Intelligence Organization, which set up a Mozambican opposition movement to retaliate by proxy against the newly independent Frelimo government for its support of Zimbabwean national liberation movements.[97] Renamo's support later shifted to apartheid South Africa, and the insurgent movement engaged in a brutal war that destroyed much of Mozambique in the 1980s. By the mid-1980s Renamo had turned most of the countryside into a free-fire zone and Frelimo's authority barely extended outside Maputo.

Renamo's leaders concluded that resources and patronage would be necessary to operate in the new context of peace and electoral competition. During the negotiations Renamo tried to extract material benefits from those interested in sponsoring the peace (and generally succeeded), most notably Italy but also private companies with interests in Mozambique such as Lonrho.[98] UN special representative Aldo Ajello stated that "it was necessary to help Renamo to achieve a minimum level that could allow the functioning of the whole mechanism" of the peace agreement.[99] Renamo insisted that there could be "no democracy without money," and Ajello agreed: "Democracy has a cost and we must pay that cost."[100]

Dhlakama, the Renamo leader, emphasized lack of resources as the key constraint: "This transition is a hard task, because the means we need have changed. During the war, we could attack an enemy position and capture enough material. In this work of transition things have changed; we need offices, fax machines, financing. And the means we have are not sufficient. The only problem we have in transforming ourselves is this one, of resources."[101] After initial concerns from donors reluctant to fund a party with a particularly brutal reputation, a $19 million fund was established to help Renamo transform itself into a political party. These resources allowed it to "buy off" high-level military officers most worried about their future in a peaceful Mozambique and to recruit new party officials (often recently returned exiles). Some of the delay in implementing the peace agreement was due to Renamo's desire to have more time to complete its transformation into a political party prior to voting.[102]

In addition to resources, Renamo sought legitimacy and recognition, and this desire could be used to increase its acceptance of democratic norms. As Stedman has suggested, Ajello initiated a process to "socialize RENAMO into the rules of democratic competition, and to make its legitimacy contingent on fulfilling its commitment to peace."[103] Regional heads of state set aside their deep antagonism to Renamo and met with its leaders, demonstrating that respect and legitimacy were possible if the party adhered to the rules of the transition. To fill the many posts in interim institutions, Renamo recruited new, better-educated officials who, over the period of the transition, became more influential. The slate of parliamentary candidates represented this younger, civilian group and included few wartime leaders.[104]

The ruling Frelimo party went through its own transformation. The party began as a liberation movement, drawing strength from diverse elements of Mozambican society during the struggle against Portuguese colonialism, then transformed itself into a Marxist-Leninist vanguard party with restricted membership after independence in 1975.[105] At its Fifth Party Congress in 1989, Frelimo abandoned Marxism-Leninism and transformed itself into a broad "democratic socialist" organization. The party went on to endorse a new multiparty constitution in 1990.[106] This transition created tensions within Frelimo and the "move from party-state to simple party, and from Marxist-Leninist vanguard party to mass-based party affected both the ideals and interests, for the leadership and the party base alike."[107] It was this new political organization, rather than the Marxist-Leninist party that had fought the civil war earlier in the 1980s, that made peace with Renamo and engaged in the postconflict elections.

In Mozambique, therefore, processes to transform both Renamo and Frelimo from organizations they had been during the war into political parties able to compete in multiparty elections were critical to the peace implementation process. The institutions that had developed during the war were not the same as the organizations that participated in the 1994 elections. The demilitarization of politics and the development of political parties helped create the conditions for postconflict elections to mark the transition to sustainable peace and democratization.

El Salvador. Similarly, in El Salvador one of the keys to the success of the peace process was the insurgent FMLN's ability to successfully convert itself into a legal political party capable of winning significant votes.[108] The United Nations stated that the FMLN's "transformation into a political party and the full reintegration of its members . . . into the civil, political, and institutional life of the country, are at the very core of the Peace Accords."[109] The ruling ARENA party also reformed itself during the period leading up to the 1994 elections, changing from an organization engaging in violent repression to protect the privileges of landowners into a political party able to mobilize new constituencies through peaceful means.

The FMLN's conversion to an organization seeking electoral strategies to pursue its political goals began prior to the conclusion of the peace talks. During the late 1980s the coalition explored opportunities to engage in electoral politics, and some perceived new possibilities with the electoral successes of Rubén Zamora and the leftist Convergencia Democrática party. As the FMLN became more engaged in international diplomacy in the late 1980s, it developed links to social democratic parties and others who urged it to pursue electoral strategies.[110] The insurgents began to create autonomous *poder de doble cara* (two-faced power) structures to organize the countryside in a semiclandestine, semilegal manner. By 1989 the FMLN was systematically building up its political capacity and establishing links with labor and other urban mass organizations. Top FMLN organizers explained that they were exploring alternatives for wide participation and popular democracy for after the war.[111]

As the negotiations progressed and resulted in a cease-fire agreement, FMLN leaders became increasingly convinced that political processes were more likely than military campaigns to advance their agenda. As they assessed the opportunities and risks, they concluded that the incentives for electoral strategies were higher and the risks lower than remaining engaged in protracted civil war. The peace implementation processes and participation in such joint decision-making bodies as COPAZ reinforced this perception. By the end of the transition the FMLN leaders believed that they could protect their core constituencies and advance their political agenda whether they won the elections or not. Joaquin Villalobos, a key FMLN leader, explained this perspective: "Our political forces will be participating [in the elections] with the aim of preventing the taking of land from the peasants, the reversal of judicial reform and the politicization of the training of the new police force. . . . The question of majority or minority electoral support does not matter. In El Salvador, it is important that we continue to reach an agreement whether we are in the majority or in the minority. The confrontation ended only months ago. Perhaps, once it is further behind us, we can embark upon a path of more democratic norms."[112] As the election neared and as confidence in the peace process grew, the FMLN concentrated its resources on creating a national network of party activists and building alliances with other parties on the left. In response to changing opportunities and incentives, the FMLN made the "shift from the armed left to the democratic left."[113]

At the same time that the FMLN was moving away from its origins as a Marxist guerrilla movement, the incumbent ARENA party shifted its base of support and its strategy to retain power. Initially founded by individuals closely associated with the repression of the left to protect large landowners, it evolved in the late 1980s into an effective political party that represented a broad range of landowners, bankers, merchants, and industrialists.[114] Leadership of ARENA shifted from Roberto D'Aubuisson, who had ties to right-wing death squads, to the more moderate, probusiness Alfredo Cristiani. As one analyst argued, "With the creation of ARENA, and its evolution into a successful electoral competitor, the upper classes and their political allies no longer needed the military to act as a political guarantor and interlocutor."[115] According to another, "In the 1980s, the ARENA Party integrated—in a remarkably short time—a wide range of political resources into an effective party organization with a broad political base."[116] ARENA's ability to win votes in elections convinced the economic elite that it could break its links to death squads without risking the loss of its economic position.

Postconflict elections in Mozambique and El Salvador therefore provided the opportunity for both insurgents and incumbents involved in the civil wars to make the transformation from warring factions into political organizations. The creation of political parties able to represent key constituencies and compete effectively in an electoral process is an important component of any democratic transition. In a transition following civil war, the viability of political parties plays an additional role with relation to war termination. To the extent that powerful military leaders and their followers perceive that they have the option to operate as a political party rather than as an insurgency or military government, the chances of a successful transition increase. Demilitarizing politics through the transformation of military organizations into political parties therefore promotes both war termination and democratization.

Unreconstructed Parties and Postconflict Elections

In some cases insurgents or the incumbent regime remain unreconstructed and retain their institutional structure throughout the transition. Such failure to demilitarize politics makes it likely that the transition will end in an election that reaffirms the power and enhances the authority of those groups and leaders that developed during the war. Such an outcome may lead to war termination in the short run but may make a transition to long-term, sustainable peace difficult. The peace implementation process in such circumstances is unlikely to build the incentives or create the opportunities to entice militarized organizations to transform themselves into political/electoral organizations.

In some cases unreformed militarized organizations have tried to derail the peace process and refused to accept the transition to electoral competition. UNITA in Angola and the Khmer Rouge in Cambodia did not make the transition to political parties during the period of peace implementation and used violence to disrupt the peace process (successfully in Angola, unsuccessfully in Cambodia). In these cases the challenges of developing democratic and electoral processes while military actors remain powerful are particularly clear.

Some observers expected UNITA to make the transition from insurgency to political party. UNITA's "sophisticated, versatile organization with proven resilience and discipline" would make the transition relatively easily, according to some. An early preelection assessment by the US-based International Republican Institute stated that "given standard indicators for organizational effectiveness— chain of command, responsiveness of policy decisions to local as well as national demands, resilience and regeneration in the face of disruptions, etc.—UNITA ranked favorably against established political parties in Central and South America, the Caribbean, Central Europe, and the Balkans."[117] But in the end UNITA did not transform itself and participated in the elections as a military organization. UNITA leader Jonas Savimbi demonstrated he was an "all-or-nothing" player and held on to his determination to accept nothing less than the presidency. Poorly designed and implemented demobilization programs, a weak UN peacekeeping operation, and UNITA's ability to tap into resources such as diamonds to rearm and remain in the field resulted in UNITA perceiving more attractive alternatives than accepting the role of loyal opposition following electoral defeat.

In Liberia, Bosnia-Herzegovina, and Tajikistan militarized organizations competed in and won postconflict elections. In a context in which politics had not been demilitarized and where insecurity and fear remained pervasive, militarized organizations had the capacity to mobilize significant constituencies and form the postconflict government. It remains uncertain whether any would have acted as spoilers, like UNITA, if they had lost. In the case of Bosnia-Herzegovina, it is unclear how a potential spoiler might have acted if international peacekeeping had been less powerful.

According to Andreas, some of the militarized institutions and private armies of Bosnia-Herzegovina retained their power and influence through the transitional period in part by retaining links to criminal networks and black-market channels that had been crucial during the war. These smuggling arrangements proved to be the most profitable and attractive means to gain access to key resources and support an organization. As Andreas argued, "Key players in the covert acquisition and distribution of supplies during wartime have emerged as a nouveau riche 'criminal elite' with close ties to the government and nationalist political parties."[118] From breaking sanctions and engaging in arms trafficking during the war, these networks and their political allies moved into smuggling, tax evasion, and trafficking in women and stolen cars.

Charles Taylor's National Patriotic Party (NPP), a mass-mobilizing political organization, was a direct descendant (or a fresh incarnation) of his insurgent National Patriotic Front for Liberia (NPFL). The NPP essentially provided a civilian platform to compete for votes, but the organization remained fundamentally unreconstructed and continued to derive power through military might and the manipulation of fear. The NPP was an effective instrument of the NPFL in that it mobilized the countryside to support Taylor in the 1997 elections. As an institution capable of mobilizing large numbers of people, if not as a democratic organization responsive to popular wishes, the NPP demonstrated enormous capacity.

In Cambodia the CPP behaved during the transition not as a political party in a multiparty context but as the "governing apparatus of Cambodia," complete with village cells and a highly organized nationwide network of cadres. As one report concluded, "The CPP clearly prefers to stick to the age-old strategy of patronage and intimidation, rather than real reform, to ensure popular support."[119] The CPP retained key advantages of incumbency throughout the transition, including control over a vast array of state institutions, from the army and state media through low-level civil and political organizations in the distant communes.[120] All the major political parties emerged from militarized organizations and shared what one Cambodian leader called the "violent and undemocratic tradition of the past."[121]

Other unreconstructed military parties participated in elections but lost the poll and consequently became less relevant in the postconflict state. The United Tajik Opposition won few seats and became a less important player in Tajikistan after the elections. In Liberia other military factions failed to make the transition to political party that the NPFL made. Some, such as the LPC or ULIMO militias, tried but failed, demonstrating that their constituencies were limited in peacetime. ULIMO-K brought in some exiled politicians to lead the political campaign of its newly created ALCOP party, but these new leaders never gained sufficient power to transform the militia into a party or to mobilize significant numbers outside its small ethnic base among the Mandingo of Lofa County.[122] The Liberian Peace Council and the United Liberation Movement of Liberia for Democracy crumbled as rank-and-file soldiers and all but a few top commanders recognized that they had no future in the new party, which was unlikely to win power and hence access to patronage.[123] Postconflict elections may promote new institutional alignments by weakening organizations that fail to demonstrate the ability to mobilize constituencies in the context of electoral competition.[124]

Postconflict elections play an important role in creating processes whereby certain parties tied to the incentives of war are unable to make the transformation to political parties able to survive the different incentives of peace and electoral competition and are thus weakened and marginalized. One of the most important changes that took place in the context of peace implementation in Cambodia, for example, was the marginalization and eventual collapse of the Khmer Rouge. Unable or unwilling to undertake the reforms necessary to compete in elections, the Khmer Rouge boycotted the process. Without a base within the new postconflict governing structures in Phnom Penh, the Khmer Rouge eventually lost its role as a significant actor in political struggles. Berdal and Leifer concluded that the Khmer Rouge "had repudiated the electoral process but failed to disrupt it with an effective military challenge."[125] The residual power of the Khmer Rouge, and the resources it controlled along the Thai border, remained important for a time, but the Khmer Rouge's institutional capacity to play an active role in political competition faded.

Conclusions

The period between the signing of a peace accord and the final implementation of the settlement through elections provides a number of opportunities to demilitarize politics and increase the chances that the voting will advance the goals of peacebuilding and democratization. The institutions made powerful by the war—insurgents and military governments—will be the most powerful parties at the time of the cease-fire. Powersharing pacts, slower transitions, and electoral-system engineering are unlikely to alter these dynamics based in power and the incentives of violence and fear. The militarized organizations will continue to dominate the postconflict elections unless processes to demilitarize politics are put in place.

Some peace implementation processes—El Salvador, Mozambique, and at least in part Cambodia—developed opportunities to demilitarize politics during the transitional period so that postconflict elections marked the transition to sustainable peace and democratization. Others—such as the processes of peace implementation in Angola, Bosnia-Herzegovina, Liberia, and Tajikistan—failed to encourage this transformation prior to elections. Demilitarization of politics includes building strong interim institutions built around joint problem-solving processes and consultation. In particular, the manner in which a postconflict electoral administration is organized will provide key opportunities to build confidence in the peace process and encourage the demilitarization of politics. The transformation of militarized organizations into political parties will increase the incentives to play by democratic electoral rules while simultaneously reducing the prospects for a return to war.

Notes

1. See Timothy D. Sisk and Andrew Reynolds, "Democratization, Elections, and Conflict Management in Africa," in Timothy D. Sisk and Andrew Reynolds, eds., *Elections and Conflict Management in Africa* (Washington, D.C.: United States Institute of Peace Press, 1998), p. 14; Krishna Kumar and Marina Ottaway, "General Conclusions and Priorities for Policy Research," in Krishna Kumar, ed., *Postconflict Elections, Democratization, and International Assistance* (Boulder, Colo.: Lynne Rienner, 1998).

2. Robert L. Rothstein, "Fragile Peace and Its Aftermath," in Robert L. Rothstein, ed., *After the Peace: Resistance and Reconciliation* (Boulder, Colo.: Lynne Rienner Publishers, 1999), p. 225.

3. Susan L. Woodward, statement to the Senate Foreign Relations Committee, Hearings on the Midterm Assessment of the Dayton Accords in Bosnia and Herzegovina, September 10, 1996.

4. Terrence Lyons, *Voting for Peace: Postconflict Elections in Liberia* (Washington, D.C.: Brookings Institution Press, 1999).

5. Terry Lynn Karl, "Dilemmas of Democratization in Latin America," *Comparative Politics* 23 (1990): 1–21; Guillermo O'Donnell and Philippe Schmitter, *Transitions from Authoritarian Rule: Tentative Conclusions About Uncertain Democracies* (Baltimore, Md.: Johns Hopkins University Press, 1986), pp. 37–47; Frances Hagopian, "Democracy by Undemocratic Means? Elites, Political Pacts, and Regime Transition in Brazil," *Comparative Political Studies* 23 (1990): 147–170; Giuseppe Di Palma, *To Craft Democracies: An Essay on Democratic Transitions* (Berkeley: University of California Press, 1990), pp. 86–90.

6. David A. Lake and Donald Rothchild, "Containing Fear: The Origins and Management of Ethnic Conflict," *International Security* 21 (1996): 41–75; Adam Przeworski et al., *Sustainable Democracy* (Cambridge: Cambridge University Press, 1995), pp. 24–30.

7. J. 'Bayo Adekanye, "Power-Sharing in Multi-Ethnic Political Systems," *Security Dialogue* 39 (1998): 33.

8. Dennis Jett, the U.S. ambassador to Mozambique, urged the parties to accept a postelection powersharing pact, but "the government-owned press, and even the independent media, vehemently condemned any such notion." Dennis Coleman Jett, "Cementing Democracy: Institution-Building in Mozambique," *Harvard International Review* 17 (1995): 24. Synge noted that "concerted efforts by members of the international community to force the government into forming a postelection pact with Renamo were unsuccessful." Richard Synge, *Mozambique: UN Peacekeeping in Action, 1992–94* (Washington, D.C.: United States Institute of Peace, 1997), p. 116.

9. Susan L. Woodward, "Bosnia and Herzegovina: How Not to End Civil War," in Barbara F. Walter and Jack Snyder, eds., *Civil Wars, Insecurity, and Intervention* (New York: Columbia University Press, 1999), p. 94.

10. Kenneth D. McRae, "Theories of Power-Sharing and Conflict Management," in Joseph Montville, ed., *Conflict and Peacemaking in Multiethnic Societies* (Lexington, Mass.: Lexington Books, 1990).

11. Sisk and Reynolds, "Democratization, Elections, and Conflict Management in Africa," pp. 3–4. Ben Reilly and Andrew Reynolds, "Electoral Systems and Conflict in Divided Societies," in Paul C. Stern and Daniel Druckman, eds., *International Conflict Resolution After the Cold War* (Washington, D.C.: National Academy Press, 2000), p.1, similarly argue that "electoral systems can be powerful levers for shaping the content and practice of politics in divided societies" if the design is sensitive to context.

12. Donald Horowitz, *Ethnic Groups in Conflict* (Berkeley: University of California Press, 1985).

13. On consociationalism, see Arend Lijphart, *Democracy in Plural Societies: A Comparative Exploration* (New Haven, Conn.: Yale University Press, 1977).

14. Donald L. Horowitz, *A Democratic South Africa? Constitutional Engineering in a Divided Society* (Berkeley: University of California Press, 1991); Timothy Sisk, "Electoral System Choice in South Africa: Implications for Intergroup Moderation," *Nationalism and Ethnic Politics* 1 (July 1995): 178–204.

15. Stephen John Stedman, "Negotiations and Mediation in Internal Conflict," in Michael E. Brown, ed., *The International Dimensions of Internal Conflict* (Cambridge, Mass., Massachusetts Institute of Technology Press, 1996), p. 370.

16. John Blacken and Terrence Lyons, *Mozambique: From Post-Conflict to Municipal Elections* (Washington, D.C.: Management Systems International for the United States Agency for International Development, April 1999).

17. Some of the classic accounts of negotiations to end wars argue along similar rational-actor lines. See Paul R. Pillar, *Negotiating Peace: War Termination as a Bargaining Process* (Princeton, N.J.: Princeton University Press, 1983).

18. Matthew Soberg Shugart, "Guerrillas and Elections: An Institutionalist Perspective on the Costs of Conflict and Cooperation," *International Studies Quarterly* 36 (1992): 121.

19. Nancy Bermeo, "What the Democratization Literature Says—or Doesn't Say—About Postwar Democratization," *Global Governance* 9:2 (April-June 2003): 159–177.

20. Herbert C. Kelman, "Transforming the Relationship Between Former Enemies: A Social-Psychological Analysis," in Robert L. Rothstein, ed., *After the Peace: Resistance and Reconciliation* (Boulder, Colo.: Lynne Rienner, 1999), p. 203.

21. Carrie Manning, "Conflict Management and Elite Habituation in Postwar Democracy: The Case of Mozambique," *Comparative Politics* 35:1 (2002): 63–84.

22. Yossi Shain and Juan J. Linz, *Between States: Interim Governments and Democratic Transitions* (Cambridge: Cambridge University Press, 1995), pp. 3–21.

23. United Nations Security Council Resolution 696 (1991). UNAVEM began as a mission to monitor the withdrawal of Cuban forces from Angola as part of the Namibian settlement but had its mandate expanded several times.

24. Virginia Page Fortna, "Success and Failure in Southern Africa: Peacekeeping in Namibia and Angola," in Donald C.F. Daniel and Bradd C. Hayes, eds., *Beyond Traditional Peacekeeping* (New York: St. Martin's Press, 1995), p. 290; Alex Vines, *One Hand Tied: Angola and the UN* (London: Catholic Institute for International Relations Briefing Paper, June 1993), p. 12.

25. Fen Osler Hampson, *Nurturing Peace: Why Peace Settlements Succeed or Fail* (Washington, D.C.: United States Institute of Peace Press, 1996), p. 110; Keith Somerville, "Angola—Groping Towards Peace or Slipping Back Towards War?" in William Gutteridge and J. E. Spence, eds., *Violence in Southern Africa* (London: Frank Cass, 1997), p. 28.

26. Juan Rial, Dennis Culkin, and Roberto Lima Siqueira, *Angola: A Pre-election Assessment* (Washington, D.C.: International Foundation for Elections Systems, March 1992).

27. Radio Nacional de Angola, December 10, 1991, cited in Keith Somerville, "The Failure of Democratic Reform in Angola and Zaire," *Survival* 35:3 (Autumn 1993): 62.

28. Marina Ottaway, "Angola's Failed Elections," in Krishna Kumar, ed., *Postconflict Elections, Democratization, and International Assistance* (Boulder, Colo.: Lynne Rienner, 1998), p. 147.

29. Lyons, *Voting for Peace*.

30. David Chandler, *Bosnia: Faking Democracy After Dayton,* 2nd ed. (London: Pluto Press, 2000), p. 61; Elizabeth M. Cousens and Charles K. Cater, *Toward Peace in Bosnia: Implementing the Dayton Accords* (Boulder, Colo.: Lynne Rienner for the International Peace Academy, 2001), p. 43.

31. Chandler, *Bosnia: Faking Democracy After Dayton*, p. 65.

32. Rashid G. Abdullo, "Implementation of the 1997 General Agreement: Successes, Dilemmas, and Challenges," in Kamoludin Abdullaev and Catherine Barnes, eds., *Politics of Compromise: The Tajikistan Peace Process* (London: Accord, March 2001), http://www. c-r.org/accord/tajik/accord10/implement.shtml.

33. Rahmatillo Zoir and Scott Newton, "Constitutional and Legislative Reform," in Kamoludin Abdullaev and Catherine Barnes, eds., *Politics of Compromise: The Tajikistan Peace Process* (London: Accord, March 2001), http://www.c-r.org/accord/tajik/accord10/constitute.shtml.

34. Burkhard Conrad, "The Problem of Small Arms and Light Weapons in Tajikistan," *Strategic Analysis* 24:8 (November 2000), http://www.idsa.india.org.

35. Michael W. Doyle, "Strategy and Transitional Authority," in Stephen John Stedman, Donald Rothchild, and Elizabeth Cousens, eds., *Ending Civil Wars: The Implementation of Peace Agreements* (Boulder, Colo.: Lynne Rienner, 2002), pp. 71–88.

36. Steven Ratner, "The Cambodian Settlement Agreements," *American Journal of International Law* 87:1 (January 1993): 1–41.

37. Frederick Z. Brown, "Cambodia's Rocky Venture in Democracy," in Krishna Kumar, ed., *Postconflict Elections, Democratization, and International Assistance* (Boulder, Colo.: Lynne Rienner, 1998), p. 90; Steve Heder and Judy Ledgerwood, "Politics of Violence: An Introduction," in Steve Heder and Judy Ledgerwood, eds., *Propaganda, Politics, and Violence in Cambodia: Democratic Transition Under United Nations Peacekeeping* (Armonk, N.Y.: M. E. Sharpe, 1996), p. 10; Sorpong Peou, *Conflict Neutralization in the Cambodia War* (Kuala Lumpur: Oxford University Press, 1997), p. 43.

38. Mats Berdal and Michael Leifer, "Cambodia," in James Mayall, ed., *The New Interventionism, 1991–1994: United Nations Experience in Cambodia, Former Yugoslavia, and Somalia* (Cambridge: Cambridge University Press, 1996), p. 20.

39. Michael W. Doyle, "War and Peace in Cambodia," in Barbara F. Walter and Jack Snyder, eds., *Civil Wars, Insecurity, and Intervention* (New York: Columbia University Press, 1999), pp. 203, 205.

40. David W. Roberts, *Political Transition in Cambodia, 1991–99: Power, Elitism, and Democracy* (New York: St. Martin's Press, 2001), p. 75.

41. Patricia Weiss Fagen, "El Salvador: Lessons in Peace Consolidation," in Tom Farer, ed., *Beyond Sovereignty: Collectively Defending Democracy in the Americas* (Baltimore, Md.: Johns Hopkins University Press, 1996), p. 219; Hugh Byrne, *El Salvador's Civil War: A Study of Revolution* (Boulder, Colo.: Lynne Rienner, 1996), p. 192.

42. Tommie Sue Montgomery, *Revolution in El Salvador: From Civil Strife to Civil Peace,* 2nd ed. (Boulder, Colo.: Westview Press, 1995), pp. 233–234. Holiday and Stanley criticized COPAZ for its slow and cumbersome decisionmaking, which compelled endless rounds of negotiations among parties. However, from the perspective of building new norms to demilitarize politics, such continuous discussion is a strong asset. See David Holiday and William Stanley, "Building the Peace: Preliminary Lessons from El Salvador," *Journal of International Affairs* 46:2 (Winter 1993): 427–429.

43. William Stanley and David Holiday, "Peace Mission Strategy and Domestic Actors: UN Mediation, Verification, and Institution-Building in El Salvador," *International Peacekeeping* 4:2 (Summer 1997): 22–49.

44. Elisabeth J. Wood, "The Peace Accords and Postwar Reconstruction," in James K. Boyce, ed., *Economic Policy for Building Peace: The Lessons of El Salvador* (Boulder, Colo.: Lynne Rienner, 1996), 101–102.

45. Cameron Hume, *Ending Mozambique's War* (Washington, D.C.: United States Institute of Peace Press, 1994), pp. 138–139. Synge wrote that

the "construction of a lasting peace . . . required still more negotiation and planning." See Synge, *Mozambique,* p. 52.

46. J. Michael Turner, Sue Nelson, and Kimberly Mahling-Clark, "Mozambique's Vote for Democratic Governance," in Krishna Kumar, ed., *Postconflict Elections, Democratization, and International Assistance* (Boulder, Colo.: Lynne Rienner, 1998). Not all of the joint bodies served the purpose of confidence building through joint decisionmaking. The Commission for Reintegration, for example, met only once, in part because donor programs for demobilization and reintegration were in place before the commission was formed. See Chris Alden, "Lessons from the Reintegration of Demobilized Soldiers in Mozambique," *Security Dialogue* 33:3 (September 2002): 341–356.

47. Carrie L. Manning, *The Politics of Peace in Mozambique: Post-Conflict Democratization, 1992–2000* (Westport, Conn.: Praeger, 2002), p. 20.

48. Chris Alden, *Mozambique and the Construction of the New African State: From Negotiations to Nation Building* (New York: Palgrave, 2001), pp. 61–62.

49. Terrence Lyons, "Postconflict Elections and the Process of Demilitarizing Politics: The Role of Electoral Administration," *Democratization* 11:3 (June 2004): 1–27.

50. Robert A. Pastor, "A Brief History of Electoral Commissions," in Andreas Schedler, Larry Diamond, and Marc F. Plattner, eds., *The Self-Restraining State: Power and Accountability in New Democracies* (Boulder, Colo.: Lynne Rienner, 1999), p. 75; Peter Harris, "Building an Electoral Administration," in Peter Harris and Ben Reilly, eds., *Democracy and Deep-Rooted Conflict* (Stockholm: International IDEA, 1998), p. 310.

51. O'Donnell and Schmitter. *Transitions from Authoritarian Rule,* pp. 57–64.

52. Guy S. Goodwin-Gill, *Free and Fair Elections in International Law* (Geneva: Inter-Parliamentary Union, 1994), p. 88.

53. There is an extensive literature on election observation. See Jennifer McCoy, Larry Garber, and Robert Pastor, "Pollwatching and Peacemaking," *Journal of Democracy* 2:3 (Fall 1991): 102–114; Thomas Carothers, "The Observers Observed," *Journal of Democracy* 8:3 (July 1997): 17–32; Jørgen Elklit and Palle Svensson, "What Makes Elections Free and Fair?" *Journal of Democracy* 8:3 (July 1997): 32–47; Thomas Carothers, *Aiding Democracy Abroad: The Learning Curve* (Washington, D.C.: Carnegie, 1999), pp. 281–302. For a reaction, see Robert A. Pastor, "Mediating Elections," *Journal of Democracy* 9:1 (January 1998): 154–163.

54. Marina Ottaway and Theresa Chung, "Toward a New Paradigm," *Journal of Democracy* 10:4 (1999): 99–113.

55. This list is by no means exhaustive. For a more specific list, see Robert A. Pastor, "The Role of Electoral Administration in Democratic Transitions: Implications for Policy and Research," *Democratization* 6:4 (Winter 1999/2000): 1–27; Yonhyok Choe and Staffan Darnolf, "Evaluating

the Structure and Functional Role of Electoral Administration in Contemporary Democracies: Building 'Free and Fair Election Index (FEEI)' and 'Effective Election Index (EEI),'" paper presented at the ninety-fifth annual meeting of the American Political Science Association, Atlanta, Georgia, September 2–5, 1999.

56. Jørgen Elklit and Andrew Reynolds, *The Impact of Election Administration on the Legitimacy of Emerging Democracies: A New Research Agenda* (Notre Dame, Ind.: The Helen Kellogg Institute for International Studies, University of Notre Dame, Working Paper no. 281, September 2000), p. 2.

57. Shaheen Mozaffar and Andreas Schedler, "The Comparative Study of Electoral Governance," *International Political Science Review* 23 (2002): 5–27.

58. Pastor, "The Role of Electoral Administration in Democratic Transitions."

59. Peter Harris and Ben Reilly, eds., *Democracy and Deep-Rooted Conflict: Options for Negotiators* (Stockholm: International IDEA, 1998); Timothy D. Sisk and Andrew Reynolds, eds., *Elections and Conflict Management in Africa* (Washington, D.C.: United States Institute of Peace Press, 1998); Ben Reilly and Andrew Reynolds, "Electoral Systems and Conflict in Divided Societies," in Paul C. Stern and Daniel Druckman, eds., *International Conflict Resolution After the Cold War* (Washington, D.C.: National Academy Press, 2000).

60. Pippa Norris, "The Politics of Electoral Reform," *International Political Science Review* 16:1 (1995): 4; Pippa Norris, *Electoral Engineering: Voting Rules and Political Behavior* (Cambridge: Cambridge University Press, 2004).

61. Marina Ottaway, "Angola's Failed Elections," in Krishna Kumar, ed., *Postconflict Elections, Democratization, and International Assistance* (Boulder, Colo.: Lynne Rienner, 1998); Margaret Joan Antsee, *Orphan of the Cold War: The Inside Story of the Collapse of the Angolan Peace Process, 1992–93* (New York: St. Martin's Press, 1996).

62. Rial, Culkin, and Siqueira, *Angola;* Tom Bayer, *Angola: Presidential and Legislative Elections, September 29–30, 1992* (Washington, D.C.: International Foundation on Electoral Systems, n.d.).

63. Ottaway, "Angola's Failed Elections," p. 140.

64. Hampson, *Nurturing Peace,* p. 113.

65. In May 1991 U.S.-based democratization promotion groups concluded that the "prospects for conducting meaningful elections as scheduled for September 29 and 30, 1992, are dubious." National Democratic Institute and International Republican Institute, "Angola Briefing Paper, Pre-assessment Mission, May 21–27, 1991."

66. Vines, *One Hand Tied,* p. 133.

67. *The Dayton Accords and Bosnian Elections,* Balkan Institute Reference Series No. 4, March 31, 1996, www.balkaninstitute.org/reference/Rs4elect.html.

68. The PEC established subsidiary bodies such as the Election

Appeals Sub-Commission and the Independent Media Commission. See Cousens and Cater, *Toward Peace in Bosnia*, p. 113.

69. International Crisis Group, *Elections in Bosnia and Herzegovina*, September 22, 1996, www.intl-crisis-group.org/projects/bosnia/reports/bh16rep1.htm.

70. Carl Bildt, *Peace Journey: The Struggle for Peace in Bosnia* (London: Weidenfeld and Nicolson, 1998), pp. 256–257.

71. Steven L. Burg and Paul S. Shoup, *The War in Bosnia-Herzegovina: Ethnic Conflict and International Intervention* (Armonk, N.Y.: M. E. Sharpe, 1999). Susan L. Woodward, "Implementing Peace in Bosnia and Herzegovina: A Post-Dayton Primer and Memorandum of Warning" (Washington, D.C.: Brookings Institution, May 1996), p. 55.

72. "Liberia: Talking of Votes," *Africa Confidential* 38:7 (March 28, 1997): 5–6.

73. Terrence Lyons, "Peace and Elections in Liberia," in Krishna Kumar, ed., *Postconflict Elections, Democratization, and International Assistance* (Boulder, Colo.: Lynne Rienner, 1998).

74. See Inter-Party Working Group, "Statement of Political Parties of the Republic of Liberia on the Prescribed Preconditions for the Holding of Free, Fair and Democratic Elections," May 1, 1997. This group consisted of eleven registered political parties (but not Taylor's NPP).

75. Agence France-Presse, "Only ECOWAS Can Change Elections Date: Ikimi," April 27, 1997.

76. Monica Whitlock, "Despatches: Tajik Opposition Withdraws Cooperation," BBC News, January 15, 1998; BBC, "Tajik Opposition Walks Out of Power-Sharing Deal," September 26, 1998; BBC, "Tajik Opposition Suspends Cooperation with Government," October 18, 1999; Rafis Abazov, "Battling in Peace," *Tajikistan Annual Report 1999*, http://archive/tol.ca/countries/tajar99.html.

77. BBC, "Tajik Elections Under Threat," October 15, 1999.

78. Human Rights Watch, *Human Rights Watch Press Backgrounder on Tajikistan*, October 5, 2001, www.hrw.org/backgrounder/eca/tajikbkg1005.htm. Abazov, "Battling in Peace." The IRP leader Davlat Usmon, who was put on the ballot against his wishes, claimed that the results had been falsified in the "Soviet tradition." See BBC, "Tajik Election Victory Is Challenged," November 7, 1999.

79. Organization for Security and Cooperation in Europe (OSCE) Office for Democratic Institutions and Human Rights (ODIHR), *The Republic of Tajikistan: Elections to the Parliament, 27 February 2000* (Warsaw: ODIHR, May 17, 2000), pp. 1, 22. See also OSCE/ODIHR, "Joint Statement Issued on Tajikistan Parliamentary Elections," press release, February 28, 2000. The United Nations concluded that the election "did not meet minimum standards." *Interim Report of the Secretary-General on the Situation in Tajikistan*, S/2000/214, March 14, 2000, para. 10.

80. International Crisis Group, *Central Asia: Crisis Conditions in Three States* (ICG Asia Report no. 7, August 7, 2000).

81. Doyle, "War and Peace in Cambodia," pp. 203, 205.

82. Doyle, "Strategy and Transitional Authority," p. 82.

83. James A. Schear and Karl Farris, "Policing Cambodia: The Public Security Dimensions of U.N. Peace Operations," in Robert B. Oakley, Michael J. Dziedzic, and Eliot M. Goldberg, eds., *Policing the New World Disorder: Peace Operations and Public Security* (Washington, D.C.: National Defense University Press, 1998), p. 96.

84. Manning, *The Politics of Peace in Mozambique*, p. 180.

85. When Renamo leader Dhlakama charged fraud and announced a boycott of the election, the Renamo representatives on the CNE joined their colleagues in rejecting it unanimously.

86. Turner, Nelson, and Mahling-Clark, "Mozambique's Vote for Democratic Governance," p. 158.

87. Montgomery, *Revolution in El Salvador*, pp. 248–259; Enrique A. Baloyra, "El Salvador: From Reactionary Despotism to *Partidocracia*," in Krishna Kumar, ed., *Postconflict Elections, Democratization, and International Assistance* (Boulder, Colo.: Lynne Rienner, 1998), p. 21; Tommie Sue Montgomery with Ruth Reitan, "The Good, the Bad, and the Ugly: Observing Elections in El Salvador," in Tommie Sue Montgomery, ed., *Peacemaking and Democratization in the Western Hemisphere* (Miami, Fla.: University of Miami North-South Center Press, 2000), pp. 139–163.

88. Ian Johnstone, *Rights and Reconciliation: UN Strategies in El Salvador* (Boulder, Colo.: Lynne Rienner for the International Peace Academy, 1995), p. 51.

89. Tommie Sue Montgomery, "Getting to Peace in El Salvador: The Roles of the United Nations Secretariat and ONUSAL," *Journal of Interamerican Studies and World Affairs* 37:4 (Winter 1995): 153.

90. Stanley and Holiday, "Peace Mission Strategy and Domestic Actors," pp. 22–49.

91. Montgomery, *Revolution in El Salvador*, p. 247.

92. For classic accounts of political parties, see Maurice Duverger, *Political Parties: Their Organization and Activity in the Modern States* (New York: John Wiley and Sons, 1954); Robert Michels, *Political Parties: A Sociological Study of the Oligarchical Tendencies of Modern Democracy* (New Brunswick, N.J.: Transaction Publishers, 1999); Joseph LaPalombara and Myron Weiner, eds., *Political Parties and Political Development* (Princeton, N.J.: Princeton University Press, 1966). For an account that analyzes parties as organizations, see Angelo Panebianco, *Political Parties: Organizations and Power* (Cambridge: Cambridge University Press, 1988).

93. Samuel Huntington, *Political Order in Changing Societies* (New Haven, Conn.: Yale University Press, 1968), p. 405.

94. For exceptions that do focus on parties, see Manning, *The Politics of Peace in Mozambique;* Scott Mainwaring and Timothy R. Scully, *Building Democratic Institutions: Party Systems in Latin America* (Palo Alto, Calif.: Stanford University Press, 1995); Scott Mainwaring, "Party Systems in the Third Wave," *Journal of Democracy* 9:3 (1998): 67–81.

95. Sidney Tarrow, *Power in Movement: Social Movements and*

Contentious Politics, 2nd ed. (Cambridge: Cambridge University Press, 1998), p. 7.

96. Mayer N. Zald and John D. McCarthy, eds., *Social Movements in an Organizational Society* (New Brunswick, N.J.: Transaction, 1987), p. 122.

97. Ken Flowers, *Serving Secretly: An Intelligence Chief on Record, Rhodesia into Zimbabwe, 1964–1981* (London: John Murray, 1987).

98. Alex Vines, *Renamo: From Terrorism to Democracy in Mozambique?* (London: James Currey, 1996), pp. 143–145. See also "Mozambique: Renamo Plays for Time," *Africa Confidential* 34:15 (July 30, 1993): 3.

99. A. Ajello, "O Papel da ONUMOZ no Processo de Democratização," in B. Mazula, ed., *Moçambique: Eleições, Democracia e Desenvolvimento* (Maputo: Inter-Africa Group, 1995), p. 127, cited in Martinho Chachiua and Mark Malan, "Anomalies and Acquiescence: The Mozambican Peace Process Revisited," *African Security Review* 7:4 (1998): 22.

100. Vines, *Renamo,* p. 146; "Mozambique: Funding for Peace," *Africa Confidential* 34:10 (May 14, 1993): 4.

101. "AWEPA, the European Parliamentarians for Southern Africa," *Mozambique Peace Process Bulletin,* September 1993.

102. Manning, *The Politics of Peace in Mozambique.*

103. Stephen John Stedman, "Spoiler Problems in Peace Processes," *International Security* 22:2 (Fall 1977): 41.

104. Manning, *The Politics of Peace in Mozambique.*

105. David Ottaway and Marina Ottaway, *Afrocommunism* (New York: Africana, 1981).

106. Mark Simpson, "Foreign and Domestic Factors in the Transformation of Frelimo," *Journal of Modern African Studies* 31:2 (1993): 309–337.

107. Manning, *The Politics of Peace in Mozambique,* p. 125. Manning added that this transition took the party "down a peg or two. Frelimo is no longer in the vanguard of Mozambique's struggle for political and socioeconomic liberation. It is now just one among several parties vying for political support," p. 133.

108. Gerardo L. Munck, "Beyond Electoralism in El Salvador: Conflict Resolution Through Negotiated Compromise," *Third World Quarterly* 14:1 (1993): 87.

109. Further report of the Secretary-General on the United Nations Observer Mission in El Salvador (ONUSAL), S/26005 (June 29, 1993), para. 11.

110. Geoff Thale, "Incentives and the Salvador Peace Process," in David Cortright, ed., *The Price of Peace: Incentives and International Conflict Prevention* (Lanham: Md.: Rowman and Littlefield for the Carnegie Commission on Preventing Deadly Conflicts, 1997), p. 190.

111. Sara Miles and Bob Ostertag, "The FMLN: New Thinking," in Anjali Sundaram and George Gelber, eds., *A Decade of War: El Salvador*

Confronts the Future (New York: Monthly Review Press, 1991), p. 231; Byrne, *El Salvador's Civil War,* pp. 132–136.

112. Quoted in Leonard Wantchekon, "Strategic Voting in Conditions of Political Instability: The 1994 Elections in El Salvador," *Comparative Political Studies* 32:7 (October 1999): 828.

113. Gerardo L. Munck and Dexter Boniface, "Political Processes and Identity Formation in El Salvador: From Armed Left to Democratic Left," in Ronaldo Munck and Purnaka L. de Silva, eds., *Postmodern Insurgencies: Political Violence, Identity Formation, and Peacemaking in Comparative Perspective* (New York: St. Martin's Press, 2000), p. 46.

114. Carlos Acevedo, "El Salvador's New Clothes: The Electoral Process, 1982–1989," and Chris Norton, "The Hard Right: ARENA Comes to Power," both in Anjali Sundaram and George Gelber, eds., *A Decade of War: El Salvador Confronts the Future* (New York: Monthly Review Press, 1991), pp. 19–37, 189–202.

115. William Stanley, *The Protection Racket State: Elite Politics, Military Extortion, and Civil War in El Salvador* (Philadelphia, Pa.: Temple University Press, 1996), pp. 220, 254–255. See also Sara Miles and Bob Ostertag, "D'Aubuisson's New ARENA," *NACLA Report on the Americas* 23 (July 1989): 14–38.

116. Elisabeth Jean Wood, *Forging Democracy from Below: Insurgent Transitions in South Africa and El Salvador* (Cambridge: Cambridge University Press, 2000), p. 75.

117. Robert E. Henderson and Edward B. Stewart, *UNITA After the Cease-Fire: The Emergence of a Party* (Washington, D.C.: National Republican Institute for International Affairs, June 17, 1991), p. 9.

118. Peter Andreas, "The Clandestine Political Economy of War and Peace in Bosnia," *International Studies Quarterly* 48:1 (March 2004): 44.

119. International Crisis Group, *Cambodia: The Elusive Peace Dividend* (ICG Asia Report no. 8, August 11, 2000), pp. 6, 7.

120. Roberts, *Political Transition in Cambodia, 1991–99,* p. 75.

121. Cited in Kate Frieson, "The Politics of Getting the Vote in Cambodia," in Steve Heder and Judy Ledgerwood, eds., *Propaganda, Politics, and Violence in Cambodia: Democratic Transition Under United Nations Peace-Keeping* (Armonk, N.Y.: M. E. Sharpe, 1996), p. 183.

122. Lyons, *Voting for Peace.*

123. Demobilized soldiers from the ULIMO-K faction, for example, regularly threatened to kill the new civilian political leaders of the successor party, All Liberian Coalition Party (ALCOP), unless they received severance packages.

124. The Mandingo constituency, however, remained unincorporated into the postconflict dispensation and soon formed another insurgent group, Liberians United for Reconciliation and Democracy, as noted in Chapter 6.

125. Berdal and Leifer, "Cambodia," p. 25.

5

Demobilization and Security Sector Reform

C hapter 4 analyzed how increasing incentives to build political and electoral institutions can demilitarize politics and thereby increase the potential for sustainable peace. This chapter will analyze closely related themes but with a focus on the military and other security institutions rather than political institutions. Demilitarizing politics entails increasing the incentives to adopt political/electoral strategies while simultaneously decreasing the incentives to retain military/violent strategies. The military must be depoliticized at the same time that politics is demilitarized for peacebuilding to be sustainable, and the two processes are closely intertwined. As detailed in Chapter 2, militarized institutions develop and displace or transform civilian institutions during protracted civil war. Reversing this process and creating the conditions for sustainable peacebuilding therefore entails reinforcing and strengthening political institutions while eroding and weakening the power of militarized institutions. "Pull factors" encourage the demilitarization of politics by building viable political alternatives for the parties to the conflict (discussed in Chapter 4). "Push factors" make unreformed militarized organizations less useful instruments to gain or retain political power (the focus of this chapter). If incentives for playing by the rules of the political game increase while incentives to pursue violent strategies decrease during peace implementation, then power-seeking individuals and institutions will shift their strategies and behavior accordingly. This change in the incentives and opportunity structures thereby create the conditions for successful postconflict elections and long-term peacebuilding.

Demobilization and Demilitarization of Politics

Demobilization and reform of the security sector are core challenges of all civil war settlements. "A basic goal of any civil war settlement is to re-establish a legitimate state monopoly over the use of force in society, under terms agreeable to the parties to conflict" according to Call and Stanley.[1] Successful demobilization has a number of positive effects on postconflict peacebuilding, including the reallocation of public expenditures from the military to civilian use (the "peace dividend"), reducing the threat of violence and increasing personal security, and providing individual and collective incentives that reinforce the transition from war to peace. Such processes also shape the political process of shifting power and authority away from armed groups and violence and toward civil institutions and electoral politics. As Berdal argued, there is "interplay, a subtle interaction, between the dynamics of a peace process and the manner in which the disarmament, demobilization and reintegration provisions associated with that process are organized, funded and implemented."[2] Spear's point with regard to disarmament is true of demobilization as well: "Disarmament is designed to fulfill two interactive roles: (1) the removal of the means by which civil wars have been prosecuted, thus preventing the reignition of conflict; and (2) the creation of a stable environment, thus strengthening confidence- and security-building among combatants."[3]

Successful demobilization will reduce the opportunities of those who might be inclined to act as spoilers and use violence to sabotage a peace process. As demobilization proceeds apace and as the dividends of peace deepen, actors may become trapped in a politics of moderation whereby the attractiveness of maintaining the peace rises and the rewards for returning to war shrink, resulting in a higher probability of successful peace implementation.[4]

Demobilization is inherently a contentious process fraught with danger for parties to the conflict. Although the peace process is still uncertain, ex-combatants must give up unilateral forms of security and rely upon untested new institutions. Under these circumstances, security dilemmas often generate pressures to remain mobilized for security. Stedman has stated: "By signing a peace agreement, leaders put themselves at risk from adversaries who may take advantage of a settlement, from disgruntled followers who see peace as a betrayal of key values, and from excluded parties who seek either to alter the process or to destroy it."⁵ In this way, demobilization following civil war is something of a "Catch-22." Spear wrote, "Without a sense of security, fighters and noncombatants alike will not want to part with their weapons. Only when security has been achieved can effective disarmament and demobilization be achieved."⁶ Security is both an outcome of and a precondition for demobilization.

Demobilization therefore encourages the demilitarization of politics by decreasing the means, and hence the likelihood, of a return to warfare and by increasing confidence in, and hence the incentives to participate in, a political process. To the extent that the size of armed forces is reduced and brought under civilian control, leaders are encouraged to use electoral processes and other nonviolent strategies to retain power and protect their vital interests. Larger political institutions above military organizations provide a new focus for political rather than military contestation. Furthermore, demobilization can demonstrate to both rank-and-file soldiers and the general population that civilian structures are (re)assuming dominance, thereby generating public confidence in the peace process and consequently creating political will to support peacebuilding. Demobilization is an important early stage—and hence an early test—in the larger process of demilitarizing politics because managing security sets the stage for a broader set of activities. The success of demobilization programs "demonstrates the warring parties' commitment to the peace process and provides the security necessary for people affected by war to reinvest in their lives and their country."⁷ As with the administration of postconflict elections, demobilization provides an early context to initiate processes to demilitarize politics and thereby create the institutional support for long-term peacebuilding.

Reducing the size of the armed forces is one aspect of demobilization, but in the context of peacebuilding demobilization must be broadened to include the challenges of sustainable reintegration and the political imperative to create civilian control over all security forces. Demobilization and security sector reform should not only reduce the size of the armed forces but also separate the roles played by the military (external security of the state) from those of the police (internal security of the individual). According to Berdal, the basic goal of demobilization is twofold: to "reduce the size of the armed forces while redefining their proper role in society alongside, although constitutionally and functionally separate from, the police and security services."[8] These changes should increase civilian control over both the armed forces and the police.

Demobilization is often managed through programs labeled as demobilization, disarmament, and reintegration (DDR) in order to emphasize the importance of returning ex-soldiers to civilian life. To simply expel an individual from the military without providing support often leads to increased insecurity as demobilized but unreintegrated solders are ready recruits for spoilers, criminal gangs, or general banditry.[9] The international community developed significant experience in assisting DDR in the 1990s, and a growing technical literature has been published on the lessons learned and best practices.[10] DDR programs generally involve a demobilization phase (consisting of disarmament, discharge, orientation, and relocation), a reinsertion phase (marked by the provision of a transitional safety net of cash and/or in-kind payments), and a social and economic reintegration phase (provision of economic assets in the form of land and/or capital and training and employment).

In general there are two broad models of demobilization following civil war: the "military merger" model and the "demilitarization" model.[11] In the first, the two (or more) warring parties are integrated into a new national armed force with some formula for the distribution of positions and leadership posts. This was the model in Mozambique, for example, where a new 12,000-strong military recruited from both Renamo and Frelimo was envisioned in the peace agreement (see details later in the chapter). Similar military merger plans were included in the Angola and Liberia (as well as South Africa, Zimbabwe, and Sierra Leone) peace agreements. Such integrated forces help overcome security dilemmas (since each party has some residual military capacity in the event that the other defects and attacks) and also ease the transition by providing jobs and resources to at least some of the insurgent fighters.[12] Alternatively, the peace agreement may call for demilitarization by disbanding certain units, reforming others, and generally reducing the size of the armed forces. This model was pursued in El Salvador (as well as Guatemala and Namibia). There are other models as well. The Paris Accord in Cambodia called for demobilization but was silent on the nature of the postconflict armed forces. In the Dayton Accords for Bosnia-Herzegovina, a military buildup to create a balance of power between the armed forces under the control of the Bosniac and Croatian forces on one hand

and Serbian forces on the other pointed to a different model of security sector reform.

During times of protracted internal conflict the lines between the roles appropriately played by the military and those best suited for civilian police forces inevitably become blurred.[13] During wartime the authority, power, and resources of military institutions tend to expand at the expense of civilian institutions. A key dimension of peacebuilding therefore is the separation of the external security function from the internal law and order function. Mani referred to this separation as "de-securitizing" and "re-civilianizing" the police.[14] Scholars of Latin America speak of "political armies" and how they must be depoliticized for democracy to be consolidated.[15] In some cases order has broken down and the state has failed to the extent that its monopoly of legitimate organized violence disintegrates. Public security becomes privatized as warlords, mafias, and paramilitary groups fill the space no longer occupied by the state security apparatus.[16] Whether characterized as demilitarizing politics or depoliticizing security, the critical issue is separating political institutions from security organizations.

A critical component of security sector reform and a defining attribute of democratic society is the extension of civilian rule over the military.[17] This is important not only for control over insurgents and paramilitary forces but also for the militarized state's forces, where the military and the ruling party are often thoroughly interpenetrated and hence less accountable. Security sector reform is not solely about reforming groups with a mandate to use force (such as the military and police) but is also about creating or strengthening those institutions that manage and monitor the security sector (civilian ministries, parliaments, and nongovernmental organizations) and those bodies responsible for guaranteeing the rule of law (the judiciary, the penal system, human rights organizations). As Hendrickson argued, "Security-sector problems are not fundamentally about the military, but about questions of governance more generally."[18]

Demobilization is sometimes contentious when ex-combatants receive earmarked resources while others—refugees, displaced populations, and civilians in general—also have significant needs. In fact, the number of refugees and displaced persons in need of reintegration assistance is often greater than the number of demobilized soldiers. Those noncombatants who suffered under the violence resent the fact that the perpetrators of violence receive earlier and possibly better assistance than they do. In addition, groups of soldiers often perceive that other factions receive more aid than they do. Kamajor ex-combantants in Sierra Leone, for example, believed that the ex–Revolutionary United Front soldiers who had committed many war atrocities received most of the international demobilization assistance.[19] Competition for demobilization benefits often replicates wartime social divisions.

Demobilized soldiers are regarded as a special category deserving special attention, given their potential to revert to the use of the gun as bandits or as soldiers on behalf of a spoiler if civilian life offers no prospects. As one review of demobilization experience in postwar countries suggested, "Without support, demobilized soldiers and guerrilla fighters might have great difficulties in reestablishing themselves in civilian life, and frustrated ex-combatants may threaten the peace and development process by becoming involved in criminal activities or violent political opposition."[20] In most cases international donors have tried to structure demobilization support through community-based programs to minimize resentment by civilians. Assessments of comparative demobilization programs indicate that "successful reintegration depends to a considerable extent on the support that ex-combatants receive from their families and communities."[21]

From the perspective of rank-and-file soldiers, the rationale for demobilization is often the exchange of arms for jobs or an agreement to leave the position of combatant and accept a position in the civilian world. In many cases soldiers have joined one or another armed force in search of security and the means of survival. The imperative to use the skills and tools gained in the military to protect one's own livelihood remain critical during the process of demobilization and reintegration. As stated by a government soldier in Mozambique, "Guns make good business. . . . Frelimo was never going to pay us for the years we were made to fight. We have to look after ourselves." An insurgent Renamo soldier echoed this instrumental understanding of the role of weapons: "Guns can mean food. . . . Business is good with a gun."[22] Disarmament without programs to provide alternative means to support ex-combatants is unlikely to succeed. More broadly, demobilization in the context of a peace agreement represents the exchange of military capacity for political benefits and opportunities.[23]

More important than disarmament and demobilization themselves in terms of numbers of guns decommissioned or soldiers returned to civilian life is the extent to which new rules are put in place with regard to cooperative and transparent processes to manage military and security questions.[24] Demobilization provides opportunities to begin the process of building new institutions and attitudes that will reinforce democratization. Looking forward and building security in a way that leads the leadership and rank-and-file of all parties to change their expectations and perceive that they will not be vulnerable to violence is critical, though not tied to any specific level of demobilization or disarmament. Aldo Ajello, the special representative in charge of the UN operation in Mozambique, realistically appraised the options. When challenged with the statement that disarmament was a failure because all parties were hedging their bets and hiding weapons, Ajello responded, "I know very well that they will give us old and obsolete material, and they will have here and there something hidden. I don't care. What I do is create the political situation in which the use of those guns is not the question. So that they stay where they are."[25]

As with many aspects of peacebuilding, the imperative for security in a context still distorted by the legacies of fear in the short term has the potential to undermine longer-term processes of democratization and security sector reform. Call and Barnett illustrated the different roles that are needed in the short-term peacekeeping phase and the longer-term peacebuilding phase in relation to police reforms.[26] In general, the short-term imperative to reestablish security and keep the peace often requires co-opting the militarized forces that are potentially unstable. Deals must be made with militia leaders to protect their interest in order to win their cooperation with the peace process. In the longer term, institutions that can support sustainable peacebuilding and democratization are necessary; these institutions will undermine military leaders' hold on power. As a result, the short-term imperative to co-opt the forces of violence and the longer-term agenda of eroding their support are in tension, if not conflict.[27]

A review of the cases of peace implementation suggests that in some cases (Mozambique, El Salvador) demobilization succeeded in reducing the incentives for violence whereas in other cases (Angola, Cambodia, Liberia, Tajikistan) military factions retained their military options over the course of peace implementation. The peace process in Bosnia-Herzegovina had contradictory provisions with regard to demobilization, with some provisions designed to create a balance of power by building up the military capacity of Bosnian Muslim forces while other provisions sought to reform the security sector. A large international peacekeeping force in Bosnia-Herzegovina has determined security since 1996 rather than the demobilization and security sector provisions of the Dayton Agreement. In Mozambique and El Salvador demobilization combined with related processes to promote political/electoral strategies helped demilitarize politics, thereby providing greater opportunities for sustainable peacebuilding. In Cambodia weak demobilization was balanced in part by effective interim administration and electoral provisions. In Angola, Liberia, Tajikistan, and Bosnia-Herzegovina parties to the conflict retained unilateral military options at the time of the postconflict elections.

Reducing the Incentives for Violence

Mozambique. Mozambique demonstrated how successful demobilization and reintegration can support demilitarization of politics and reinforce a process of peacebuilding. Frelimo wanted to demobilize and reintegrate Renamo soldiers into civilian life, whereas Renamo representatives to the Rome peace talks insisted on creating an integrated army with soldiers from both parties. Renamo saw the integrated army both as a security guarantee and as a way to provide jobs for its ex-combatants.[28] The Rome peace plan called for a cantonment of 63,000 government troops and 20,000 insurgent troops in forty-nine assembly areas. The agreement, however, was silent on encampment of the government's police and militias. In addition, lack of time and infrastructure made the task of setting up and managing the assembly areas beyond the capacity of the state and the donors. Assembly areas were often poorly prepared, riots broke out as demobilized soldiers protested the lack of promised benefits, and deadlines had to be extended. Demobilization worked to reinforce processes to demilitarize politics not because it was clearly or realistically specified in the agreement but because the parties worked together and with the international community to build a credible process during the interim period.[29]

Reducing the overall size of the two armed forces proved to be easy. More soldiers demobilized than the Rome Agreement envisioned as thousands from both sides spontaneously left the military. Although the accord specified 63,000 government and 20,000 Renamo troops, the United Nations Development Program calculated that 71,000 government and 22,000 Renamo combatants were demobilized.[30] Delays in demobilization, due both to the slow development of international programs and to each party's efforts to obtain maximum leverage, led many soldiers to spend more time in cantonment than was tolerable. Many resorted to taking UN camp personnel hostage, blocking roads, and commandeering vehicles in order to get out of camps and "self-demobilize."[31] War-weariness and harsh conditions without pay in the military made civilian life, even under the difficult circumstances of a war-ravaged economy, more attractive.

The UN operation in Mozambique, UNOMOZ, recognized that "demobilization was the most difficult and dangerous phase of pacification" and increased its support.[32] The donors eventually provided some $95 million for the exercise and developed an expansive and expensive package for reintegration. The cost per soldier totaled slightly more than $1,000, and this cost did not include the burden carried by families and local communities in caring for ex-combatants.[33] The reintegration and support scheme provided subsidies for all ex-combatants that were paid out over time through the many rural branches of the Banco Popular de Desinvolvimento. In this way the demobilization process dispersed ex-combatants, provided them with cash subsidies to discourage them from preying on civilian society, and gave the peace process time to develop. This scheme therefore provided the "two things that were most likely to facilitate reintegration into society: time and money."[34]

Most ex-soldiers in Mozambique returned to rural areas and shared the general poverty of the people there. Local-level community processes were a key component of reintegration and fostered the acceptance of ex-combatants back into village social structures. A significant portion of demobilization money was spent by ex-combatants on gifts to village elders, thereby assisting them in building social networks and reintegrating into village life. One traditional chief explained, "We gave our daughters in marriage to ex-soldiers, so they could settle here with us and help to feed our children. They are our sons now, and are doing good so far."[35] Many local communities and traditional leaders conducted reconciliation and healing and purification rituals to promote integration of ex-combatants into peaceful community life.[36] Reintegration succeeded in part due to resources made available by the international community, in part due to the collapse of the armed forces of both Renamo and Frelimo, and finally in part due to rural social structures willing and able to reintegrate ex-combatants.

The General Peace Agreement called for a new national army, the Armed Forces for the Defense of Mozambique (Forças Armadas de Defensa de Moçambique, FADM), with 30,000 troops recruited equally from Renamo and government soldiers. Britain, France, and Portugal agreed to train the new army, which represented aspects of both the integration model and the demilitarization model of post–civil war demobilization. The FADM had dual leadership, with Renamo and Frelimo officers in joint command. The actual force, however, numbered only 6,000 at the time of the 1992 elections, as most ex-soldiers from both sides had preferred to reintegrate into civilian life after the war.[37] The collapse of both parties' military capacity reinforced the imperative to work through mechanisms of peaceful, democratic competition.

El Salvador. In El Salvador extensive programs to rebuild the police force and to install new mechanisms of accountability over security forces formed critical components of the peace process and the transition to democracy.[38] The peace agreement called for 100 percent demobilization of the insurgent FMLN and a 50 percent reduction of the government's Armed Forces of El Salvador (FAES), cutting the force from some 60,000 soldiers to 30,000. Initially the phased demobilization of the FMLN was scheduled to take place between February and October 1992, and the accord had an intricate and carefully crafted set of implementation mechanisms regarding this key and contentious matter. In the end, with the UN helping to renegotiate the calendar of demobilization, the demobilization of the last of the FMLN's 12,362 troops took place on December 15, 1992.[39]

As one observer noted, "The centrality of these reforms reflected the importance of the flawed public security forces in contributing to the conflict in the first place. . . . Profound reform of this system was a *sine qua non* for achieving peace."[40] The peace accords promised land in exchange for FMLN demobilization, but implementation of this key provision was slow and uneven. Ex-guerrillas often were left with poor-quality land and without the agricultural supplies needed to farm it.[41] During the transitional period the government delayed its implementation of the military provisions with regard to the demobilization of the National Guard and Treasury Police. The FMLN delayed scheduled demobilization when it perceived a lack of compliance and when it wanted additional leverage for land reform.

The old National Guard, implicated in some of the worst human rights abuses during the war, was to be completely disbanded and a new, reformed National Civilian Police created. The peace agreement therefore stipulated a large demobilization of all forces (all of the FMLN, all of the National Police, 50 percent of the FAES) and followed something of an integration model for the new National Civilian Police (20 percent FMLN, 20 percent former National Police, 60 percent new).

The period of peace implementation had a mixed balance sheet of both successes and failures with regard to demobilization and security sector reform. The cease-fire held, the FMLN was disarmed, and the FAES was reduced to half its previous size. These were significant accomplishments in the context of the previous decade of civil war. However, there were a series of delays in the dissolution of the old police, and FMLN arms caches were discovered after the deadline for disarmament. The demobilization of the FMLN was delayed, in part due to delays in land reform, which remained mired in contentious debates. Overall, however, the key transformation of the security forces from an instrument of intimidation to an institution under civilian control allowed the peacebuilding process to continue and elections to be held.[42]

Summary. In Mozambique and El Salvador, demobilization and reintegration helped shift incentives away from the use of force and toward political strategies. In both cases significant portions of the forces of both the insurgents and the government were demobilized. In addition, new security forces (the new armed forces in Mozambique and the new National Civilian Police in El Salvador) were created by combining members of the formerly warring factions. These processes of security sector reforms not only reduced the chances of a return to war by shrinking the armed forces, they also created new institutions within which ex-combatants engaged in joint administration. Demobilization and security sector reform thereby promoted demilitarization of politics and advanced the prospects for sustainable peacebuilding.

Unsuccessful Demobilization

In contrast to the relatively successful cases of Mozambique and El Salvador, demobilization and security sector reform did little to promote the demilitarization of politics in Angola, Cambodia, Liberia, or Tajikistan. The peace agreements in each of these four cases had provisions for demobilization, but the plans were incomplete, poorly designed and supported, or not implemented by one or another party. As a result postconflict elections in these cases took place in a context in which at least some organizations retained military capacities, thereby providing options to pursue goals through nondemocratic means. Poor processes of demobilization may fail to develop opportunities to demilitarize politics and hence may not increase the prospects for sustainable peacebuilding.

Angola. The Bicesse Agreement called for the demobilization of large numbers of soldiers from both UNITA and the MPLA, along with the creation of a new Armed Forces of Angola composed of 20,000 from each side. Demobilization lagged behind schedule from the beginning. Planning and logistics broke down, leaving many camps in violent disarray. Rather than completely reintegrating, significant numbers of soldiers remained encamped and therefore were easily remobilized. By June 1992, ten months after the scheduled completion of the process, 85 percent of UNITA and 37 percent of MPLA forces remained in camps.[43]

The failure to demobilize UNITA allowed the insurgent movement to play the spoiler role and return the country to war after it lost the election. Overall, many analysts conclude that UNITA gained a military advantage during the demobilization process. UNITA used the transitional period to relocate many of its forces to more favorable strategic locations and kept an estimated 25,000 of its best troops in the bush. Jonas Savimbi and other top UNITA leaders retained command and control over their soldiers in the demobilization camps, and many weapons remained uncollected.[44]

The Bicesse Agreement called for the creation of a new, integrated army composed of 20,000 from the MPLA and 20,000 from UNITA. All other armies would be illegal. By election day in September 1992, however, only 8,800 soldiers were in the new national army. Only 45 percent of government troops and 24 percent of UNITA troops had been demobilized, and some 10,000 to 20,000 of the government's troops had been converted into a special paramilitary "riot police" force.[45] In the view of most civilians Angola remained a highly militarized state, and the shift from army to paramilitary police provided little reassurance that the days of violent conflict were ending.

Cambodia. According to the Paris Agreements, 70 percent of the existing armies of all four factions—approximately 200,000 soldiers—were to be cantoned and disarmed by September 1992, prior to the elections. Delays in the deployment of UN peacekeepers and resistance by the Khmer Rouge, however, derailed this demobilization plan.[46] Even before the Khmer Rouge ended its cooperation with the peace process, the early demobilization efforts raised questions. The United Nations suspected that many of those entering the demobilization centers were "untrained teenagers with old, often useless weapons, while superior forces and caches of weapons remained in the field."[47] As security concerns increased in the lead-up to election day and as the Khmer Rouge continued to threaten the process, the UN abandoned its demobilization plans. The collapse of the military provisions of the peace agreement meant that less than 5 percent of the estimated 200,000 troops from the four factions had been cantoned by the September 1992 target date.[48]

With demobilization and disarmament a failure, and in the face of Khmer Rouge intransigence, the UN returned weapons to the other factions on the grounds that they had the right to self-defense.[49] UNTAC worked in partnership with the armed forces of the other parties to provide security. Although demobilization programs failed in Cambodia, the overall peace implementation process marginalized the Khmer Rouge's military capacity to act as a spoiler. In addition, the electoral process provided a means for Funcinpec to increase its influence through political rather than military means. The state of Cambodia's military, under the control of the CPP, began and ended the peace implementation period as the dominant armed force in the country and was able to use its military advantages to force its way into a larger role in government after the elections.

Liberia. Although demobilization and disarmament began slowly in Liberia, the process gained momentum in early 1997. The West African peacekeeping force collected large quantities of weapons; for the first time in years guns were not visible on the streets except in the hands of the peacekeepers, and factional roadblocks became rare in most areas. According to official figures, 21,315 fighters (including 4,306 children) were demobilized and some 10,000 weapons recovered.[50] Even after the deadline ECOMOG regularly announced that it had found new arms caches and in March 1997 briefly detained Al-Haji Kromah, the head of ULIMO-K, after large quantities of heavy weapons were discovered in his Monrovia home.[51]

Although arms were collected, demobilization in terms of breaking the command and control structures over fighters was far less complete. Demobilization remained a difficult problem to manage, due in part to the nature of the fighting forces in Liberia and the large numbers of "casual fighters" and child soldiers.[52] Scarce resources and poor planning reduced demobilization to a twelve-hour process whereby ex-combatants simply turned in a weapon (or even a handful of bullets), received a registration card, and then were left on their own. Observers called the level of planning for disarmament, demobilization, and reintegration "frighteningly inadequate" and the entire process "hollow."[53] Many of the weapons turned in were not serviceable, and few doubted that the most reliable fighters avoided demobilization while the young and inexperienced went through the process in the hope of obtaining social services or other benefits.

The United Nations Development Program and the U.S. Agency for International Development (USAID) created some programs to engage ex-combatants in public works such as road repair and ditch clearance, but these were not long-term employment programs, and few social reintegration packages were developed. Groups of young unemployed ex-combatants congregated on street corners throughout the transitional period, ready to be remobilized rapidly. Furthermore, some quick jobs programs hired entire units intact, including commanders, thereby sustaining the old factional command and control structures.

As in Angola, Tajikistan, and Cambodia, the peace implementation process in Liberia did not demobilize or reform the security sector in a meaningful way. The NPFL/NPP, the most powerful military faction at the beginning of the peace implementation process, remained the most powerful actor at the end of the process and thereby dominated the post-transition government. Postconflict elections in Liberia took place in a context in which armed factions, not civilian structures, dominated politics.

Tajikistan. In Tajikistan, the demobilization and disarmament provisions of the peace agreement also were ignored. The agreement called for the demobilization of all insurgent forces and their incorporation into the state's armed forces. Demobilization, disarmament, and reintegration fell within the mandate of the Commission of

National Reconciliation (CNR), but continual struggles between the government and the opposition created an atmosphere of crisis that inhibited collaborative implementation of the demobilization provisions. The United Tajik Opposition (UTO) declared in 1999 that it was no longer a military organization, but few ex-fighters were included in the state's military, and few weapons were collected, as called for by the agreement. The United Nations Mission of Observers in Tajikistan (UNMOT) monitored the demobilization and disarmament process and noted that while the government claimed that a number of ex-UTO fighters had joined the armed forces, "few of the fighters have actually integrated in the chain of command or are being provided salaries, uniforms, food or accommodation."[54] Furthermore, the agreement left a number of independent and regionally based militias outside the formal security structures.[55] With regard to disarmament, UNMOT reported, "It is believed that the majority of serviceable weapons remain in the hands of former UTO fighters, other groups, and the population at large and that the total number of weapons in storage fluctuates on a daily basis."[56] Tajikistan therefore held its postconflict elections with its armed factions powerful and unreformed.

Creating a New Balance of Power: Security Sector Reform in Bosnia-Herzegovina

Demobilization and disarmament following the war in Bosnia-Herzegovina had multiple and contradictory objectives (reflecting the overall tensions and ambiguities within the Dayton Agreements). First and foremost, there was a large international peacekeeping force to maintain security in the short term. Second, the agreement envisioned a kind of balance of power between conflicting groups to maintain peace. The United States sought to build up the military capacity of the combined Muslim-Croat federation to balance the power of the separate Serbian Republika Srpska force. Richard Holbrooke stated during Senate hearings in December 1995 that the United States had given Bosnian leaders assurances that they would have the arms necessary "to defend themselves adequately when IFOR leaves."[57] Rather than a reduction of military forces, implementation of the Dayton Agreement entailed a military buildup for the federation's forces along with a strong international peacekeeping presence. In addition to the armed forces of the main parties, a plethora of paramilitary, informal, and criminal organizations operated, sometimes in alliance with the main parties and sometimes driven by parochial motives or simple predation. In addition to the Bosnian Serb force, the Bosnian Croat force, and the Bosnian Muslim force, there were by one count seventeen armed factions in Bosnia and Herzegovina.[58]

The fundamental challenge with regard to demobilization was that the Dayton Peace Agreement recognized two separate armies—the BiH Federation Army and the Republika Srpska army. To make matters even more difficult, the Federation Army never integrated the Croat and Bosnian Muslim forces. As a result, Bosnia-Herzegovina had three effective armed forces, each with a separate ethnic and partisan identity, creating a general sense of fragility and uncertainty over security questions.[59] Furthermore, private forces and criminal organizations remained active, often with the protection of one or another of the entities.

Each armed force had its own foreign military support. The Bosnian army received assistance from the United States, Turkey, Saudi Arabia, and other Muslim states and training from the private U.S.-based Military Professionals Resources Inc. (MPRI). The Croatian army also benefited from the U.S. Train and Equip program. The Republika Srpska force received financial assistance and arms from Belgrade before the Dayton Agreement and allegedly maintained some ties after the agreement.[60] Demobilization and security sector reform in Bosnia-Herzegovina suffered from the inherent tension in the Dayton Agreement between provisions that sought to encourage integration and those that reinforced separation. Rather than demobilization, the peace process envisioned the creation of a rough balance of power. That balance, along with the crucial participation of the large NATO force charged with peace enforcement, prevented the renewal of large-scale violence. It also, however, created the highly militarized context for postconflict elections.

Conclusions: Demobilization and Demilitarization of Politics

Demobilization and security sector reforms are designed to reduce the power of military institutions and to increase civilian authority over the legitimate use of violence. These processes can promote the demilitarization of politics in two principal ways. First, by reducing the size and power of the military they reduce the prospects for major actors to revert to the use of armed forces to pursue their goals. As military capacity shrinks, alternatives to armed strategies become more attractive. Second, demobilization offers powerful opportunities to use joint verification and collaborative processes to manage this inevitably contentious process. If joint commissions such as COPAZ in El Salvador and the Supervisory and Monitoring Commission in Mozambique are responsible for demobilization, norms and expectations will change, and confidence in the peace process will be built. In both El Salvador and Mozambique, the peace process created significant elements of the postconflict security force (the National Civilian Police in El Salvador and the Mozambique Armed Defense Forces) by merging elements from the two warring parties. In this way, security dilemmas are minimized and the leaders of the two formerly warring parties can provide jobs to at least some of their supporters. As with interim administration, electoral administration, and processes to transform militarized organizations into political parties, demobilization is not sufficient by itself to create sustainable peacebuilding. This comparison of relatively successful cases of peace implementation (El Salvador, Mozambique) and less successful cases (Angola, Liberia, Tajikistan) suggests that carefully designed and supported processes of demobilization can help alter the incentives and provide additional opportunities for parties to make the transition from war to peace.

Notes

1. Charles T. Call and William Stanley, "Military and Police Reform After Civil Wars," in John Darby and Roger Mac Ginty, eds., *Contemporary Peacemaking: Conflict, Violence, and Peace Processes* (Hampshire, UK: Palgrave Macmillan, 2003), p. 212.
2. Mats R. Berdal, *Disarmament and Demobilisation After Civil Wars* (London: International Institute for Strategic Studies Adelphi Paper no. 303, 1996), p. 73.
3. Joanna Spear, "Disarmament and Demobilization," in Stephen John Stedman, Donald Rothchild, and Elizabeth M. Cousens, eds., *Ending Civil Wars: The Implementation of Peace Agreements* (Boulder, Colo.: Lynne Rienner, 2002), p. 142.
4. Marie-Joëlle Zahar, "Reframing the Spoiler Debate in Peace

Processes," in John Darby and Roger Mac Ginty, eds., *Contemporary Peacemaking: Conflict, Violence and Peace Processes* (Hampshire, UK: Palgrave MacMillan, 2003).

5. Stephen John Stedman, "Spoiler Problems in Peace Processes," *International Security* 22:5 (Fall 1997): 5. Walter similarly has written that peace agreements in civil wars ask opponents "to do what they consider unthinkable. At a time when no legitimate government and no legal institutions exist to enforce a contract, they are asked to demobilize, disarm, and disengage their military forces and prepare for peace." Barbara F. Walter, "The Critical Barrier to Civil War Settlement," *International Organization* 51:3 (Summer 1997): 335–336.

6. Spear, "Disarmament and Demobilization," p. 147.

7. Nat J. Colletta, Markus Kostner, and Ingo Wiederhofer, "Disarmament, Demobilization, and Reintegration: Lessons and Liabilities in Reconstruction," in Robert I. Rotberg, ed., *When States Fail: Causes and Consequences* (Princeton, N.J.: Princeton University Press, 2004), p. 170.

8. Berdal, *Disarmament and Demobilisation After Civil War*, p. 5. Spear makes a similar point: "Peace requires breaking the command and control structures operating over rebel fighters—thus making it more difficult for them to return to organized armed rebellion—and reforming or integrating new state armies to act in the interest of the entire citizenry." Spear, "Disarmament and Demobilization," p. 141.

9. Colletta, Kostner, and Wiederhofer, "Disarmament, Demobilization, and Reintegration," p. 171.

10. Nicole Ball, "Demobilization and Reintegrating Soldiers: Lessons from Africa," in Krishna Kumar, ed., *Rebuilding Societies After Civil War: Critical Roles for International Assistance* (Boulder, Colo.: Lynne Rienner, 1997), p. 87. See also Nat J. Colletta, Markus Kostner, and Ingo Wiederhofer, *The Transition from War to Peace in Sub-Saharan Africa* (Washington D.C.: The World Bank Directions in Development Series, 1996); Kees Kingma, ed., *Demobilization in Sub-Saharan Africa: The Development and Security Impacts* (New York: St. Martin's Press, 2000); Herbert Wulf, ed., *Security Sector Reform* (Bonn: Bonn International Centre for Conversion Brief no. 15, June 2000); Natalie Pauwels, ed., *War Force to Work Force: Global Perspectives on Demobilization and Reintegration* (Baden-Baden: Nomos Verlagsgesellschaft, 2000).

11. Charles T. Call and William Stanley, "Protecting the People: Public Security Choices After Civil Wars," *Global Governance* 7 (2001): 151–172; Call and Stanley, "Military and Police Reform After Civil Wars."

12. Katherine Glassmyer and Nicholas Sambanis, "Rebel-Military Integration and Civil War Termination," paper presented at the American Political Science Association meeting, Philadelphia, Pa., August 2003.

13. Alice Hills, *Policing Africa: Internal Security and the Limits of Liberalization* (Boulder, Colo.: Lynne Rienner, 2000).

14. Rama Mani, "Contextualizing Police Reform: Security, the Rule of Law and Post-Conflict Peacebuilding," *International Peacebuilding* 6 (1999): 9–26.

15. Paul Chevigny, *Edge of the Knife: Political Violence in the Americas* (New York: The New Press, 1995); Kees Koonings, "Political Armies, Security Forces and Democratic Consolidation in Latin America," in Gavin Cawthra and Robin Luckham, eds., *Governing Insecurity: Democratic Control of Military and Security Establishments in Transitional Democracies* (London: Zed Books, 2003), pp. 124–151.

16. Mary Kaldor, *New and Old Wars: Organized Violence in a Global Era* (London: Polity, 1999).

17. Neil Cooper and Michael Pugh, *Security-Sector Transformation in Post-conflict Societies* (London: The Conflict, Security, and Development Group at the Centre for Defence Studies, Kings College, University of London, Working Paper, February 2002); Wulf, *Security Sector Reform.*

18. Dylan Hendrickson, "A Review of Security-Sector Reform," (London: The Conflict, Security, and Development Group at the Centre for Defence Studies, Kings College, University of London, Working Paper, September 1999), p. 29. See also Jane Chanaa, *Security Sector Reform: Issues, Challenges, and Prospects* (London: International Institute for Strategic Studies Adelphi Paper no. 344, 2002).

19. Danny Hoffman, "The Civilian Target in Sierra Leone and Liberia: Political Power, Military Strategy, and Humanitarian Intervention," *African Affairs* 103 (2004): 211–226. In fact, most of the demobilization assistance went to the Civilian Defense Forces, of which the kamajors were a major component.

20. Kees Kingma, *Demobilisation and Reintegration of Ex-combatants in Post-war and Transition Countries: Trends and Challenges of External Support* (Eschborn, Germany: Deutsche Gesellschaft für Technische Zusammenarbeit, 2001), p. 14.

21. Kees Kingma, "Post-war Societies," in Natalie Pauwels, ed., *War Force to Work Force: Global Perspectives on Demobilization and Reintegration* (Baden-Baden: Nomos Verlagsgesellschaft, 2000), p. 223. This was seen clearly in the Mozambique case.

22. Both quoted in Alex Vines, "Disarmament in Mozambique," *Journal of Southern African Studies* 24:1 (March 1998): 192–193.

23. Annika S. Hansen and Lia Brynjar, *The Role of International Security Assistance in Support of Peace Agreements in War-Torn Societies* (Kjeller, Norway: Forsvarets Forskingsinstitut [Norwegian Defence Research Establishment], FFI Rapport no. 98/05291, December 1998). For a similar discussion in the context of Kosovo, see Robert Neil Cooper, *Demilitarisation and (Lack of?) Transformation in Kosovo*, The Geneva Centre for Security Policy Working Paper, 1999–2000, available on Columbia International Affairs Online, www.ciaonet.org/wps/cor06.

24. Fred Tanner, "Post-conflict Weapons Control: In Search of Normative Interactions," paper presented at the International Studies Association Meeting, Washington, D.C., February 1999, p. 2.

25. Quoted in Brian Hall, "Blue Helmets, Empty Guns," *New York Times Sunday Magazine,* January 2, 1994, p. 24.

26. Chuck Call and Michael Barnett, "Looking for a Few Good Cops:

Peacekeeping, Peacebuilding, and CIVPOL," *International Peacekeeping* 6 (1999): 43–68.

27. For a similar argument in a context without a peace agreement, see Terrence Lyons and Ahmed Samatar, *Somalia: State Collapse, Multilateral Intervention, and Strategies for Political Reconstruction* (Washington, D.C.: Brookings Institution Press, 1995).

28. Cameron Hume, *Ending Mozambique's War* (Washington, D.C.: United States Institute of Peace Press, 1994), p. 59.

29. Chris Alden, "Lessons from the Reintegration of Demobilized Soldiers in Mozambique," *Security Dialogue* 33:3 (September 2002): 341–356; Chris Alden, "Political Violence in Mozambique: Past, Present, and Future," in William Gutteridge and J. E. Spence, eds., *Violence in Southern Africa* (London: Frank Cass, 1997).

30. Cited in Iraê Baptista Lundin, Marinho Chachiua, António Gaspar, Habiba Guebuza, and Guilherme Mbilana, "'Reducing Costs Through an Expensive Exercise': The Impact of Demobilization in Mozambique," in Kees Kingma, ed., *Demobilization in Sub-Saharan Africa: The Development and Security Impacts* (New York: St. Martin's Press, 2000), p. 182.

31. Colletta, Kostner, and Wiederhofer, "Disarmament, Demobilization, and Reintegration," p. 173.

32. United Nations, *The United Nations and Mozambique, 1992–1995* (New York: The United Nations Department of Public Information, 1995), p. 38.

33. Lundin, Chachiua, Gaspar, Guebuza, and Mbilana, "'Reducing Costs Through an Expensive Exercise,'" p. 186. This cost is high but is comparable to the cost per soldier in similar demobilization schemes in Uganda and Eritrea. See Kees Kingma, "The Impact of Demobilization," in Kees Kingma, ed., *Demobilization in Sub-Saharan Africa: The Development and Security Impacts* (New York: St. Martin's Press, 2000), pp. 218–219.

34. Alden, "Lessons from the Reintegration of Demobilized Soldiers in Mozambique," p. 341–356.

35. Cited in Lundin, Chachiua, Gaspar, Guebuza, and Mbilana, "'Reducing Costs Through an Expensive Exercise,'" pp. 189–190.

36. Carolyn Nordstrom, *A Different Kind of War Story* (Philadelphia: University of Pennsylvania Press, 1997).

37. Kees Kingma, "Demobilization and Reintegration Experiences in Africa," in Natalie Pauwels, ed., *War Force to Work Force: Global Perspectives on Demobilization and Reintegration* (Baden-Baden: Nomos Verlagsgesellschaft, 2000), p. 309. The Mozambican government had to reintroduce the very unpopular conscription, another indication of war fatigue and alternatives within the population.

38. On the demobilization process in El Salvador, see William Stanley and Charles T. Call, "Building a New Civilian Police Force in El Salvador," in Krishna Kumar, ed., *Rebuilding Societies After Civil War: Critical Roles for International Assistance* (Boulder, Colo.: Lynne Rienner, 1997), pp. 107–134; A. Douglas Kincaid, "Demilitarization and Security in El Salvador and Guatemala: Convergences of Success and Crisis," *Journal of*

Interamerican Studies and World Affairs 42 (Winter 2000): 4–43; Denise Spencer, *Demobilization and Reintegration in Central America* (Bonn: Bonn International Center for Conversion Paper 8, February 1997); Johanna Oliver, "Seeking a Return to Normalcy for Central America's Ex-Combatants," in Natalie Pauwels, ed., *War Force to Work Force: Global Perspectives on Demobilization and Reintegration* (Baden-Baden: Nomos Verlagsgesellschaft, 2000), p. 277; Alejandro Bendaña, *Demobilization and Reintegration in Central America: Peace-Building Challenges and Responses* (Managua, Nicaragua: Centro de Estudios Internacionales, 1999).

39. Cynthia J. Arnson and Dinorah Azpuru, "From Peace to Democratization: Lessons from Central America," in John Darby and Roger Mac Ginty, eds., *Contemporary Peacemaking: Conflict, Violence, and Peace Processes* (Hampshire, UK: Palgrave Macmillan, 2003), pp. 200–201.

40. William Stanley and Robert Loosle, "El Salvador: The Civilian Police Component of Peace Operations," in Robert B. Oakley, Michael J. Dziedzic, and Eliot M. Goldberg, eds., *Policing the New World Disorder: Peace Operations and Public Security* (Washington, D.C.: National Defense University Press, 1998), pp. 106, 107.

41. Colletta, Kostner, and Wiederhofer, "Disarmament, Demobilization, and Reintegration," p. 176.

42. Charles T. Call, "Assessing El Salvador's Transition from Civil War to Peace," in Steven John Stedman, Donald Rothchild, and Elizabeth Cousens, eds., *Ending Civil Wars: The Implementation of Peace Agreements* (Boulder, Colo.: Lynne Rienner, 2002), pp. 383–420.

43. World Bank, *Demobilization and Reintegration of Military Personnel in Africa* (Washington, D.C.: World Bank, October 1993), cited in Marina Ottaway, "Angola's Failed Elections," in Krishna Kumar, ed., *Postconflict Elections, Democratization, and International Assistance* (Boulder, Colo.: Lynne Rienner, 1998), p. 138.

44. "Angola II: Winner Does Not Take All," *Africa Confidential* (September 11, 1992), p. 6; Human Rights Watch, *Angola: Arms Trade and Violations of the Laws of War Since the 1992 Elections* (New York: Human Rights Watch Arms Project and Human Rights Watch/Africa, 1994).

45. Keith Somerville, "Angola—Groping Towards Peace or Slipping Back Towards War?" in William Gutteridge and J. E. Spence, eds., *Violence in Southern Africa* (London: Frank Cass, 1997), p. 28.

46. David W. Roberts, *Political Transition in Cambodia, 1991–99: Power, Elitism, and Democracy* (New York: St. Martin's Press, 2001), p. 88; Jianwei Wang, *Managing Arms in Peace Processes: Cambodia* (Geneva: United Nations Institute for Disarmament Research, 1996).

47. Mats Berdal and Michael Leifer, "Cambodia," in James Mayall, ed., *The New Interventionism, 1991–1994: United Nations Experience in Cambodia, Former Yugoslavia, and Somalia* (Cambridge: Cambridge University Press, 1996), p. 43.

48. According to UN Document S/24286, July 14, 1992, as of July 10 9,003 Cambodian People's Armed Forces troops had been cantoned, 3,187 from Funcinpec, 1,322 from the KPNLF, and none from the Khmer Rouge.

This represented less than 5 percent of the estimated 200,000 troops. Cited in Sorpong Peou, *Conflict Neutralization in the Cambodia War* (Kuala Lumpur: Oxford University Press, 1997), p. 63.

49. Sorpong Peou, *Conflict Neutralization in the Cambodia War* (Kuala Lumpur: Oxford University Press, 1997), p. 66.

50. United Nations, "Twenty-Second Progress Report of the Secretary-General on the United Nations Observer Mission in Liberia," UN Document S/1997/237, March 19, 1997, para. 13; United Nations, "Final Report of the Secretary-General on the United Nations Observer Mission in Liberia," UN Document S/1997/712, September 12, 1997, para. 5.

51. Despite Kromah's clear violation of the Abuja agreements, ECO-MOG allowed him to participate in the election after he apologized publicly. Agence France-Presse, "Kromah Apologizes for Hoarding Arms, Ammunition," March 14, 1997.

52. Max Ahmadu Sesay, "Politics and Society in Post-War Liberia," *Journal of Modern African Studies* 34:3 (1996): 405–409.

53. Friends of Liberia, "Liberia: Opportunities and Obstacles for Peace," unpublished report, December 1996, p. 5; Victor Tanner, "Liberia: Railroading Peace," *Review of African Political Economy* 25:75 (March 1998): 137.

54. United Nations, *Report of the Secretary-General on the Situation in Tajikistan,* UN Document S/1999/1127 (November 4, 1999), para. 18.

55. Muzaffar Olimov and Ksenia Gonchar, "Consolidating Peace in Tajikistan—Reconciliation, Reinsertion, and Reintegration," in Natalie Pauwels, ed., *War Force to Work Force: Global Perspectives on Demobilization and Reintegration* (Baden-Baden: NOMOS Verlagsgesellschaft, 2000), pp. 335–346.

56. United Nations, *Report of the Secretary-General on the Situation in Tajikistan,* para. 17; Burkhard Conrad, "The Problem of Small Arms and Light Weapons in Tajikistan," *Strategic Analysis* 24:8 (November 2000); John Heathershaw, Emil Juraev, Michael von Tangen Page, and Lada Zimina, *Small Arms Control in Central Asia* (London: International Alert Monitoring the Implementation of Small Arms Controls, Eurasia Series no. 4, 2004).

57. Cited in Lenard J. Cohen, "Bosnia and Herzegovina: Fragile Peace in a Segmented State," *Current History* (March 1996): 110.

58. Barbara Ekwall-Uebelhart and Andrei Raevsky, *Managing Arms in Peace Processes: Croatia and Bosnia-Herzegovina* (Geneva: United Nations Institute for Disarmament Research, 1996), p. 10.

59. Jeremy King and A. Walter Dorn, with Matthew Hodes, *An Unprecedented Experiment: Security Sector Reform in Bosnia and Herzegovina* (London: Saferworld, September 2002), p. 15.

60. Mary Kaldor, "Security Structures in Bosnia and Herzegovina," in Gavin Cawthra and Robin Luckham, eds., *Governing Insecurity: Democratic Control of Military and Security Establishments in Transitional Democracies* (London: Zed, 2003), p. 214.

6

Sustaining Peace and Democracy

This study has focused on the relatively short time frame between the signing of peace agreements to end protracted civil wars and the elections held to mark the end of the transition. In El Salvador, Mozambique, and Cambodia these brief interregnums launched the early stages of processes to demilitarize politics, improving prospects for sustainable peacebuilding and democratic consolidation in the long term. In Angola, Bosnia-Herzegovina, Liberia, and Tajikistan, by contrast, the organizations made powerful by the war remained dominant at the time of postconflict elections, diminishing the potential for the poll to promote peace and democratization. The outcomes of processes to implement peace agreements therefore depend in part on whether politics is demilitarized during the brief transitional period between cease-fire and elections.

Peacebuilding and democratic consolidation are inherently long-term processes, all the more so following protracted civil war. Any assessment just a year or two after a cease-fire or after a single election must be made with considerable caution and qualification. In the seven cases analyzed here, at best only the very first, partial, and tentative steps in the much longer-term processes of peacebuilding and democratization have been possible given the legacies of war. These first steps, however, are critical. If demilitarization of politics can begin during the transitional period leading up to postconflict elections, then the prospects for sustainable peace and democratization are enhanced. This chapter briefly reviews whether peace and democratization have been sustained in these seven cases. In El Salvador, Mozambique, and Cambodia at least elements of a process to demilitarize politics were in place prior to the elections, and elections have been held regularly. In Angola, Liberia, and Tajikistan even narrowly defined war-termination goals have not been met, and in Bosnia-Herzegovina the overwhelming presence of international peacekeeping forces makes it difficult to judge the state of internal political processes.

Sustainable Peace and Democratization

Mozambique

Peace in Mozambique has held for over ten years since the 1992 Rome Peace Agreements and the 1994 national elections. This is a remarkable achievement in an era characterized by so many failed peace processes and by so much conflict in Africa in particular. With regard to democratization, Mozambique followed up its 1994 post-conflict elections with local elections in 1998 and national elections in 1999 and 2004. The incumbent Frelimo party has won each of these elections, and Renamo has consistently made charges of electoral fraud, but each national election has been actively contested. Numerous challenges remain with regard to consolidating democracy: voter turnout, for example, has declined from 5.4 million in 1994 to 4.9 million in 1999 to an estimated 3.3 million in 2004.[1] Despite these rather typical difficulties of a new democracy in a poor region, the 1992–1994 peace process successfully ended the civil war of the 1980s and early 1990s.[2] Processes to demilitarize politics prior to the 1994 elections supported this transition to sustainable peace and democratization.

After the 1994 elections Renamo eventually accepted its role as opposition in the parliament and played a constructive role in questioning government policies. Joachim Chissano and the ruling Frelimo party often continued to govern without consultation, but over time parliament's role incrementally broadened. For its part Renamo took additional steps to make its transition from an insurgent organization into a national political party. In 1998, for example, Joao Alexandre became its first secretary-general who had joined the party after the cessation of hostilities, suggesting further demilitarization of the party.[3]

In 1998 Renamo objected to its exclusion from the National Elections Committee (CNE) and the Technical Secretariat for

Election Administration (STAE) and boycotted the local elections. Although other parties and independents did compete, only a handful of urban areas had local seats up for competition, turnout was only 15 percent, and the poll did little to deepen democratization.[4] The national elections of 1999 reaffirmed the divisions within Mozambique suggested by the 1994 results. Frelimo again received the most votes, polling 48.5 percent (up slightly from the 44.3 percent of 1994), and Renamo (this time allied with some minor parties) received 38.8 percent (up from the 33.7 percent of 1994). Chissano won the presidency with 52.3 percent of the vote over Afonso Dhlakama's 47.7 percent.[5] As in 1994, Renamo's support came from the six central and northern provinces. Renamo had expected to do better and protested the results to the Mozambique Supreme Court, which upheld the results. Renamo yet again threatened to boycott the new parliament but participated in the end.

In December 2004 Mozambique held its third set of elections following the Rome Peace Agreement. Chissano did not run for a third term, and Armando Guebuza was the ruling Frelimo party's candidate. Dhlakama ran for a third time as Renamo's candidate, and Raul Domingos, who had recently been expelled from Renamo, ran as the leader of the Party of Peace, Democracy, and Development. Guebuza won 64 percent of the vote (increasing Frelimo's percentage from 52 percent in 1999), Dhlakama's percentage fell from 48 percent in 1999 to 32 percent in 2004, and Domingos won just 2 percent.[6] The election was well run and peaceful, but turnout was quite low (estimated at approximately 50 percent), particularly in areas that had voted strongly for Renamo in previous years. Frelimo continued to demonstrate its organizational capacity to mobilize its supporters, in part by using the advantages of incumbency, while Renamo seemed to weaken as a political party.

Elections have become an integral part of the competition for power in Mozambique, and the prospect of a return to civil war seems small. Both Renamo and Frelimo have made uneven but steady progress in evolving away from their respective military origins toward typical patron-client parties in the developing world. The 2004 results suggest that incumbency remains an important tool of political party-building and that opposition parties that do not gain a share of power tend to fade, but these are problems common to new democracies and suggest that Mozambique has made the transition from civil war to a difficult process of democratization.

El Salvador

Stability and democratization also have been maintained in El Salvador for the ten years since the peace process ended the civil war. Tensions within the FMLN coalition led to splits within months of the 1994 elections, and the Popular Revolutionary Army and the National Resistance components formed their own Democratic Party (PD) with a centrist social democratic position. The harder-line elements retained the FMLN banner.[7]

The next opportunity to test the resilience of the political institutions and processes created through the 1992–1994 transitional process came in the March 1997 elections for the Legislative Assembly and mayors. In the legislative contest, the ruling Nationalist Republican Alliance (ARENA) won 28 seats, down from the 39 won in the 1994 elections, while the FMLN won 27 seats, up from the 21 it won in 1994. ARENA also lost ground to the FMLN in the mayoral contests, with the former insurgent party winning the mayor's office in the capital, San Salvador. Turnout, however, was very low: Only 37 percent participated, down from 54 percent in March 1994.

The FMLN seemed to have made the transition from a liberation movement to a populist socialist/social democratic party. Following its victories in 1997, it served as the major opposition party within the parliament. In subsequent elections in 2000 and 2004, ARENA maintained its hold on the presidency, but the FMLN won significant support both in the countryside and in the major cities. Since 1993 politics in El Salvador has focused on questions of economic performance and probity rather than war and peace. The country remains closely divided between ARENA and FMLN supporters, but both operate as political parties pursuing electoral strategies rather than as militarized institutions, "reflecting a remarkable transformation of the armed conflict to the electoral arena."[8]

Cambodia

Since the United Nations Transitional Authority for Cambodia (UNTAC) departed shortly after the elections in 1993, Cambodia has experienced political instability, governmental disarray, and violence. The royalist Funcinpec coalition never formed a government but rather was forced to enter into a coalition with the defeated Cambodian People's Party (CPP) that reflected the actual distribution of power rather than the electoral mandate. The new government had two prime ministers: Prince Ranariddh of Funcinpec and Hun Sen of CPP. Powersharing was a necessity given that the CPP refused to surrender its control over the state (which was particularly strong in the countryside) and that Funcinpec was unprepared to govern despite having won the vote. Sam Rainsy, then economics and finance minister for Funcinpec, admitted that his party had "neither the time nor the political means to bring the provinces under central control . . . [Funcinpec] central control had very little knowledge—not even to speak of control—but knowledge of the provinces."[9] The new government had difficulties extending its authority to the entire territory, and the Khmer Rouge remained a threat for a time.[10]

Pervasive governmental corruption and increasing evidence that major international criminal syndicates and drug traffickers were protected in Cambodia threatened to undermine the inchoate democratic institutions created during the peace implementation period.[11] Some analysts labeled Phnom Penh "Medellín on the Mekong" and detailed the number of journalists critical of the regime who had been threatened or killed.[12] Corruption and private deals to exploit Cambodia's forests and gems, often in collaboration with the remnants of the Khmer Rouge and such regional warlords as Ieng Sary, prevented the demilitarization of the economy.[13] Funcinpec never developed into an effective political party, despite the natural advantage of its links to the monarchy in a deeply traditional society, and its links to the countryside remained loose.[14] Funcinpec and the CPP competed for the loyalty (and resources) of fragments of the disintegrating Khmer Rouge, and defectors were often richly rewarded. Wide-scale civil war did not return, but pervasive corruption and a divided administration created a tense stalemate.

In the lead-up to the next round of elections, scheduled for 1998, a confrontation between Funcinpec and the CPP seemed inevitable. Armed clashes broke out in Phnom Penh for two days in July 1997, and Funcinpec prime minister Ranariddh was removed from power and went into exile with a number of his supporters. Funcinpec eventually split into factions, with one remaining in the government, now thoroughly dominated by CPP prime minister Hun Sen. Elections eventually were held in July 1998 in an atmosphere of violence and accusations of partisan administration.[15] Representatives of US-based NGOs described the preelection process as "fundamentally flawed."[16] The CPP won 64 seats (41 percent of the vote) to

Funcinpec's 43 (32 percent of the vote), with the Sam Rainsy Party (led by the former finance minister, a vocal critic of corruption) winning the remaining 15 (14 percent of the vote).[17] The elections were followed by a series of opposition protests, allegations of fraud, and demands for a recount.

Cambodia remained on the brink of crisis, with week after week of civil disobedience, violent protest, and political deadlock, until the main political parties reached an agreement in November 1998, with King Norodom Sihanouk's help, to form a new coalition government. As before the July 1997 resurgence of fighting, Funcinpec and the CPP shared power in a shaky alliance of parties that perceive themselves as rivals rather than partners. CPP leader Hun Sen became prime minister, Funcinpec leader Ranariddh became speaker of the National Assembly, and other ministries were divided evenly (with shared responsibility for Defense and Interior). Sam Rainsy took up his position as head of the parliamentary opposition.

A similar story played out following the 2003 elections. The CPP won just under 50 percent of the seats, and although Funcinpec's share fell sharply, Hun Sen again struck a deal with Ranariddh to form a coalition government. In a sign of relative stability, Cambodia went through a smooth transition from longtime king Norodom Sihanouk to his son Norodom Sihamoni in October 2004.

Despite high tensions and persistent violence, Cambodia did not fall back into wide-scale civil war. A longtime Western observer noted in 1999 that "this is probably the most peaceful period, in terms of military confrontation, in Cambodia in the last 32 years"; peace has held since then.[18] As in so many states in the developing world, Cambodia has regular elections but is far from a consolidated democracy. Partial steps to demilitarize politics during the 1992–1994 transition allowed progress on war termination, but power continues to be allocated by nonelectoral mechanisms and democracy remains constrained.

Summary

Looking back over the decade since the conclusion of the peace implementation processes in Mozambique, El Salvador, and Cambodia suggests that, although each faces continuing serious problems with democratic consolidation and violence remains high, significant progress toward sustainable peacebuilding and democratization has occurred. The promise of demilitarization of politics in the brief interim between the signing of a peace accord and the culminating postconflict elections is not to end all conflict and to leap from war to consolidated democracy all at once. It is rather to take the first critical steps on this long, contentious, and often uncertain path to peace—first steps that are particularly critical because they establish the early precedents and incentives that organizations will pursue. In El Salvador, Mozambique, and Cambodia, the peace processes ended periods of protracted civil war and at least opened up possibilities for democratization (if only tentatively in Cambodia). In each of these three cases the institutions made powerful by the war—ARENA and FMLN, Frelimo and Renamo, the CPP and Funcinpec (if not the Khmer Rouge)—have found ways to transform themselves so that they remain as vital in the postconflict political game as they had been in the violent civil war.

War Termination Without Sustainable Democracy

In contrast to El Salvador, Mozambique, and Cambodia, other cases indicate that some peace processes may end in elections that at best serve to advance war-termination goals with ambiguous and quite possibly negative implications for long-term democratization. In Bosnia-Herzegovina, Tajikistan, and for a rather brief period in Liberia, the new authorities empowered by postconflict elections managed to prevent a renewal of civil war (with the critical assistance of international forces in Bosnia-Herzegovina). These authorities, however, remained essentially unreconstructed war parties at the time of the first postconflict elections. Demilitarization of politics was limited at best, and the organizations made powerful by the civil war—the nationalist parties in Bosnia-Herzegovina, the incumbent People's Democratic Party and its allied regional strongmen in Tajikistan, and the National Patriot Party machine of the military strongman Charles Taylor in Liberia—continued to derive their power by responding to the old incentives of violence, polarization, and predation rather than democratic incentives of peaceful political competition.

In the years since these agreements, stability has been maintained in Bosnia-Herzegovina, where the international community remains an overwhelmingly forceful presence. This stability, along with critical transitions in Croatia and Serbia, has allowed for some slow processes of reform that may represent the early stages of democratization and peacebuilding. In Tajikistan the state is becoming less and less relevant as external dynamics from Afghanistan, the global war against terrorism, and the international narcotics trade drive developments. In Liberia another wave of civil war with many of the same actors and issues broke out in 2000. Military pressure by insurgent factions, along with strong regional and international pressure, eventually forced Taylor into exile. A new peace agreement and international peacekeeping force maintain security in the context of another set of postconflict elections set for 2005. These cases illustrate that in the absence of processes to demilitarize politics, war termination and stability may be possible, but sustainable peacebuilding and democratization are much more difficult.

Bosnia-Herzegovina

After the September 1996 elections, the OSCE organized and monitored four more sets of elections in Bosnia-Herzegovina between 1996 and 1998. In September 1997 the postponed municipal elections were held. As in 1996, nationalist parties manipulated where voters registered in order to pack strategic towns with their preferred ethnic composition, thereby reinforcing some of the war's ethnic polarization.[19] Subsequent elections showed steadily improving electoral administration, but nationalist parties continued to dominate and the international community continued to manage the process.

Stalemate among the ethnic leaders and the international community led the Office of the High Representative (OHR) to make contentious decisions unilaterally. Following the Bonn meeting of the Peace Implementation Council in December 1997, the OHR intervened in local political life by removing mayors and even dismissing the president of the Republika Srpska in March 1999. Under Carlos Westendorp the OHR imposed common license plates, a flag, and a national anthem. According to Westendorp, "In the future, I will put an end to all that endless decision making. . . . If the parties do not agree, I will tell them, no problem. I will make the decision for them. . . . And if they systematically block Dayton I will ask those who are not cooperating to resign."[20] Such actions created a pattern whereby local political leaders did not have to take responsibility for developments in the country.[21] Over time the OHR acted to erode some of the power of the nationalist parties. Some indicted war criminals finally were captured and sent to The Hague for trial, key assets such as radio stations were taken from nationalist parties, and control over criminal sources of revenue began to take effect.[22]

In addition to the High Commission's actions, regional dynamics and political transitions in Croatia and Serbia led to reduced support for nationalist leaders and parties in Bosnia-Herzegovina. The Croatian Democratic Union (HDZ) lost power following Franjo Tudjman's death in late 1999. In the January 2000 elections opposition posters urged, "Vote for Change," and Croatians, tired of the nationalist policies that had produced war and economic hardship, voted overwhelmingly to replace the HDZ.[23] In 2003, however, the HDZ returned to power. In Serbia and Montenegro, following international intervention in Kosovo, the nationalist leader Slobodan Milosevic lost elections and finally was pushed from office in 2000 by a wave of carefully organized and internationally supported strikes and demonstrations. Political violence remains high, with Serbian prime minister Zoran Djindjic assassinated in March 2003 and nationalist parties remaining powerful. In June 2004 the more moderate Boris Tadic narrowly won the election to become Serbian president over the more nationalistic Tomislav Nikolic of the Serbian Radical Party (SRS).[24]

By the late 1990s reform and greater political space for nonnationalist actors began to grow in Bosnia-Herzegovina. As security held over time, nationalist groups came under pressure and began to fragment. Biljana Plavsic, who was designated by Radovan Karadžić as his successor in the SDS, broke with Karadžić.[25] Vote shares of the nationalist parties declined as a percentage of total votes cast in Bosnia-Herzegovina. This is attributable to the rise of many small parties and the rise of moderate parties (Social Democratic Party, Party for BiH).[26] In October 2002, however, a new coalition of nationalist parties won elections and assumed power with promises to pursue economic and political reform.[27]

Although elections in Bosnia-Herzegovina have not brought to power the moderate, multiethnic democrats that many wished to see take office, the process of shifting competition from the battlefield to elections and parliamentary negotiations is significant. The state continues to face difficult challenges, and a number of questions arising from the civil war remain unanswered. Security remains heavily in the hands of the international community, and there are some who worry that violence will return if peacekeepers withdraw. The economy includes significant criminalized elements, and human rights remain problematic. Although Bosnia-Herzegovina now faces these challenges of democratic consolidation and statebuilding, the Dayton Peace Agreement was instrumental in ending the civil war of the 1990s.

Tajikistan

The peace process in Tajikistan helped reconstruct the failed state—an important accomplishment and necessary precondition for further improvements—but did not advance the longer-term peacebuilding and democratization agendas. Since the 1999–2000 and 2005 elections that confirmed the incumbent Rakhmonov in power, the state has remained extremely weak, desperately poor, and quite authoritarian (characteristics it shares with most of its neighbors in Central Asia).[28] Rakhmonov has faced challenges from former commanders from both sides of the civil war, and violent flare-ups, particularly in the first few years after the 2000 elections, were common. Widescale civil war, however, has not returned.

The Islamic Revival Party (IRP), the only legal Islamic party in Central Asia, continued to demonstrate its commitment to peace and to work within the constitution. New leaders in the IRP deemphasized the creation of an Islamic state and rather stressed their goal to inject more religious and traditional values into political life and point to Turkey as a model.[29] Although dialogue continued, the basic rules of democracy and respect for human rights were largely ignored. Large parts of the country were outside central government control, and violence remained unchecked. Political assassinations were common, foreign humanitarian workers were kidnapped, and former UTO military leaders fought with the government in the northeastern region.[30] The IRP and other opposition parties have had little influence as President Imomali Rakhmonov and his People's Democratic Party have consolidated power and continued the pre-1997 practice of excluding rival clan and regional factions from power. By one estimate, 80 percent of the postconflict government posts went to members of the Kulabi clan.[31]

In February 2005 Rakhmonov's People's Democratic Party won 74 percent of the vote in national elections, followed by the Communist Party with 13 percent and the IRP with 8 percent. The

Organization of Security and Cooperation in Europe's Office for Democratic Institutions and Human Rights (OSCE/ODIHR) concluded that the elections "failed to meet many key OSCE commitments and other international standards on democratic elections." The OSCE/ODIHR in particular noted that the composition of the election commissions was not sufficiently inclusive, that many local election commissions did not meet in public session, and that two well-known opposition leaders were prevented from running despite not having been convicted of charges filed against them.[32] The main opposition parties filed complaints charging widespread fraud and demanding new elections in Dushanbe.[33]

The civil war in the 1990s in Tajikistan has not returned, but politics remains firmly in the hands of nondemocratic institutions. Elections in 1999–2000 and 2005 did little to shift the strategies of the incumbent regime. The IRP has moved from an insurgent group to a political party but remains largely on the margins of political life in Tajikistan. The peace process and postconflict elections played a role in ending the civil war but have had little impact in generating the conditions for long-term democratization.

Return to War

In the most tragic cases the peace process either broke down immediately after the elections, as in Angola, or after a brief interregnum of authoritarian rule, as in Liberia. In these cases the failure of the peace process was clear, as even the minimal goal of war termination was not met. On the other hand, even these failed efforts to end civil war propelled transformation of the organizations engaged in the struggles and provide a new baseline—for better or worse—for subsequent efforts to build peace.

Angola

In the aftermath of the 1992 elections, renewed war between the MPLA and UNITA created another wave of immense human suffering. The period between the end of 1992 and November 1994 was the "most devastating chapter yet in the Angolan conflict," and for the first time major cities suffered prolonged sieges and artillery bombardments. An estimated 300,000 died in this horrific phase of the war.[34] The failure of demobilization under the Bicesse process left UNITA with its army intact, and access to diamonds allowed the insurgents to remain armed and funded. The MPLA government, in turn, used oil revenues to rearm and reorganize its armed forces. The government's superior resources and international sanctions imposed on UNITA eventually led to a shift in the battlefield and to the signing of the Lusaka Protocol in November 1994.

The Lusaka peace process built on the earlier Bicesse Accords but included powersharing and mandatory demobilization before elections. The peace process foundered, however, with long delays in quartering UNITA troops and foot-dragging in setting up the new interim authorities. In December 1998 the MPLA determined that UNITA could not be a partner in peace and had to be defeated militarily. UNITA began to crumble under the military onslaught, with one faction joining the government, and the movement finally collapsed when its leader Jonas Savimbi was killed in combat on February 22, 2002.

The 1991 Bicesse Accords and the subsequent elections in 1992 clearly failed to deliver either peace or democracy to Angola. The failed process, however, transformed the nature of the conflict in significant ways. The MPLA gained additional international legitimacy as a result of the elections, resulting in the government's recognition by the United States.[35] The Bicesse process served as the starting point for later negotiations, and the 1994 Lusaka Agreement included provisions on powersharing and demobilization in the hope of overcoming the weaknesses of the earlier process.[36]

Liberia

Charles Taylor and the National Patriotic Party (NPP) government reeled from crisis to crisis until Taylor flew to exile in Nigeria in August 2003. Many Liberians had hoped that appeasing Taylor and his militant faction would end the violence but soon concluded that Taylor's organization continued to rely upon violence and fear to retain power. Within weeks of assuming power as president, Taylor closed down independent radio stations, ended cooperation with ECOMOG on security sector reform, and created a plethora of unaccountable special security units loyal to him. Strategies based on the use of intimidation and fear remained the NPP's approach even after winning the elections. The December 1997 murder while in the custody of Taylor's security forces of Sam Dokie, one of Taylor's early supporters who had broken with the NPFL, led many Liberians to fear that the violence of the war years was not over yet.[37]

In addition to continuing to use violence to intimidate opposition at home, Taylor continued to interfere in neighboring states, particularly Sierra Leone, where the wartime networks of gun and diamond markets remained lucrative. Armed opposition movements soon reemerged, first operating out of Guinea and Sierra Leone, where exiles formed the Liberians United for Reconciliation and Democracy (LURD), drawing on some of the Mandingo and Krahn groups previously mobilized in the United Liberation Movement of Liberia for Democracy (ULIMO). Later the Movement for Democracy in Liberia (MODEL) organized from Côte d'Ivoire in part by mobilizing former Krahn soldiers in the Liberian Peace Council (LPC) and began putting military pressure on the Liberian government from the east. By the late 1990s most of the key armed factions of the civil war of the earlier 1990s had reemerged and were fighting once again.

In 1999 West African states engaged in the peacekeeping operation in neighboring Sierra Leone accused Taylor of supporting the Revolutionary United Front rebels there. Taylor charged that Guinea was supporting LURD and fought a series of border skirmishes in 2000. The War Crimes Tribunal in Sierra Leone indicted Taylor in June 2003. The conflict came to a head when international pressure and advances by LURD and MODEL left Taylor with no further room to maneuver. To end an increasingly violent impasse, Nigeria offered Taylor asylum, and a new interim government led by businessman Gyude Bryant was put in place and given the mandate to organize another round of postconflict elections.

The 1997 elections to implement the Abuja II agreement in Liberia therefore succeeded in bringing about only a brief interregnum between waves of civil war. Taylor's National Patriotic Front for Liberia changed its public face from an insurgent force to the National Patriotic Party political party, but the militarized institutions of the civil war remained fundamentally unreconstructed throughout the transitional process. Other militias, such as ULIMO and the LPC, failed to transform themselves into successful political parties but retained the ability to reemerge as insurgent forces (LURD and MODEL). Rather than marking a sustainable transition from war to peacebuilding and democratization, the 1997 elections initiated a rather short interlude between two phases of civil war among broadly similar forces. Politics remained militarized throughout Taylor's reign.

Summary

Creating sustainable peacebuilding and the consolidation of democracy are long-term challenges, particularly in the aftermath of protracted civil war. The early steps take place during the peace implementation period, and key precedents and norms are established through the conduct of the first postconflict elections. In those cases where demilitarization of politics took place prior to elections, electoral competition, if not consolidated democracy, seems to be well in place. Elections have been held according to the constitutional schedule in Mozambique and El Salvador, and each has had several rounds, although neither has seen alternation of power. Cambodia remains a more ambiguous and troubled case. Elections remain a critical part of political competition, but positions in the ensuing governments owe more to bargaining and power plays outside the constitutional framework.

In Angola, Bosnia-Herzegovina, Liberia, and Tajikistan the first postconflict elections were characterized by the continued dominance of the institutions made powerful by the war. Developments since those elections have failed to demonstrate the capacity to sustain peacebuilding and democratization. In Angola the 1992 elections led to renewed civil war, and subsequent elections have not taken place. The case of Bosnia-Herzegovina is more ambiguous. Although a series of elections has taken place, the question of security remains firmly in the hands of international peacekeepers, making it difficult to assess whether the peacebuilding process is sustainable. Political violence remained high in Liberia despite the 1997 elections, and full-scale civil war returned by 2000. Similarly, in Tajikistan the outcome of the 1999–2000 elections did not mark a shift to electoral competition but rather to continued domination by institutions that derive their power from the use of armed force and fear.

Consolidation of democracy has proven to be a more difficult challenge than some of the early optimism about the "third wave" of democracy suggested. The post–civil war cases face these same challenges as well as the distinct challenges of overcoming the legacies of protracted conflict. No single set of elections, and certainly not elections held to implement a peace agreement, can be expected to establish democracy. The seven cases examined in this study, however, suggest that the first critical steps in sustainable peacebuilding and the consolidation of democracy begin with processes to demilitarize politics.

Notes

1. "National Election Results," *Mozambique Political Process Bulletin*, 2004 Election Issue 31, December 29, 2004.
2. For a less optimistic view, see Jeremy M. Weinstein, "Mozambique: A Fading U.N. Success Story," *Journal of Democracy* 13:1 (January 2002): 141–156.
3. See Mozambique News Agency, "New Renamo Secretary-General Appointed," *AIM Reports* 125 (January 12, 1998), http://www.poptel.org.uk/mozambique-news/newsletter/aim125.html. The facts that Dhlakama made the change unilaterally rather than through the election process required by Renamo statutes and that the former secretary-general José de Castro was sacked after storming the Renamo radio station in October 1997 further suggest that the transformation of a militia into a political party is a gradual and uneven process. See "Mozambique: Peace Pains," *Africa Confidential* 39:2 (January 23, 1998): 7.
4. John Blacken and Terrence Lyons, *Mozambique: From Post-Conflict to Municipal Elections* (Washington, D.C.: Management Systems International for the United States Agency for International Development, April 1999).
5. http://www.ifes.org/eguide/resultsum/mozambiqueres.htm.
6. "National Election Results," *Mozambique Political Process Bulletin*, 2004 Election Issue 31, December 29, 2004.
7. Charles T. Call, "Assessing El Salvador's Transition from Civil War to Peace," in Steven John Stedman, Donald Rothchild, and Elizabeth Cousens, eds., *Ending Civil Wars: The Implementation of Peace Agreements* (Boulder, Colo.: Lynne Rienner, 2002), p. 409.
8. Ibid., p. 409.
9. Cited in David W. Roberts, *Political Transition in Cambodia, 1991–99: Power, Elitism, and Democracy* (New York: St. Martin's Press, 2001), p. 122. See also William Shawcross, *Cambodia's New Deal* (Carnegie Endowment for International Peace Contemporary Issues Paper no. 1, 1994), p. 41.
10. Roberts, *Political Transition in Cambodia*.
11. Shawcross, *Cambodia's New Deal*.
12. Nate Thayer, cited in William Shawcross, "Tragedy in Cambodia," *New York Review of Books*, November 14, 1996.
13. See Global Witness, *Forest, Famine, and War—The Key to Cambodia's Future* (March 1995) and subsequent Global Witness reports available at www.globalwitness.org.
14. International Crisis Group, *Cambodia: The Elusive Peace Dividend* (ICG Asia Report no. 8, August 11, 2000), p. 9.

15. MacAlister Brown, "Election Observers in Cambodia, 1998: What Can We Learn?" *Government and Opposition* 35 (Winter 2000): 77–89.

16. National Democratic Institute and International Republican Institute, "Preliminary Statement on Elections in Cambodia," July 28, 1998.

17. One member of the electoral commission called the vote an "administrative triumph, political failure." Kassie Neou with Jeffrey C. Gallup, "Conducting Cambodia's Elections," *Journal of Democracy* 10:2 (April 1999): 160. For an election observer's perspective, see Brown, "Election Observers in Cambodia," pp. 77–89.

18. Cited in Keith B. Richburg, "Cambodia Comes to Peace with Itself," *Washington Post,* January 31, 1999, p. A23.

19. Christopher Bennett, "No Flying Colors for Dayton—Yet," *Transitions* 4:7 (December 1997): 39.

20. Lenard J. Cohen, "Whose Bosnia? The Politics of Nation Building," *Current History* (March 1998): 109–110.

21. International Crisis Group, *Whither Bosnia?* ICG Europe Report no. 43 (September 1998): 8.

22. Mary Kaldor, "Security Structures in Bosnia and Herzegovina," in Gavin Cawthra and Robin Luckham, eds., *Governing Insecurity: Democratic Control of Military and Security Establishments in Transitional Democracies* (London: Zed, 2003).

23. "All Change in Croatia," *Economist,* January 6, 2000, http://www. economist.com/archive/view.cgi; "Croatia's Democratic Message," *New York Times,* January 6, 2000, p. A24.

24. International Crisis Group, *Serbia's Changing Political Landscape* (ICG Europe Briefing, July 22, 2004).

25. Cohen, "Whose Bosnia?" pp. 105–106.

26. Carrie Manning and Miljenko Antić, "Lessons from Bosnia and Herzegovina: The Limits of Electoral Engineering," *Journal of Democracy* 14:3 (July 2003): 48.

27. International Crisis Group, *Bosnia's Nationalist Governments: Paddy Ashdown and the Paradoxes of State Building* (ICG Balkans Report no. 146, July 22, 2003).

28. For assessments, see International Crisis Group, *Tajikistan: An Uncertain Peace* (ICG Asia Report No. 30, December 24, 2001); International Crisis Group, "Tajikistan's Politics: Confrontation or Consolidation?" (ICG Asia Briefing, May 19, 2004); Nasrin Dadmehr, "Tajikistan: Regionalism and Weakness," in Robert I. Rotberg, ed., *State Failure and State Weakness in a Time of Terror* (Washington D.C.: Brookings Institution Press, 2003); Kathleen Collins, "Tajikistan: Bad Peace Agreements and Prolonged Civil Conflict," in Chandra Lekha Sriram and Karin Wermester, eds., *From Promise to Practice: Strengthening UN Capacities for the Prevention of Violent Conflict* (Boulder, Colo.: Lynne Rienner, 2003).

29. "Islam in Central Asia: Religion, Politics and Moderation," *Economist,* May 17, 2003, p. 39.

30. Human Rights Watch, *Tajikistan,* October 5, 2001, http://www.hrw. org/press/2001/10/tajik1005.htm.

31. Irina Zviagelskaya, "The Tajik Conflict: Problems of Regulation," in Mohammad-Reza Djalili, Frédéric Grare, and Shirin Akiner, eds., *Tajikistan: The Trials of Independence* (New York: St. Martin's Press, 1997), cited in Collins, "Tajikistan," p. 282.

32. The Organization of Security and Cooperation in Europe's Office for Democratic Institutions and Human Rights (OSCE/ODHR) Election Observation Mission, "Statement of Preliminary Findings and Conclusions, Republic of Tajikistan Parliamentary Elections—First Round, 27 February 2005."

33. Bagila Bukharbayeva, "Opposition Says Tajikistan Elections Unfair," Associated Press, February 28, 2005.

34. Tony Hodges, *Angola from Afro-Stalinism to Petro-Diamond Capitalism* (Oxford: James Currey, 2001), p. 15.

35. Norrie MacQueen, "Peacekeeping by Attrition: The United Nations in Angola," *Journal of Modern African Studies* 36:3 (1998): 399–422.

36. Paul Hare, *Angola's Last Best Chance for Peace* (Washington, D.C.: United States Institute of Peace Press, 1998).

37. Dokie and his wife, sister, and cousin were found near Gbarnga, decapitated and burned after his arrest by Taylor's Special Security Service. See Agence France-Presse, "Liberian Police Arrest Four After Murder of Politician," December 10, 1997.

7

Encouraging the Demilitarization of Politics

Creating the conditions for sustainable peace following protracted civil war is one of the most difficult and important challenges of contemporary politics. In recent years elections have been designated as a key mechanism in negotiated peace settlements with the expectation that the poll will bring to power new leaders and legitimize new institutions that can maintain peace and democratization. The results, however, have been mixed, and important aspects of these transitions remain underanalyzed. This book has argued that demilitarizing politics during the interim period is key to sustainable peace and democratization. Elections themselves do not end wars but can provide the context and incentives for critical institutional transformations. If politics is demilitarized during the transitional peace implementation period, then new organizations capable of sustaining peace will be in place at the time of the elections.

Elections served as a key, culminating event in peace implementation processes in many of the negotiated settlements of the 1990s, including Angola (1992), Cambodia (1993), Mozambique (1994), El Salvador (1994), Bosnia-Herzegovina (1996), Liberia (1997), and Tajikistan (1999–2000). These cases suggest that transitions ending in elections sometimes result in new political leadership and institutions capable of both preserving the peace and initiating democratization. This was the result in El Salvador, Mozambique, and to a more limited extent Cambodia. In other cases the move toward elections precipitated renewed conflict, as in Angola. In Bosnia-Herzegovina, Liberia, and Tajikistan elections served more as a mechanism of war termination with only a secondary, limited, and perhaps damaging relationship to long-term democratization. In El Salvador, Mozambique, and Cambodia, relatively effective processes to demilitarize politics were in place during the period between cease-fire and elections while in Angola, Bosnia-Herzegovina, Liberia, and Tajikistan the institutions of war remained powerful throughout the transitional period and hence dominated the postconflict elections.

The literature on political and economic change suggests that institutional legacies of the past play powerful roles in shaping transitional processes. In cases of post–civil war transition, the most immediate and salient legacies will be the organizations and structures that emerged during the period of violence, insecurity, and fear. Protracted and violent conflicts distort and shatter peacetime social structures while they engender particular institutions that meet the demands and incentives of violence. These wartime institutions— insurgent groups, paramilitaries, militarized governments, black-market networks and humanitarian economies, and social groups polarized by fear—will be key actors during the war and will remain powerful during the peace implementation process. If the institutions of war are demilitarized and transformed into organizations that can respond to the different incentives of peace—political parties, open-market economies, and civil society—then sustainable peace and democratization are more likely. If the institutions of war remain unreconstructed during the peace implementation period and retain their dominance through the postconflict elections, then limited war termination may be possible but sustainable peacebuilding and democratization difficult.

Demilitarization of politics focuses on the imperative to transform the institutions of war as a necessary initial component of sustainable peacebuilding. Efforts to negotiate powersharing pacts, to delay elections until conditions are "right," to engineer inclusive electoral systems, or to offer third-party "guarantees" are likely to fail in the most difficult and protracted cases of civil war. The powerful actors that developed during a protracted civil war cannot be wished away; neither can the enabling environment for peaceful political competition be proclaimed into existence. To the extent that politics is demilitarized during the transitional period, postconflict elections are more likely to result in a new political order that can sustain peace and democracy.

Demilitarization of politics is a set of processes whereby strategies and behavior of military organizations change in response to new incentives and opportunities. Three aspects of demilitarizing politics are particularly important: (1) the construction of effective interim administrations, particularly the creation of credible electoral commissions; (2) the transformation of insurgents, paramilitaries, and military regimes into competitive political parties; and (3) the development of processes of demobilization and security sector reform, which reduces the likelihood of a return to war while building confidence in the political process. This transformation is more likely when interim administration—including the critical election management body—is embedded in processes of joint decisionmaking, consultation, and collaborative problem-solving. It is in this institutional context that expectations develop and recently warring parties decide whether to adopt strategies suitable for peaceful democratic competition or to retain their fighting capacities and strategies. Demilitarization of politics creates opportunities and increases the incentives for parties to alter their strategies from violence and the manipulation of fear to peaceful mobilization and electoral competition. Politics is demilitarized both by increasing the incentives for institutions to adopt political and electoral strategies and by decreasing incentives and opportunities for violence.

In El Salvador, Mozambique, and Cambodia interim institutions helped create the context for successful elections, while in Liberia, Bosnia-Herzegovina, Tajikistan, and Angola weak interim governments left the structures of war in place and failed to alleviate the legacies of fear prior to elections. To the extent that transitional regimes operate on the basis of joint decisionmaking and collaborative problem-solving, they can build confidence in the peace process, create opportunities for political rather than military competition, and provide an institutional context that encourages successful elections. Such strong interim regimes can alter conflicting parties' perceptions and incentives—and hence strategies—during peace implementation, thereby encouraging the demilitarization of politics and effective postconflict elections.

Demilitarization of politics also includes processes to transform militarized institutions such as insurgent movements and military regimes into political parties able to compete effectively in an electoral environment. In Mozambique, for example, Renamo transformed itself from a violent insurgent group into a political party able to compete effectively in multiparty elections. Similar processes took place within both the ruling ARENA party and the insurgent FMLN in El Salvador. In the less successful or failed cases, militarized groups retained their capacity to operate as military forces and continued to respond to the still dominant incentives of war, weakening the capacity of postconflict elections to mark a transition to civilian rule. Such militarized parties often do well in a postconflict context still distorted by fear and insecurity, as in Bosnia-Herzegovina, Liberia, and Tajikistan, but the prospects for sustainable democratization and long-term peacebuilding are limited in such cases. In Angola and eventually in Liberia, the militarized parties that remained powerful throughout the peace implementation process returned to war.

Finally, demobilization and security sector reform are at the heart of peace implementation and provide important opportunities to demilitarize politics. Reducing the number of soldiers under the command of the leaders of the competing parties will increase the prospects for effective postconflict elections by reducing the potential for a return to war. Furthermore, if demobilization is organized around collaborative decisionmaking, then the process will promote new institutions and norms appropriate for democratization as well as reducing the capacity for armed conflict.

The demilitarization of politics therefore focuses attention on the processes by which the former parties to the conflict relate to one another during the peace implementation process following civil war and how these interactions may promote the adoption of strategies that can support peacebuilding. At the time of the initial cease-fire, organizations made powerful by the war will dominate the political landscape. During the transitional period leading up to postconflict elections, a new context can shift the incentives and opportunities organizations face and thereby encourage the transformation of institutions whose origins previously lay in violent conflict into institutions whose future lies in democratic competition. In this way postconflict elections are both the context in which demilitarization of politics takes place and the event that will demonstrate the extent to which that transformation has been successful.

Postconflict elections have become a ubiquitous component of civil war settlements supported by the international community since the end of the Cold War. In recent years there has been a vigorous policy debate about whether elections are useful in such difficult cases as Afghanistan, Iraq, and the Democratic Republic of Congo.[1]

Yet elections remain a core component of the transitional plans in these cases. Despite the widely recognized limits to elections and the potential for elections to exacerbate postconflict tensions, there seem to be few alternatives to this mechanism of peace implementation. Postconflict elections often are criticized for failing to advance democratization. This is often true but misses the potential for such elections to promote important war-termination goals even if they fail to promote democratization. Policymakers seeking to address the challenges of postconflict reconstruction cannot afford to make democratization their one and only goal and must accept that in many of the difficult cases war termination is the only available short-term option that provides at least the potential for long-term stability and eventual transition to democracy.[2]

This book has argued that attention should be focused on what kinds of institutional transformations may take place in the period between the signing of the peace accord and the postconflict election. In the most difficult cases, such as Angola, El Salvador, Cambodia, Mozambique, Bosnia-Herzegovina, Liberia, and Tajikistan—as well as Iraq, Afghanistan, and the Democratic Republic of Congo—there will be few opportunities to promote peacebuilding and democratization through powersharing pacts, electoral-system engineering, or delaying the elections until security is firmly established. Even these difficult cases, however, often have openings to advance the demilitarization of politics by encouraging the transformation of the institutions of war into institutions that can support peace.

For the international community, the peace implementation process following civil war presents a number of opportunities. Greater emphasis should be placed on the processes that shape how the parties to the conflict relate to each other during the transition rather than to elements in the peace agreement itself or international peacekeeping policy. By emphasizing the internal dynamics among parties and institutions during the interim phase rather than power-sharing arrangements in the peace agreement or international guarantees, the issue of what policies support successful implementation shifts. Rather than asking for additional provisions in the peace accord or trying to negotiate a postelection powersharing pact (a difficult challenge given the imperatives to negotiate a cease-fire), it is more useful to ask how the implementation process can strengthen patterns of cooperation and trust and overcome insecurity. Rather than placing responsibility on the international community to "guarantee" compliance (a guarantee that is rarely credible), successful peace processes have developed institutions that create expectations among the parties to encourage them to abide by their agreement. The peace agreement becomes the starting point for another series of negotiations, bargaining, and institution-building rather than a blueprint to be enacted. The interim period will represent a fluid period during which parties and leadership change, expectations are formed, and the fears and interests that motivated the initial cease-fire agreement are transformed. The outcome of this period of continued bargaining and maneuvering for advantage provides the context for postconflict elections more than the initial agreement or the international community.

To the extent that a process to demilitarize politics can be initiated, the precedents and institutional basis for sustainable peace and democratization can be supported. Donor support for strong and effective interim administrations, particularly those based on consultation and collaborative problem-solving, can help create a new institutional context that bridges the structures of war to structures that can sustain peace and democracy. In particular, donors and international organizations should examine electoral commissions and recognize them as opportunities not only to administer good elections but also as openings for confidence-building and potential models for new forms of cooperation and peaceful competition. The transformation of militarized institutions into political parties has enormous potential to bolster both the war termination and democratization agendas of postconflict elections. Finally, demobilization and security sector reform provide opportunities not only to reduce the potential for a return to war but also to build institutions that will encourage ex-combatants to change their evaluation of their future prospects and pursue electoral strategies.

The process of implementing peace and promoting democracy following civil war is difficult, but recent experience suggests that processes to demilitarize politics can—and must—begin during the transitional period.

Notes

1. See, for example, Marina Ottaway and Thomas Carothers, "The Right Road to Sovereignty in Iraq," Carnegie Endowment for International

Peace Policy Brief 27, October 2003. See Roland Paris, *At War's End: Building Peace After Civil Conflict* (Cambridge: Cambridge University Press, 2004).

2. For more on the multiple roles of postconflict elections, see Terrence Lyons, "The Role of Postsettlement Elections," in Stephen John Stedman, Elizabeth Cousens, and Donald Rothchild, eds., *Ending Civil Wars: The Implementation of Peace Agreements* (Boulder, Colo.: Lynne Rienner, 2002).

Acronyms

AFL	Armed Forces of Liberia
ALCOP	All Liberian Coalition Party
ARENA	National Republican Alliance (Alianza Republicana Nacionalists)
ASEAN	Association of Southeast Asian Nations
CCF	Cease-Fire Commission
CCPM	Joint Political and Military Commission
CD	Democratic Convergence (Convergencia Democrática)
CDR	Coalition for the Defense of the Republic (Coalition pour la Défense de la République)
CIM	Coordinator for International Monitoring
CNR	Commission of National Reconciliation
COPAZ	National Commission for the Consolidation of Peace (Comisión Nacional para la Consolidación de la Paz)
CPP	Cambodian People's Party
CSC	Supervisory and Monitoring Commission
DDR	demobilization, disarmament, and reintegration
ECOMOG	ECOWAS Cease-fire Monitoring Group
ECOWAS	Economic Community of West African States
ETA	Basque Homeland and Liberty (Euskadi Ta Askatasuna)
FADM	Armed Forces for the Defense of Mozambique (Forças Armadas de Defensa de Moçambique)
FAES	Armed Forces of El Salvador
FARC	Armed Revolutionary Forces of Columbia (Fuerzas Armadas Revolucionarias de Colombia)

FMLN	Farabundo Martí Front for National Liberation (Frente Farabundo Martí para la Liberación Nacional)
FNLA	National Front for the Liberation of Angola (Frente Nacional de Libertação de Angola)
Frelimo	Front for the Liberation of Mozambique (Frente da Libertação de Moçambique)
Funcinpec	National Union Front for an Independent, Neutral, Peaceful, and Cooperative Cambodia (Font Uni National pour une Cambodge Indépendent, Neutre, Pacifique et Coopératif)
HB	Herri Batasuna
HDZ	Croatian Democratic Party
HOS	Croatian Defense Forces
HSP	Croatian Party of Rights
HVO	Croatian Defense Council
IECOM	Independent Electoral Commission
IFOR	Implementation Force
IRP	Islamic Revival Party
KPNLF	Khmer People's National Liberation Front
LPC	Liberia Peace Council
LURD	Liberians United for Reconciliation and Democracy
MODEL	Movement for Democracy in Liberia
MPLA	Popular Movement for the Liberation of Angola (Movimento Popular de Libertação de Angola)
MPRI	Military Professionals Resources Inc.
MRND	National Republican Movement for Development (Mouvement Republicain National pour le Developpement)
NATO	North Atlantic Treaty Organization
NDPL	National Democratic Party of Liberia
NPFL	National Patriotic Front for Liberia
NPP	National Patriotic Party
OHR	Office of the High Representative
ONUMOZ	United Nations Operation in Mozambique
ONUSAL	United Nations Observer Mission in El Salvador
OSCE	Organization for Security and Cooperation in Europe
PD	Democratic Party
PDC	Christian Democratic Party
PDK	Party of Democratic Kampuchea
PDP	People's Democratic Party

PKK	Kurdistan Worker's Party
Renamo	Mozambique National Resistance (Resistência Nacional Moçambicana)
SBiH	Party for Bosnia and Herzegovina
SDA	Party of Democratic Action
SDS	Serbian Democratic Party
SNC	Supreme National Council
STAE	Technical Secretariat for Election Administration
TSE	Supreme Electoral Tribunal
ULIMO	United Liberation Movement of Liberia for Democracy
UNAVEM	United Nations Verification Mission
UNITA	National Union for the Total Independence of Angola (União Nacional para a Independência Total de Angola)
UNMOT	United Nations Mission of Observers in Tajikistan
UNOMIL	United Nations Observer Mission in Liberia
UNPROFOR	UN Protection Force
UNTAC	UN Transitional Authority in Cambodia
USAID	U.S. Agency for International Development
UTO	United Tajik Opposition

Bibliography

Abazov, Rafis. "Battling in Peace." *Tajikistan Annual Report 1999*. http://archive/tol.ca/countries/tajar99.html.

Abdullaev, Kamoludin, and Catherine Barnes, eds. *Politics of Compromise: The Tajikistan Peace Process*. London: Conciliation Resources, March 2001.

Abdullo, Rashid G. "Implementation of the 1997 General Agreement: Successes, Dilemmas, and Challenges." In Kamoludin Abdullaev and Catherine Barnes, eds. *Politics of Compromise: The Tajikistan Peace Process*. London: Accord, March 2001.

Abrahamsson, Hans, and Anders Nilsson. *Mozambique: The Troubled Transition from Socialist Construction to Free Market Capitalism*. London: Zed, 1995.

Acevedo, Carlos. "El Salvador's New Clothes: The Electoral Process 1982–1989." In Anjali Sundaram and George Gelber, eds. *A Decade of War: El Salvador Confronts the Future*. New York: Monthly Review Press, 1991, pp. 19–37.

Adebajo, Adekeye. "Dog Days in Monrovia." *West Africa* (April 22–28, 1996): 622–623.

———. *Liberia's Civil War: Nigeria, ECOMOG, and Regional Security in West Africa*. Boulder, Colo.: Lynne Rienner, 2002.

Adekanye, J. Bayo. "Power-Sharing in Multi-Ethnic Political Systems." *Security Dialogue* 39 (1998): 33.

Advic, Senad. "The Limits of the Landslide." Institute for War and Peace Reporting, October 1996, www.iwpr.net/index.pl?archive/war/war_46_199610_01.txt.

Agence France-Presse. "Kromah Apologizes for Hoarding Arms, Ammunition." March 14, 1997.

———. "Liberian Police Arrest Four After Murder of Politician." December 10, 1997.

———. "Only ECOWAS Can Change Elections Date: Ikimi." April 27, 1997.

Africa Confidential. "Angola: Luanda Shoot Out." *Africa Confidential* 33:22 (November 6, 1992): 8.

————. "Angola: Two Elephants Fight." *Africa Confidential* 33:13 (July 3, 1992): 1.

————. "Angola II: Winner Does Not Take All." *Africa Confidential* 33:18 (September 11, 1992): 5.

————. "Liberia: Talking of Votes." *Africa Confidential* 38:7 (March 28, 1997): 5–6.

————. "Mozambique: Funding for Peace." *Africa Confidential* 34:10 (May 14, 1993): 4.

————. "Mozambique: Peace Pains." *Africa Confidential* 39:2 (January 23, 1998): 7.

————. "Mozambique: Renamo Plays for Time." *Africa Confidential* 34:15 (July 30, 1993): 3.

————. "Mozambique: The Freelance Warriors." *Africa Confidential* 33:19 (September 23, 1994): 3.

————. "Mozambique: The People for Peace." *Africa Confidential* 35:22 (November 4, 1994): 1.

————. "Politics of Vengeance and Victory for UNITA." *Africa Confidential* 33:13 (July 3, 1992): 2.

African Rights. *Death, Despair, and Defiance*. London: African Rights, 1994.

Africa Recovery. "Mozambique Accords Aid Relief Effort." *Africa Recovery* (December 1992–February 1993): 25.

Ajello, A. "O Papel da ONUMOZ no Processo de Democratização." In B. Mazula, ed. *Moçambique: Eleições, Democracia e Desenvolvimento* (Maputo, Mozambique: Inter-Africa Group, 1995).

Alden, Chris. "Lessons from the Reintegration of Demobilized Soldiers in Mozambique." *Security Dialogue* 33:3 (September 2002): 341–356.

————. *Mozambique and the Construction of the New African State: From Negotiations to Nation Building*. New York: Palgrave, 2001.

————. "Political Violence in Mozambique: Past, Present, and Future." In William Gutteridge and J. E. Spence, eds. *Violence in Southern Africa*. London: Frank Cass, 1997.

Alexander, Jocelyn. "The Local State in Post-War Mozambique: Political Practice and Ideas About Authority." *Africa* 67 (Winter 1997): 1–26.

Anderson, Mary B. *Do No Harm: How Aid Can Support Peace—or War*. Boulder: Lynne Rienner, 1999.

Andreas, Peter. "The Clandestine Political Economy of War and Peace in Bosnia." *International Studies Quarterly* 48:1 (March 2004): 29–52.

Antsee, Margaret Joan. *Orphan of the Cold War: The Inside Story of the Collapse of the Angolan Peace Process, 1992–93*. New York: St. Martin's Press, 1996.

Apter, David. *The Gold Coast in Transition*. Princeton, N.J.: Princeton University Press, 1955.

Arnson, Cynthia J., and Dinorah Azpuru. "From Peace to Democratization: Lessons from Central America." In John Darby and Roger Mac Ginty, eds. *Contemporary Peacemaking: Conflict, Violence, and Peace Processes*. Hampshire, UK: Palgrave Macmillan, 2003, pp. 197–211.

Austin, Dennis. *Democracy and Violence in India and Sri Lanka*. New York: Council on Foreign Relations Press, 1995.

Austin, Reginald. "Democracy and Democratisation." In William Maley, Charles Sampford, and Ramesh Thakur, eds. *From Civil Strife to Civil Society: Civil and Military Responsibilities in Disrupted States.* Tokyo: United Nations University Press, 2003, pp. 180–204.

Azar, Edward E. "The Analysis and Management of Protracted Conflicts." In William Maley, Charles Sampford, and Ramesh Thakur, eds. *The Psychodynamics of International Relationships.* Lexington, Mass.: Lexington Books, 1991.

Balkan Institute. *The Dayton Accords and Bosnian Elections.* Balkan Institute Reference Series No. 4, March 31, 1996, www.balkaninstitute.org/reference/Rs4elect.html.

Ball, Nicole. "Demobilization and Reintegrating Soldiers: Lessons from Africa." In Krishna Kumar, ed. *Rebuilding Societies After Civil War: Critical Roles for International Assistance.* Boulder, Colo.: Lynne Rienner, 1997, pp. 85–105.

Baloyra, Enrique A. "El Salvador: From Reactionary Despotism to 'Partidocracia.'" In Krishna Kumar, ed. *Postconflict Elections, Democratization, and International Assistance.* Boulder, Colo.: Lynne Rienner, 1998, pp. 15–37.

Barak, Oren. "Lebanon: Failure, Collapse and Resuscitation." In Robert I. Rotberg, ed. *State Failure and State Weakness in a Time of Terror.* Washington, D.C.: Brookings Institution/World Peace Foundation, 2003, pp. 305–339.

Bardi, Luciano, and Leonardo Morlino. "Italy: Tracing the Roots of the Great Transformation." In Richard S. Katz and Peter Mair, eds. *How Parties Organize: Change and Adaptation in Party Organizations in Western Democracies.* London: Sage, 1994, pp. 242–277.

Barnes, Samuel H. "The Contribution of Democracy to Rebuilding Postconflict Societies." *American Journal of International Law* 95:1 (January 2001): 86–101.

Bartoli, Andrea. "Mediating Peace in Mozambique: The Role of the Community of Sant'Egidio." In Chester A. Crocker, Fen Osler Hampson, and Pamela Aall, eds. *Herding Cats: Multiparty Mediation in a Complex World.* Washington, D.C.: United States Institute of Peace, 1999, pp. 245–274.

Bayer, Tom. *Angola: Presidential and Legislative Elections, September 29–30, 1992.* Washington, D.C. International Foundation on Electoral Systems, n.d.

Bendaña, Alejandro. *Demobilization and Reintegration in Central America: Peace-Building Challenges and Responses.* Managua, Nicaragua: Centro de Estudios Internacionales, 1999.

Bender, Gerald J. *Angola Under the Portuguese: The Myth and the Reality.* Berkeley: University of California Press, 1978.

Bennett, Christopher. "No Flying Colors for Dayton Yet." *Transitions* 4:7 (December 1997): 34–43.

———. "Voting Early, Voting Often." Institute for War and Peace Reporting, October 1996, www.iwpr.net/index.pl?archive/war/war_46_199610_02.txt.

Berdal, Mats R. *Disarmament and Demobilisation After Civil Wars.* London: International Institute for Strategic Studies Adelphi Paper 303, 1996.

Berdal, Mats, and Michael Leifer. "Cambodia." In James Mayall, ed. *The New Interventionism, 1991–1994: United Nations Experience in Cambodia, Former Yugoslavia, and Somalia.* Cambridge: Cambridge University Press, 1996, pp. 25–57.

Berkeley, Bill. *The Graves Are Not Yet Full: Race, Tribe, and Power in the Heart of Africa.* New York: Basic Books, 2001.

Bermeo, Nancy. "What the Democratization Literature Says—or Doesn't Say—About Postwar Democratization." *Global Governance* 9:2 (April-June 2003): 159–177.

Bildt, Carl. *Peace Journey: The Struggle for Peace in Bosnia.* London: Weidenfeld and Nicolson, 1998.

Blacken, John, and Terrence Lyons. *Mozambique: From Post-Conflict to Municipal Elections.* Washington, D.C.: Management Systems International for the United States Agency for International Development, April 1999.

Bojičić, Vesna, and Mary Kaldor. "The 'Abnormal' Economy of Bosnia-Herzegovina." In Carl-Ulrik Schierup, ed. *Scramble for the Balkans: Nationalism, Globalism, and the Political Economy of Reconstruction.* New York: St. Martin's Press in association with the Centre for Research in Ethnic Relations, University of Warwick, 1999.

Borden, Anthony, and Hedl Drago. "How the Bosnians Were Broken: Twenty-One Days at Dayton." *War Report* 39 (February-March 1996): 26–42.

Borden, Anthony, Slavenka Drakulic, and George Kenny. "Bosnia's Democratic Charade." *Nation* 263:8 (September 23, 1996): 14.

Bracamonte, José Angel Moroni, and David E. Spencer, *Strategy and Tactics of the Salvadoran FMLN Guerrillas: Last Battle of the Cold War, Blueprint for Future Conflicts.* Westport, Conn.: Praeger, 1995.

Bratton, Michael, and Nicholas van de Walle. *Democratic Experiments in Africa: Regime Transitions in Comparative Perspective.* Cambridge: Cambridge University Press, 1997.

British Broadcasting Corporation (BBC). "Tajik Elections Under Threat." October 15, 1999.

———. "Tajik Election Victory Is Challenged." November 7, 1999.

———. "Tajik Opposition Suspends Cooperation with Government." October 18, 1999.

———. "Tajik Opposition Walks Out of Power-sharing Deal." September 26, 1998.

Brown, Bess A. "The Civil War in Tajikistan, 1992–1993." In Mohammad-Reza Djalili, Frédéric Grare, and Shirin Akiner, eds. *Tajikistan: The Trials of Independence.* New York: St. Martin's Press, 1997, pp. 86–96.

Brown, Frederick Z. "Cambodia's Rocky Venture in Democracy." In Krishna Kumar, ed. *Postconflict Elections, Democratization, and International Assistance.* Boulder, Colo.: Lynne Rienner, 1998, pp. 87–109.

Brown, MacAlister. "Election Observers in Cambodia, 1998: What Can We Learn?" *Government and Opposition* 35 (Winter 2000): 77–89.

Brown, Mark Malloch. "Democratic Governance: Toward a Framework for Sustainable Peace." *Global Governance* 9 (2003): 147–152.

Buckley, Stephen. "Liberia Tries Peace After 5-Year Civil War." *Washington Post*, September 10, 1995, p. A28.

Budalic, Radivoje, and Mark Wheeler. "Press War by Other Means." *War Report* 42 (June 1996), http://www.iwpr.net/index.pl?archive/war/war_42_199606_3.txt.

Bukharbayeva, Bagila. "Opposition says Tajikistan Elections Unfair." Associated Press, February 28, 2005.

Burg, Steven L., and Paul S. Shoup. *The War in Bosnia-Herzegovina: Ethnic Conflict and International Intervention.* Armonk, N.Y.: M. E. Sharpe, 1999.

Byrne, Hugh. *El Salvador's Civil War: A Study of Revolution.* Boulder, Colo.: Lynne Rienner, 1996.

Cahen, Michel. "Dhlakama e Maninque Nice: An Atypical Former Guerrilla in the Mozambican Presidential Race." *L'Afrique Politique* (1995).

Call, Charles T. "Assessing El Salvador's Transition from Civil War to Peace." In Steven John Stedman, Donald Rothchild, and Elizabeth Cousens, eds. *Ending Civil Wars: The Implementation of Peace Agreements.* Boulder, Colo.: Lynne Rienner, 2002, pp. 383–420.

Call, Charles T., and William Stanley. "Civilian Security." In Steven John Stedman, Donald Rothchild, and Elizabeth Cousens, eds. *Ending Civil Wars: The Implementation of Peace Agreements.* Boulder, Colo.: Lynne Rienner, 2002, pp. 303–326.

———. "Military and Police Reform After Civil Wars." In John Darby and Roger Mac Ginty, eds. *Contemporary Peacemaking: Conflict, Violence, and Peace Processes.* Hampshire, UK: Palgrave Macmillan, 2003, pp. 212–223.

———. "Protecting the People: Public Security Choices After Civil Wars." *Global Governance* 7 (2001): 151–172.

Call, Chuck, and Michael Barnett. "Looking for a Few Good Cops: Peacekeeping, Peacebuilding, and CIVPOL." *International Peacekeeping* 6 (1999): 43–68.

Carothers, Thomas. *Aiding Democracy Abroad: The Learning Curve.* Washington, D.C.: Carnegie Endowment for International Peace, 1999.

———. "The End of the Transition Paradigm." *Journal of Democracy* 13:1 (2002): 1–21.

———. "The Observers Observed." *Journal of Democracy* 8:3 (July 1997): 17–32.

Chachiua, Martinho, and Mark Malan. "Anomalies and Acquiescence: The Mozambican Peace Process Revisited." *African Security Review* 7:4 (1998), http://www.iss.co.za/PUBS/ASR/7No4/Anomalies.html.

Chan, Stephen, and Moises Venancio. *War and Peace in Mozambique.* London: Macmillan, 1998.

Chanaa, Jane. *Security Sector Reform: Issues, Challenges, and Prospects.* Adelphi Paper no. 344. London: International Institute for Strategic Studies, 2002.

Chandler, David P. *The Tragedy of Cambodian History: Politics, War and Revolution Since 1945.* New Haven, Conn.: Yale University Press, 1991.

———. *Bosnia: Faking Democracy After Dayton.* 2nd ed. London and Sterling, Va.: Pluto Press, 2000.

Chernick, Marc W. "Negotiated Settlement to Armed Conflict: Lessons from the Colombian Peace Process." *Journal of Interamerican Studies and World Affairs* 30:4 (Winter 1988–1989): 53–88.

Chevigny, Paul. *Edge of the Knife: Political Violence in the Americas.* New York: The New Press, 1995.

Chiahemen, John. "Liberians Vote in Peace Against War." Reuters, July 19, 1997.

Child, Jack. *The Central American Peace Process, 1983–1991: Sheathing Swords, Building Confidence.* Boulder, Colo.: Lynne Rienner, 1992.

Chingono, Mark. *The State, Violence and Development: The Political Economy of War in Mozambique, 1975–92.* Aldershot, UK: Averbury, 1996.

Chiozza, Giacomo, and H. E. Goemans. "Avoiding Diversionary Targets." Paper presented at the American Political Science Association meeting. Philadelphia, Pa., August 2003.

Choe, Yonhyok, and Staffan Darnolf. "Evaluating the Structure and Functional Role of Electoral Administration in Contemporary Democracies: Building 'Free and Fair Election Index (FEEI)' and 'Effective Election Index (EEI).'" Paper presented at the ninety-fifth annual meeting of the American Political Science Association. Atlanta, Georgia, September 2–5, 1999.

Cigar, Norman. "Serb War Effort and the Termination of the War." In Branka Magaŝ and Ivo Žanić, eds., *The War in Croatia and Bosnia-Herzegovina, 1991–1995.* London: Frank Cass, 2001.

Clapham, Christopher. *Africa and the International System: The Politics of State Survival.* Cambridge: Cambridge University Press, 1996.

———. "Introduction: Analysing African Insurgencies." In Christopher Clapham, ed. *African Guerrillas.* Bloomington: Indiana University Press, 1998, pp. 1–18.

———. "Rwanda: The Perils of Peacemaking." *Journal of Peace Research* 35:2 (1998): 193–210.

Cohen, Lenard J. "Bosnia and Herzegovina: Fragile Peace in a Segmented State." *Current History* (March 1996): 103–112.

———. "Whose Bosnia? The Politics of Nation Building." *Current History* (March 1998): 103–112.

Coleman, James S., and Carl G. Rosberg Jr. *Political Parties and National Integration in Tropical Africa.* Berkeley: University of California Press, 1964.

Colletta, Nat, Markus Kostner, and Ingo Wiederhofer. *Case Studies in War-to-Peace Transitions: Demobilization and Reintegration of Ex-Combatants in Ethiopia, Namibia, and Uganda.* Washington D.C.: World Bank Africa Technical Department Working Paper, 1996.

———. "Disarmament, Demobilization, and Reintegration: Lessons and Liabilities in Reconstruction." In Robert I. Rotberg, ed. *When States Fail: Causes and Consequences.* Princeton, N.J.: Princeton University Press, 2004, pp. 170–181.

———. *The Transition from War to Peace in Sub-Saharan Africa.* Washington D.C.: The World Bank Directions in Development Series, 1996.

Collier, Paul. "Doing Well out of War: An Economic Perspective." In Mats Berdal and David M. Malone, eds. *Greed and Grievance: Economic Agendas in Civil Wars.* Boulder, Colo.: Lynne Rienner for the International Peace Academy, 2000, pp. 90–111.

Collier, Paul, and Anke Hoeffler. "Greed and Grievances in Civil War." World Bank Working Paper, October 21, 2001.

Collins, Kathleen. "Clans, Pacts, and Politics in Central Asia." *Journal of Democracy* 13:3 (July 2002): 137–152.

———. "Tajikistan: Bad Peace Agreements and Prolonged Civil Conflict." In Chandra Lekha Sriram and Karin Wermester, eds. *From Promise to Practice: Strengthening UN Capacities for the Prevention of Violent Conflict.* Boulder, Colo.: Lynne Rienner, 2003, pp. 267–306.

Conrad, Burkhard. "The Problem of Small Arms and Light Weapons in Tajikistan." *Strategic Analysis* 24:8 (November 2000), Columbia International Affairs Online, http://www.idsa-india.org/.

Constable, Pamela. "At War's End in El Salvador." *Current History* 92:572 (March 1993).

Cooper, Neil, and Michael Pugh, *Security-Sector Transformation in Post-conflict Societies.* London: The Conflict, Security, and Development Group at the Centre for Defence Studies, Kings College, University of London, Working Paper, February 2002.

Cooper, Robert Neil. *Demilitarisation and (Lack of?) Transformation in Kosovo.* The Geneva Centre for Security Policy Working Paper, 1999–2000, Columbia International Affairs Online, www.ciaonet.org/wps/cor06.

Coser, Lewis. *The Functions of Social Conflict.* Glencoe, Ill.: Free Press,1956.

Cousens, Elizabeth M. "Building Peace in Bosnia." In Elizabeth M. Cousens and Chetan Kumar, with Karin Wermester, eds. *Peacebuilding as Politics: Cultivating Peace in Fragile Societies.* Boulder, Colo.: Lynne Rienner for the International Peace Academy, 2001, pp. 113–152.

Cousens, Elizabeth M., and Charles K. Cater. *Toward Peace in Bosnia: Implementing the Dayton Accords.* Boulder, Colo.: Lynne Rienner for the International Peace Academy, 2001.

Crocker, Chester. *High Noon in Southern Africa.* New York: W. W. Norton, 1992.

Da Costa, Peter. "Liberia: Peace Postponed." *Africa Report* 37:3 (May-June 1992): 52.

Dadmehr, Nasrin. "Tajikistan: Regionalism and Weakness." In Robert I. Rotberg, ed. *State Failure and State Weakness in a Time of Terror.* Washington, D.C.: Brookings Institution Press, 2003.

Darby, John, and Roger Mac Ginty. "Introduction: What Peace? What Process?" In John Darby and Roger Mac Ginty, eds. *Contemporary Peacemaking: Conflict, Violence, and Peace Processes.* Hampshire, UK: Palgrave Macmillan, 2003, pp. 1–6.

De Figueiredo, Rui J. P., Jr., and Barry R. Weingast. "The Rationality of Fear: Political Opportunism and Ethnic Conflict." In Barbara F. Walter and Jack Snyder, eds. *Civil Wars, Insecurity, and Intervention.* New York: Columbia University Press, 1999, pp. 261–302.

Demetriou, Spyros. "Rising from the Ashes? The Difficult (Re)Birth of the Georgian State." *Development and Change* 33:4 (2002): 859–883.

Deng, Francis M. *War of Visions: Conflict of Identities in the Sudan.* Washington, D.C.: Brookings Institution Press, 1995.

Deng, Francis M., Sadikiel Kimaro, Terrence Lyons, Donald Rothchild, and I. William Zartman. *Sovereignty as Responsibility: Conflict Management in Africa.* Washington, D.C.: Brookings Institution Press, 1996.

Diehl, James. *Paramilitary Politics in Weimar Germany.* Bloomington: Indiana University Press, 1977.

Di Palma, Giuseppe. *To Craft Democracies: An Essay on Democratic Transitions.* Berkeley: University of California Press, 1990.

Doornbos, Martin. "African Multipartyism and the Quest for Democratic Alternatives: Ugandan Elections, Past and Present." In Jan Abbink and Gerti Hesseling, eds. *Chasing a Mirage? Observing Elections and Democratization in Africa.* New York: St. Martin's Press, 1999.

Downs, George, and Stephen John Stedman. "Evaluation Issues in Peace Implementation." In Stephen John Stedman, Donald Rothchild, and Elizabeth Cousens, eds. *Ending Civil Wars: The Implementation of Peace Agreements.* Boulder, Colo.: Lynne Rienner, 2002, pp. 43–70.

Doyle, Michael W. "Strategy and Transitional Authority." In Steven John Stedman, Donald Rothchild, and Elizabeth Cousens, eds. *Ending Civil Wars: The Implementation of Peace Agreements.* Boulder, Colo.: Lynne Rienner, 2002, pp. 71–88.

———. "Transitional Authority." Paper prepared for the World Bank project "The Economics of Civil Violence." February 25, 2001.

———. "War and Peace in Cambodia." In Barbara F. Walter and Jack Snyder, eds. *Civil Wars, Insecurity, and Intervention.* New York: Columbia University Press, 1999, pp. 181–217.

Dudoignon, Stéphane A. "Political Parties and Forces in Tajikistan, 1989–1993." In Mohammad-Reza Djalili, Frédéric Grare, and Shirin Akiner, eds. *Tajikistan: The Trials of Independence.* New York: St. Martin's Press, 1997.

Duffield, Mark. *Global Governance and the New Wars: The Merging of Development and Security.* New York and London: Zed Books, 2001.

Duverger, Maurice. *Political Parties: Their Organization and Activity in the Modern States.* New York: John Wiley and Sons, 1954.

Eckstein, Harry. "Theoretical Approaches to Explaining Collective Political Violence." In Ted Robert Gurr, ed. *Handbook of Political Conflict: Theory and Research.* New York: Free Press, 1980.

Economist. "Bosnia: Market Shimmer." *Economist,* September 7–13, 1996, p. 48.

———. "All Change in Croatia." *Economist,* January 6, 2000, pp. 46, 76.

———. "Islam in Central Asia: Religion, Politics and Moderation." *Economist,* May 17, 2003, p. 39.

Egbert, Bill. "A Noble Act of Harmony in the Balkans." *Christian Science Monitor,* October 9, 1997, http://csmonitor.com/cgi-bin/durableRedirect. pl?/durable/1997/10/09/intl/intl.1.html.

Eide, Espen Barth. "'Conflict Entrepreneurship': On the 'Art' of Waging Civil

War." In Anthony McDermott, ed. *Humanitarian Force*. Oslo: PRIO Report 4/97, 1997.

Eisenstadt, Todd, and Daniel Garcia. "Colombia: Negotiations in a Shifting Pattern of Insurgency." In I. William Zartman, ed. *Elusive Peace: Negotiating an End to Civil Wars*. Washington, D.C.: Brookings Institution, 1995, pp. 265–298.

Eisinger, Peter K. "The Conditions of Protest Behavior in American Cities." *American Political Science Review* 67:1 (March 1973): 11–28.

Ekwall-Uebelhart, Barbara, and Andrei Raevsky. *Managing Arms in Peace Processes: Croatia and Bosnia-Herzegovina*. Geneva: United Nations Institute for Disarmament Research, 1996.

Elklit, Jørgen, and Andrew Reynolds. *The Impact of Election Administration on the Legitimacy of Emerging Democracies: A New Research Agenda*. Working Paper no. 281. Notre Dame, Ind.: The Helen Kellogg Institute for International Studies, University of Notre Dame, September 2000.

Elklit, Jørgen, and Palle Svensson. "What Makes Elections Free and Fair?" *Journal of Democracy* 8:3 (July 1997): 32–47.

Ellis, Stephen. "Liberia 1989–1994: A Study of Ethnic and Spiritual Violence." *African Affairs* 94 (1995): 165–197.

———. "Liberia's Warlord Insurgency." In Christopher Clapham, ed. *African Guerrillas*. Oxford: James Currey, 1998.

———. *The Mask of Anarchy: The Destruction of Liberia and the Religious Dimensions of an African Civil War*. New York: New York University Press, 1999.

Elwert, Georg. "Markets of Violence." In Georg Elwert, Stephan Feuchtwant, and Dieter Neubert, eds. *Dynamics of Collective Violence: Processes of Escalation and De-escalation in Violent Group Conflicts*. Berlin: Duncker and Humblot, 1999, pp. 85–102.

Elwert, Georg, Stephan Feuchtwant, and Dieter Neubert. "The Dynamics of Collective Violence—An Introduction." In Georg Elwert, Stephan Feuchtwant, and Dieter Neubert, eds. *Dynamics of Collective Violence: Processes of Escalation and De-escalation in Violent Group Conflicts*. Berlin: Duncker and Humblot, 1999, pp. 7–31.

Emery, Alan, and Rupert Taylor. "South Africa: From 'Racial Conflict' to Democratic Settlement." In Ronaldo Munck and Purnaka L. de Silva, eds. *Postmodern Insurgencies: Political Violence, Identity Formation, and Peacemaking in Comparative Perspective*. New York: St. Martin's Press, 2000, pp. 54–69.

Fagen, Patricia Weiss. "El Salvador: Lessons in Peace Consolidation." In Tom Farer, ed. *Beyond Sovereignty: Collectively Defending Democracy in the Americas*. Baltimore, Md.: Johns Hopkins University Press, 1996, pp. 213–237.

Fearon, James D., and David D. Laitin. "Violence and the Social Construction of Ethnic Identity." *International Organization* 54:4 (Autumn 2000): 845–877.

Findlay, Trevor. *Cambodia: The Legacy and Lessons of UNTAC*. SIPRI Research Report No. 9. Oxford: Oxford University Press, 1995.

Fischer, Jeff. "Post-Conflict Peace Operations and Governance in

Afghanistan: A Strategy for Peace and Political Intervention."
International Foundation for Electoral Systems White Paper, December
20, 2001.

Fisher, Ian. "Abuse of Bosnia Election Rules Is Alleged." *New York Times,*
August 24, 1996, p. A6.

Flowers, Ken. *Serving Secretly: An Intelligence Chief on Record, Rhodesia
into Zimbabwe, 1964–1981.* London: John Murray, 1987.

Fortna, Virginia Page. *Peace Time: Cease-Fire Agreements and the Durability
of Peace.* Princeton, N.J.: Princeton University Press, 2004.

———. "Scraps of Paper? Agreements and the Durability of Peace."
International Organization 57 (Spring 2003): 337–372.

———. "Success and Failure in Southern Africa: Peacekeeping in Namibia
and Angola." In Donald C.F. Daniel and Bradd C. Hayes, eds. *Beyond
Traditional Peacekeeping.* New York: St. Martin's Press, 1995, pp.
282–299.

Fox, Gregory H. "International Law and the Entitlement to Democracy After
War." *Global Governance* 9:2 (April-June 2003): 179–198.

Franck, Thomas M. "The Emerging Right to Democratic Governance."
American Journal of International Law 86 (January 1992): 46–91.

Freeman, Chas. W., Jr. "The Angola/Namibia Accords." *Foreign Affairs* 68:3
(Summer 1989): 126–141.

French, Howard W. "In Liberia, Life Returns to a Grim Normality." *New York
Times,* August 21, 1996, p. A8.

Friends of Liberia. "Liberia: Opportunities and Obstacles for Peace."
December 1996.

Frieson, Kate. "The Politics of Getting the Vote in Cambodia." In Steve Heder
and Judy Ledgerwood, eds. *Propaganda, Politics, and Violence in
Cambodia: Democratic Transition Under United Nations Peace-keeping.*
Armonk, N.Y.: M. E. Sharpe, 1996, pp. 183–207.

Frohlich, Norman, Joe A. Oppenheimer, and Oran R. Young. *Political
Leadership and Collective Goods.* Princeton, N.J.: Princeton University
Press, 1971.

Gagnon, V. P., Jr. "Ethnic Nationalism and International Conflict: The Case of
Serbia." *International Security* 19:3 (Winter 1994–1995).

Gallagher, Denis, and Anna Schowengerdt. *Refugees and Elections: A
Separate Peace.* Washington, D.C.: Refugee Policy Group, 1997.

Gamson, William A. *The Strategy of Social Protest.* Homewood, Ill.: The
Dorsey Press, 1975.

Geffray, Christian. *Les Causes des Armes au Mozambique: Anthropologie
d'une Guerre Civile.* Paris: Credu-Karthala, 1990.

Glassmyer, Katherine, and Nicholas Sambanis. "Rebel-Military Integration
and Civil War Termination." Paper presented at the American Political
Science Association meeting, Philadelphia, Penn., August 2003.

Global Witness. *Forest, Famine, and War—The Key to Cambodia's Future.*
March 1995. www.globalwitness.org.

Goodwin-Gill, Guy S. *Free and Fair Elections in International Law.* Geneva:
Inter-Parliamentary Union, 1994.

Guelke, Adrian, and Jim Smyth. "The Ballot Bomb: Terrorism and the

Electoral Process in Northern Ireland." In Leonard Weinberg, ed. *Political Parties and Terrorist Groups.* London: Frank Cass, 1992, pp. 103–124.

Gunter, Richard. "Spain: The Very Model of the Modern Elite Settlement." In John Higley and Richard Gunter, eds. *Elites and Democratic Consolidation in Latin America and Southern Europe.* Cambridge: Cambridge University Press, 1992, pp. 38–80.

Hagopian, Frances. "Democracy by Undemocratic Means? Elites, Political Pacts, and Regime Transition in Brazil." *Comparative Political Studies* 23:2 (1990): 147–170.

Hall, Brian. "Blue Helmets, Empty Guns." *New York Times Sunday Magazine,* January 2, 1994.

Hall, Margaret. "The Mozambique National Resistance (Renamo): A Study of the Destruction of an African Country." *Africa* 60:1 (1990): 39–68.

Hampson, Fen Osler. *Nurturing Peace: Why Peace Settlements Succeed or Fail.* Washington, D.C.: United States Institute of Peace, 1996.

Hansen, Annika S., and Lia Brynjar. *The Role of International Security Assistance in Support of Peace Agreements in War-Torn Societies.* FFI Rapport no. 98/05291. Kjeller, Norway: Forsvarets Forskingsinstitut (Norwegian Defence Research Establishment), December 1998.

Hare, Paul. *Angola's Last Best Chance for Peace.* Washington, D.C.: United States Institute of Peace Press, 1998.

Harris, Peter. "Building an Electoral Administration." In Peter Harris and Ben Reilly, eds. *Democracy and Deep-Rooted Conflict: Options for Negotiators.* Stockholm: International IDEA, 1998, pp. 308–319.

Harris, Peter, and Ben Reilly, eds. *Democracy and Deep-Rooted Conflict: Options for Negotiators.* Stockholm: International IDEA, 1998.

Heathershaw, John Emil Juraev, Michael von Tangen Page, and Lada Zimina. *Small Arms Control in Central Asia.* Eurasia Series no. 4. London: International Alert Monitoring the Implementation of Small Arms Controls, 2004.

Heder, Steve, and Judy Ledgerwood. "Politics of Violence: An Introduction." In Steve Heder and Judy Ledgerwood, eds. *Propaganda, Politics, and Violence in Cambodia: Democratic Transition Under United Nations Peace-keeping.* Armonk, N.Y.: M. E. Sharpe, 1996, pp. 3–49.

———, eds. *Propaganda, Politics, and Violence in Cambodia: Democratic Transition Under United Nations Peace-keeping.* Armonk, N.Y.: M. E. Sharpe, 1996.

Heininger, Janet E. *Peacekeeping in Transition: The United Nations in Cambodia.* New York: The Twentieth Century Fund Press, 1994.

Henderson, Robert E., and Edward B. Stewart. *UNITA After the Cease-Fire: The Emergence of a Party.* Washington, D.C.: National Republican Institute for International Affairs, June 17, 1991.

Hendrickson, Dylan. "A Review of Security-Sector Reform." Working Paper. London: The Conflict, Security, and Development Group at the Centre for Defence Studies, Kings College, University of London, September 1999.

Herbst, Jeffrey. "African Militaries and Rebellion: The Political Economy of

Threat and Combat Effectiveness." *Journal of Peace Research* 41:3 (2004): 357–369.

Heywood, Linda M. "UNITA and Ethnic Nationalism in Angola." *Journal of Modern African Studies* 27:1 (1989): 47–66.

Hills, Alice. *Policing Africa: Internal Security and the Limits of Liberalization.* Boulder, Colo.: Lynne Rienner, 2000.

Hislope, Robert. "Intra-Ethnic Conflict in Croatia and Serbia: Flanking and the Consequences for Democracy." *East European Quarterly* 30:4 (Winter 1996): 471–494.

Hoddie, Matthew, and Caroline Hartzell. "Civil War Settlements and the Implementation of Military Power-Sharing Arrangements." *Journal of Peace Research* 40:3 (2003): 303–320.

Hodges, Tony. *Angola from Afro-Stalinism to Petro-Diamond Capitalism.* Oxford: James Currey, 2001.

Hoffman, Danny. "The Civilian Target in Sierra Leone and Liberia: Political Power, Military Strategy, and Humanitarian Intervention." *African Affairs* 103 (2004): 211–226.

Holbrooke, Richard. *To End a War.* New York: The Modern Library, 1999.

Holiday, David, and William Stanley. "Building the Peace: Preliminary Lessons from El Salvador." *Journal of International Affairs* 46:2 (Winter 1993): 415–438.

———. "Under the Best of Circumstances: ONUSAL and the Challenges of Verification and Institution Building in El Salvador." In Tommie Sue Montgomery, ed. *Peacemaking and Democratization in the Western Hemisphere.* Miami, Fla.: University of Miami North-South Center Press, 2000, pp. 37–65.

Holsti, Kalevi. *Peace and War: Armed Conflict and International Order.* Cambridge: Cambridge University Press, 1991.

Horowitz, Donald L. *The Deadly Ethnic Riot.* Berkeley: University of California Press, 2001.

———. *A Democratic South Africa? Constitutional Engineering in a Divided Society.* Berkeley: University of California Press, 1991.

———. *Ethnic Groups in Conflict.* Berkeley: University of California Press, 1985.

Hudson, Michael C. "Power-Sharing in Post–Civil War Lebanon." *International Negotiation* 2:1 (1997): 103–122.

Human Rights Watch. *Angola: Arms Trade and Violations of the Laws of War Since the 1992 Elections.* New York: Human Rights Watch Arms Project and Human Rights Watch/Africa, 1994.

———. *Angola Unravels: The Rise and Fall of the Lusaka Peace Process.* New York: Human Rights Watch, September 1999.

———. *Divide and Rule: State-Sponsored Ethnic Violence in Kenya.* New York: Human Rights Watch, 1993.

———. *Human Rights Watch Press Backgrounder on Tajikistan.* October 5, 2001. www.hrw.org/backgrounder/eca/tajikbkg1005.htm.

Hume, Cameron. *Ending Mozambique's War.* Washington, D.C.: United States Institute of Peace, 1994.

Huntington, Samuel. *Political Order in Changing Societies.* New Haven, Conn.: Yale University Press, 1968.

Husarska, Anna. "Bosnian Elections: The 103.9% Solution." *Wall Street Journal,* October 3, 1996, p. 14.

International Crisis Group. *Bosnia's Nationalist Governments: Paddy Ashdown and the Paradoxes of State Building.* ICG Balkans Report no. 146, July 22, 2003.

———. *Cambodia: The Elusive Peace Dividend.* ICG Asia Report no. 8, August 11, 2000.

———. *Central Asia: Crisis Conditions in Three States.* ICG Asia Report no. 7, August 7, 2000.

———. *"Consensual Democracy" in Post-Genocide Rwanda: Evaluating the March 2001 District Elections.* International Crisis Group, Africa Report no. 34, October 9, 2001.

———. *Côte d'Ivoire: "The War Is Not Yet Over."* ICG Report November 2003.

———. *Elections in Bosnia and Herzegovina.* ICG Report, September 22, 1996.

———. *Serbia's Changing Political Landscape.* ICG Europe Briefing, July 22, 2004.

———. *Tajikistan: An Uncertain Peace.* ICG Asia Report no. 30, December 24, 2001.

———. "Tajikistan's Politics: Confrontation or Consolidation?" ICG Asia Briefing, May 19, 2004.

———. *Whither Bosnia?* ICG Europe Report no. 43, September 9, 1998.

Inter-Party Working Group. "Statement of Political Parties of the Republic of Liberia on the Prescribed Preconditions for the Holding of Free, Fair and Democratic Elections." May 1, 1997.

"Interview with Samuel Kofi Woods of Liberia." *African Affairs* 99 (2000): 97–111.

Isaacs, Dan. "Mozambique: Fulfilling a Dream." *Africa Report* 40:1 (January 1995): 13–21.

Jawad, Nassim, and Shahrbanou Tadjbakhsh. *Tajikistan: A Forgotten Civil War.* London: Minority Rights Group, 1995.

Jett, Dennis C. *Why Peacekeeping Fails.* New York: Palgrave, 2001.

———. "Cementing Democracy: Institution-Building in Mozambique." *Harvard International Review* 17 (1995).

Johnson, Chalmers. *Peasant Nationalism and Communist Power: The Emergence of Revolutionary China, 1937–1945.* Palo Alto, Calif.: Stanford University Press, 1962.

Johnstone, Ian. *Rights and Reconciliation: UN Strategies in El Salvador.* Boulder, Colo.: Lynne Rienner for the International Peace Academy, 1995.

Kaldor, Mary. *New and Old Wars: Organized Violence in a Global Era.* London: Polity, 1999.

———. "Security Structures in Bosnia and Herzegovina." In Gavin Cawthra and Robin Luckham, eds. *Governing Insecurity: Democratic Control of Military and Security Establishments in Transitional Democracies.* London: Zed Books, 2003.

Kandeh, Jimmy D. "Sierra Leone's Post-Conflict Elections of 2002." *Journal of Modern African Studies* 41:2 (2003): 189–216.

Kaplan, Robert. "The Coming Anarchy." *Atlantic Monthly* 273:2 (February 1994): 44–65.

Karl, Terry Lynn. "Dilemmas of Democratization in Latin America." *Comparative Politics* 22 (1990): 1–21.

———. "Imposing Consent? Electoralism vs. Democratization in El Salvador." In Paul Drake and Eduardo Silva, eds. *Elections and Democratization in Latin America, 1980–85*. San Diego, Calif.: CLAS/Center for U.S.-Mexican Studies, 1986, pp. 9–36.

Kasfir, Nelson. "Guerrillas and Civilian Participation: The National Resistance Army in Uganda, 1981–86." *Journal of Modern African Studies* 43 (June 2005): 271–296.

———. "One Full Revolution: The Politics of Sudanese Military Government, 1969–1985." In John W. Harbeson, ed. *The Military in African Politics*. Westport, Conn.: Praeger, 1987.

Keen, David. *The Economic Functions of Violence in Civil Wars*. Adelphi Paper 320. London: International Institute for Strategic Studies, 1998.

———. "Incentives and Disincentives for Violence." In Mats Berdal and David M. Malone, eds. *Greed and Grievance: Economic Agendas in Civil Wars*. Boulder, Colo.: Lynne Rienner, 2000.

Keller, Bill. "Mozambican Elections Thrown in Doubt." *New York Times*, October 28, 1994, p. A6.

Kelman, Herbert C. "Transforming the Relationship Between Former Enemies: A Social-Psychological Analysis." In Robert I. Rothstein, ed. *After the Peace: Resistance and Reconciliation*. Boulder, Colo.: Lynne Rienner, 1999, pp. 193–206.

Kim, Lucian. "Bringing Peace to Tajikistan's Mountain Fiefdoms." *Christian Science Monitor,* September 15, 1998, www.csmonitor.com/durable/1998/09/15/p6s1.htm.

Kincaid, A. Douglas. "Demilitarization and Security in El Salvador and Guatemala: Convergences of Success and Crisis." *Journal of Interamerican Studies and World Affairs* 42 (Winter 2000): 4–43.

King, Jeremy. "Too Little Too Late—The Demobilization Dilemma in Bosnia-Herzegovina." In Natalie Pauwels, ed. *War Force to Work Force: Global Perspectives on Demobilization and Reintegration*. Baden-Baden: NOMOS Verlagsgesellschaft, 2000, pp. 329–333.

King, Jeremy, and A. Walter Dorn, with Matthew Hodes. *An Unprecedented Experiment: Security Sector Reform in Bosnia and Herzegovina*. London: Saferworld, September 2002.

Kingma, Kees. "Demobilization and Reintegration Experiences in Africa." In Natalie Pauwels, ed. *War Force to Work Force: Global Perspectives on Demobilization and Reintegration*. Baden-Baden: NOMOS Verlagsgesellschaft, 2000, pp. 301–328.

———. *Demobilisation and Reintegration of Ex-combatants in Post-war and Transition Countries: Trends and Challenges of External Support*. Eschborn, Germany: Deutsche Gesellschaft für Technische Zusammenarbeit, 2001.

———. "The Impact of Demobilization." In Kees Kingma, ed. *Demobilization in Sub-Saharan Africa: The Development and Security Impacts*. New York: St. Martin's Press, 2000, pp. 198–220.

————. "Post-war Societies." In Natalie Pauwels, ed. *War Force to Work Force: Global Perspectives on Demobilization and Reintegration.* Baden-Baden: NOMOS Verlagsgesellschaft, 2000, pp. 221–233.

————, ed. *Demobilization in Sub-Saharan Africa: The Development and Security Impacts.* New York: St. Martin's Press, 2000.

Kingma, Kees, and Natalie Pauwels. "Demobilization and Reintegration in the 'Downsizing Decade.'" In Natalie Pauwels, ed. *War Force to Work Force: Global Perspectives on Demobilization and Reintegration.* Baden-Baden: NOMOS Verlagsgesellschaft, 2000, pp. 9–19.

Kitschelt, Herbert. "Political Regime Change: Structure and Process-Driven Explanations?" *American Political Science Review* 86:4 (December 1992): 1028–1034.

Koonings, Kees. "Political Armies, Security Forces and Democratic Consolidation in Latin America." In Gavin Cawthra and Robin Luckham, eds. *Governing Insecurity: Democratic Control of Military and Security Establishments in Transitional Democracies.* London: Zed Books, 2003.

Krieger, Norma. *Zimbabwe's Guerrilla War: Peasant Voices.* Cambridge: Cambridge University Press, 1992.

Kriesberg, Louis. *Constructive Conflicts: From Escalation to Resolution.* Lanham, Md.: Rowman and Littlefield, 1998.

————. "Transforming Conflicts in the Middle East and Central Europe." In Louis Kriesberg, Terrell A. Northrup, and Stuart J. Thorson, eds. *Intractable Conflicts and Their Transformation.* Syracuse, N.Y.: Syracuse University Press, 1989, pp. 109–131.

Kumar, Krishna, ed. *Postconflict Elections, Democratization, and International Assistance.* Boulder, Colo.: Lynne Rienner, 1998.

Kumar, Krishna, and Marina Ottaway. "General Conclusions and Priorities for Policy Research." In Krishna Kumar, ed. *Postconflict Elections, Democratization, and International Assistance.* Boulder, Colo.: Lynne Rienner, 1998, pp. 229–237.

Lake, David A., and Donald Rothchild. "Containing Fear: The Origins and Management of Ethnic Conflict." *International Security* 21 (1996): 41–75.

LaPalombara, Joseph, and Myron Weiner, eds. *Political Parties and Political Development.* Princeton, N.J.: Princeton University Press, 1966.

LeBillion, Philippe. "Angola's Political Economy of War: The Role of Oil and Diamonds, 1975–2000." *African Affairs* 100 (2001): 55–80.

Ledgerwood, Judy. "Patterns of CPP Political Repression and Violence During the UNTAC Period." In Steve Heder and Judy Ledgerwood, eds. *Propaganda, Politics, and Violence in Cambodia: Democratic Transition Under United Nations Peace-keeping.* Armonk, N.Y.: M. E. Sharpe, 1996, pp. 114–133.

Levy, Jack. "The Diversionary Theory of War: A Critique." In Manus I. Midlarsky, ed. *Handbook of War Studies.* New York: Unwin-Hyman, 1989, pp. 259–288.

Lichbach, Mark Irving. *The Rebel's Dilemma.* Ann Arbor: University of Michigan Press, 1998.

Lichbach, Mark I., Christian Davenport, and David A. Armstrong II. "Contingency, Inherency, and the Onset of Civil War." www.bsos.umd. edu/gvpt/davenport/cioc.pdf, December 9, 2003.

Licklider, Roy. *Stopping the Killing: How Civil Wars End.* New York: New York University Press, 1993.

Lijphart, Arend. *Democracy in Plural Societies: A Comparative Exploration.* New Haven, Conn.: Yale University Press, 1977.

Linz, Juan J., and Alfred Stepan. *Problems of Democratic Transition and Consolidation: Southern Europe, South America, and Post-Communist Europe.* Baltimore, Md.: Johns Hopkins University Press, 1996.

Lizée, Pierre P. *Peace, Power and Resistance in Cambodia: Global Governance and the Failure of International Conflict Resolution.* New York: St. Martin's Press, 2000.

Lloyd, Robert B. "Mozambique: The Terror of War, the Tensions of Peace." *Current History* 94:591 (April 1995): 152–155.

Lodge, Tom. "The ANC and the Development of Party Politics in Modern South Africa." *Journal of Modern African Studies* 42:2 (2004): 189–219.

Lundin, Iraê Baptista. "Partidos Políticos: A Leitura da Vertente Étnico-Regional no Processo Democrático." In Brazão Mazula, ed. *Moçambique: Eleições, Democracia e Desenvolvimento.* Maputo, Mozambique: Inter-Africa Group, 1995.

Lundin, Iraê Baptista, Marinho Chachiua, António Gaspar, Habiba Guebuza, and Guilherme Mbilana. "'Reducing Costs Through an Expensive Exercise': The Impact of Demobilization in Mozambique." In Kees Kingma, ed. *Demobilization in Sub-Saharan Africa: The Development and Security Impacts.* New York: St. Martin's Press, 2000, pp. 172–212.

Lyons, Terrence. "Closing the Transition: The May 1995 Elections in Ethiopia." *Journal of Modern African Studies* 34 (1996): 121–142.

———. "Diasporas and Homeland Conflict." In Miles Kahler and Barbara Walter, eds. *Globalization, Territoriality, and Conflict.* New York: Cambridge University Press, 2005.

———. "Peace and Elections in Liberia." In Krishna Kumar, ed. *Postconflict Elections, Democratization, and International Assistance.* Boulder, Colo.: Lynne Rienner, 1998, pp. 177–194.

———. "Postconflict Elections and the Process of Demilitarizing Politics: The Role of Electoral Administration." *Democratization* 11:3 (June 2004): 1–27.

———. "The Role of Post-settlement Elections." In Stephen John Stedman, Donald Rothchild, and Elizabeth M. Cousens, eds. *Ending Civil Wars: The Implementation of Peace Agreements.* Boulder, Colo.: Lynne Rienner, 2002, pp. 215–236.

———. *Voting for Peace: Postconflict Elections in Liberia.* Washington, D.C.: Brookings Institution Press, 1999.

Lyons, Terrence, and Ahmed Samatar. *Somalia: State Collapse, Multilateral Intervention, and Strategies for Political Reconstruction.* Washington, D.C.: Brookings Institution Press, 1995.

MacQueen, Norrie. "Peacekeeping by Attrition: The United Nations in Angola." *Journal of Modern African Studies* 36:3 (1998): 399–422.

Macrae, Joanna, and Anthony Zwi, eds. *War and Hunger: Rethinking International Responses to Complex Emergencies.* London: Zed Books, 1994.

Mainwaring, Scott. "Party Systems in the Third Wave." *Journal of Democracy* 9:3 (1998): 67–81.

Mainwaring, Scott, and Timothy R. Scully. *Building Democratic Institutions: Party Systems in Latin America.* Palo Alto, Calif.: Stanford University Press, 1995.

Mani, Rama. "Contextualizing Police Reform: Security, the Rule of Law and Post-Conflict Peacebuilding." *International Peacebuilding* 6 (1999): 9–26.

Manning, Carrie. "Conflict Management and Elite Habituation in Postwar Democracy: the Case of Mozambique." *Comparative Politics* 35:1 (2002): 63–84.

———. *The Politics of Peace in Mozambique: Post-Conflict Democratization, 1992–2000.* Westport, Conn.: Praeger, 2002.

Manning, Carrie, and Miljenko Antić. "Lessons from Bosnia and Herzegovina: The Limits of Electoral Engineering." *Journal of Democracy* 14:3 (July 2003): 45–59.

Marcum, John A. "Angola: War Again." *Current History* (May 1993): 218–223.

———. *The Angolan Revolution.* Cambridge: Massachusetts Institute of Technology Press, 1981.

Mason, T. David, and Dale A. Krane. "The Political Economy of Death Squads: Toward a Theory of the Impact of State-Sanctioned Terror." *International Studies Quarterly* 33 (1989): 175–198.

McClintock, Cynthia. *Revolutionary Movements in Latin America: El Salvador's FMLN and Peru's Shining Path.* Washington, D.C.: United States Institute of Peace Press, 1998.

———. "Why Peasants Rebel: The Case of Peru's Sendero Luminoso." *World Politics* 37 (October 1987): 48–84.

McCoy, Jennifer, Larry Garber, and Robert Pastor. "Pollwatching and Peacemaking." *Journal of Democracy* 2:3 (Fall 1991): 102–114.

McNeil, Donald G., Jr. "Under Scrutiny, Postwar Liberia Goes to Polls." *New York Times,* July 20, 1997.

McRae, Kenneth D. "Theories of Power-Sharing and Conflict Management." In Joseph Montville, ed. *Conflict and Peacemaking in Multiethnic Societies.* Lexington, Mass.: Lexington Books, 1990.

Michels, Robert. *Political Parties: A Sociological Study of the Oligarchical Tendencies of Modern Democracy.* New York: Free Press, 1962.

Migdal, Joel. *Peasants, Politics, and Revolution: Pressures Toward Political and Social Change in the Third World.* Princeton, N.J.: Princeton University Press, 1974.

Miles, Sara, and Bob Ostertag. "D'Aubuisson's New ARENA." *NACLA Report on the Americas* 23 (July 1989): 14–38.

———. "The FMLN: New Thinking." In Anjali Sundaram and George Gelber, eds. *A Decade of War: El Salvador Confronts the Future.* New York: Monthly Review Press, 1991.

Minter, William. *Apartheid's Contras: An Inquiry into the Roots of War in Angola and Mozambique.* London: Zed Books, 1994.

Montgomery, Tommie Sue. "Getting to Peace in El Salvador: The Roles of the

United Nations Secretariat and ONUSAL." *Journal of Interamerican Studies and World Affairs* 37:4 (Winter 1995): 139–172.
———. *Revolution in El Salvador: From Civil Strife to Civil Peace.* 2nd ed. Boulder, Colo.: Westview Press, 1995.
Montgomery, Tommie Sue, with Ruth Reitan. "The Good, the Bad, and the Ugly: Observing Elections in El Salvador." In Tommie Sue Montgomery, ed. *Peacemaking and Democratization in the Western Hemisphere.* Miami, Fla.: University of Miami North-South Center Press, 2000.
Mozaffar, Shaheen, and Andreas Schedler. "The Comparative Study of Electoral Governance—Introduction." *International Political Science Review* 23:1 (2002): 5–27.
Mozambique News Agency. "New Renamo Secretary General Appointed." *AIM Reports* no. 125 (January 12, 1998). http://www.poptel.org.uk/mozambique-news/newsletter/aim125.html.
Msabaha, Ibrahim. "Negotiating an End to Mozambique's Murderous Rebellion." In I. William Zartman, ed. *Elusive Peace: Negotiating an End to Civil Wars.* Washington, D.C.: Brookings Institution Press, 1995, pp. 204–230.
Munck, Gerardo L. "Beyond Electoralism in El Salvador: Conflict Resolution Through Negotiated Compromise." *Third World Quarterly* 14:1 (1993): 75–93.
Munck, Gerardo L., and Dexter Boniface. "Political Processes and Identity Formation in El Salvador: From Armed Left to Democratic Left." In Ronaldo Munck and Purnaka L. de Silva, eds. *Postmodern Insurgencies: Political Violence, Identity Formation, and Peacemaking in Comparative Perspective.* New York: St. Martin's Press, 2000, pp. 38–53.
Munck, Ronaldo. "Deconstructing Terror: Insurgency, Repression, and Peace." In Ronaldo Munck and Purnaka L. de Silva, eds. *Postmodern Insurgencies: Political Violence, Identity Formation, and Peacemaking in Comparative Perspective.* New York: St. Martin's Press, 2000.
National Democratic Institute (NDI) and International Republican Institute (IRI). "Angola Briefing Paper, Pre-assessment Mission, May 21–27, 1991."
Naylor, R. T. *Wages of Crime: Black Markets, Illegal Finance, and the Underworld Economy.* Ithaca, N.Y.: Cornell University Press, 2002.
Neou, Kassie, with Jeffrey C. Gallup. "Conducting Cambodia's Elections." *Journal of Democracy* 10:2 (April 1999): 152–164.
Noble, Kenneth B. "Election Makes Skeptics of Angolans." *New York Times,* June 28, 1992, p. A8.
Nordstrom, Carolyn. *A Different Kind of War Story.* Philadelphia: University of Pennsylvania Press, 1997.
Nordstrom, Carolyn, and JoAnn Martin, eds. *The Paths to Domination, Resistance and Terror.* Berkeley: University of California Press, 1992.
Norris, Pippa. "Introduction: The Politics of Electoral Reform." *International Political Science Review* 16:1 (1995): 3–8.
North, Douglass. *Institutions, Institutional Change, and Economic Performance.* Cambridge: Cambridge University Press, 1990.

Norton, Chris. "The Hard Right: ARENA Comes to Power." In Anjali Sundaram and George Gelber, eds. *A Decade of War: El Salvador Confronts the Future*. New York: Monthly Review Press, 1991.

Norwegian Helsinki Committee. *Report from the Observation of the Elections in Bosnia and Herzegovina, 14 September 1996*. Oslo: Norwegian Helsinki Committee, October 1996.

O'Donnell, Guillermo, and Philippe Schmitter. *Transitions from Authoritarian Rule: Tentative Conclusions About Uncertain Democracies*. Baltimore, Md.: Johns Hopkins University Press, 1986.

Olimov, Muzaffar, and Ksenia Gonchar. "Consolidating Peace in Tajikistan—Reconciliation, Reinsertion, and Reintegration." In Natalie Pauwels, ed. *War Force to Work Force: Global Perspectives on Demobilization and Reintegration*. Baden-Baden: NOMOS Verlagsgesellschaft, 2000, pp. 335–246.

Oliver, Johanna. "Seeking a Return to Normalcy for Central America's Ex-Combatants." In Natalie Pauwels, ed. *War Force to Work Force: Global Perspectives on Demobilization and Reintegration*. Baden-Baden: NOMOS Verlagsgesellschaft, 2000, pp. 263–296.

Olson, Mancur, Jr. *The Logic of Collective Action: Public Goods and the Theory of Groups*. Cambridge, Mass.: Harvard University Press, 1965.

Organization for Security and Cooperation in Europe (OSCE) Office for Democratic Institutions and Human Rights (ODIHR). *The Republic of Tajikistan: Elections to the Parliament, 27 February 2000*. Warsaw: ODIHR, 17 May 2000.

———. "Joint Statement Issued on Tajikistan Parliamentary Elections." Press release, 28 February 2000.

Organization for Security and Cooperation in Europe (OSCE) Office for Democratic Institutions and Human Rights (ODIHR) Election Observation Mission. "Statement of Preliminary Findings and Conclusions, Republic of Tajikistan Parliamentary Elections—First Round, 27 February 2005."

Ottaway, David, and Marina Ottaway. *Afrocommunism*. New York: Africana, 1981.

Ottaway, Marina. "Angola's Failed Elections." In Krishna Kumar, ed. *Postconflict Elections, Democratization, and International Assistance*. Boulder, Colo.: Lynne Rienner, 1998, pp. 133–152.

———. "Liberation Movements and Transition to Democracy: The Case of the A.N.C." *Journal of Modern African Studies* 29:1 (March 1991): 61–82.

———. "Promoting Democracy After Conflict: The Difficult Choices." *International Studies Perspectives* 4:3 (2003): 314–322.

———. "Rebuilding State Institutions in Collapsed States." *Development and Change* 33:5 (2002): 1001–1023.

———. *South Africa: The Struggle for a New Order*. Washington, D.C.: Brookings Institution Press, 1993.

Ottaway, Marina, and Anatol Lieven. "Peacebuilding Afghanistan: Fantasy vs. Reality." Carnegie Endowment for International Peace Policy Brief no. 12, January 2002.

Ottaway, Marina, and Theresa Chung. "Toward a New Paradigm." *Journal of Democracy* 10:4 (1999): 99–113.

Ottaway, Marina, and Thomas Carothers. "The Right Road to Sovereignty in Iraq." Carnegie Endowment for International Peace Policy Brief 27, October 2003.

Panebianco, Angelo. *Political Parties: Organization and Power.* Cambridge: Cambridge University Press, 1988.

Paris, Roland. *At War's End: Building Peace After Civil Conflict.* Cambridge: Cambridge University Press, 2004.

———. "Peacebuilding and the Limits of Liberal Internationalism." *International Security* 22:2 (Fall 1997): 54–89.

Pastor, Robert A. "A Brief History of Electoral Commissions." In Andreas Schedler, Larry Diamond, and Marc F. Plattner, eds. *The Self-Restraining State: Power and Accountability in New Democracies.* Boulder, Colo.: Lynne Rienner, 1999, pp. 75–82.

———. "Mediating Elections." *Journal of Democracy* 9:1 (January 1998): 154–163.

———. "The Role of Electoral Administration in Democratic Transitions: Implications for Policy and Research." *Democratization* 6:4 (Winter 1999): 1–27.

Pauwels, Natalie, ed. *War Force to Work Force: Global Perspectives on Demobilization and Reintegration.* Baden-Baden: Nomos Verlagsgessellschaft, 2000.

Payne, Tony. "Multi-Party Politics in Jamaica." In Vicky Randal, ed. *Political Parties in the Third World.* London: Sage, 1988.

Peceny, Mark, and William Stanley. "Liberal Social Reconstruction and the Resolution of Civil Wars in Central America." *International Organization* 55:1 (Winter 2001): 149–182.

Peou, Sorpong. *Conflict Neutralization in the Cambodia War.* Kuala Lumpur: Oxford University Press, 1997.

Pereira, Anthony W. "The Neglected Tragedy: The Return to War in Angola." *Journal of Modern African Studies* 32:1 (March 1994): 1–28.

Pillar, Paul R. *Negotiating Peace: War Termination as a Bargaining Process.* Princeton, N.J.: Princeton University Press, 1983.

Pitcher, M. Anne. *Transforming Mozambique: The Politics of Privatization, 1975–2000.* Cambridge: Cambridge University Press, 2002.

Popkin, Samuel L. *The Rational Peasant: The Political Economy of Rural Society in Vietnam.* Berkeley: University of California Press, 1979.

Posen, Barry R. "The Security Dilemma and Ethnic Conflict." In Michael E. Brown, ed. *Ethnic Conflict and International Security.* Princeton, N.J.: Princeton University Press, 1993, pp. 103–124.

Prunier, Gérald. *The Rwanda Crisis: History of a Genocide.* New York: Columbia University Press, 1995.

Przeworski, Adam. "Democracy as a Contingent Outcome of Conflicts." In Jon Elster and Rune Slagstad, eds. *Constitutionalism and Democracy.* Cambridge: Cambridge University Press, 1988, pp. 59–80.

———. "Some Problems in the Study of the Transition to Democracy." In Guillermo O'Donnell, Philippe C. Schmitter, and Laurence Whitehead, eds. *Transitions from Authoritarian Rule: Comparative Perspectives.* Baltimore, Md.: Johns Hopkins University Press, 1986, pp. 47–63.

Przeworski, Adam, et al. *Sustainable Democracy*. Cambridge: Cambridge University Press, 1995.

Pugh, Michael, and Margaret Cobble. "Non-Nationalist Voting in Bosnian Municipal Elections: Implications for Democracy and Peacebuilding." *Journal of Peace Research* 38:1 (2001): 27–47.

Pugh, Michael, and Neil Cooper, eds. *War Economies in a Regional Context: Challenges of Transformation*. Boulder, Colo.: Lynne Rienner, 2004.

Ratner, Steven. "The Cambodian Settlement Agreements." *American Journal of International Law* 87:1 (January 1993): 1–41.

———. "The United Nations in Cambodia: A Model for Resolution of Internal Conflicts?" In Lori Fisler Damrosch, ed. *Enforcing Restraint: Collective Intervention in Internal Conflicts*. New York: Council on Foreign Relations, 1993, pp. 241–273.

Reilly, Ben. "Democratic Validation." In John Darby and Roger Mac Ginty, eds. *Contemporary Peacemaking: Conflict, Violence, and Peace Processes*. Hampshire, UK: Palgrave Macmillan, 2003, pp. 174–183.

Reilly, Ben, and Andrew Reynolds. "Electoral Systems and Conflict in Divided Societies." In Paul C. Stern and Daniel Druckman, eds. *International Conflict Resolution After the Cold War*. Washington, D.C.: National Academy Press, 2000.

Reno, William "The Business of War in Liberia." *Current History* 95 (May 1996): 212–213.

———. "Foreign Firms and the Financing of Charles Taylor's NPFL." *Liberian Studies Journal* 18:2 (1993): 259–299.

———. "Reinvention of an African Patrimonial State: Charles Taylor's Liberia." *Third World Quarterly* 16:1 (1995): 109–120.

Reyntjens, Filip. "Rwanda, Ten Years On: From Genocide to Dictatorship." *African Affairs* 103 (2004): 177–210.

Rial, Juan, Dennis Culkin, and Roberto Lima Siqueira. *Angola: A Pre-election Assessment*. Washington, D.C.: International Foundation for Elections Systems, March 1992.

Richani, Nazih. *Dilemmas of Democracy and Political Parties in Sectarian Societies: The Case of the Progressive Socialist Party of Lebanon, 1949–1996*. New York: St. Martin's Press, 1998.

———. "The Political Economy of Violence: The War-System in Colombia." *Journal of Interamerican Studies and World Affairs* 39:2 (1997): 37–81.

Richburg, Keith B. "Cambodia Comes to Peace with Itself." *Washington Post*, January 31, 1999, p. A23.

———. "Ex–Rebel Group's Withdrawal Mars Mozambique's 1st Multi-Party Vote: Pullout on Eve of Election Stirs Fears of Renewed Civil War." *Washington Post*, October 28, 1994, p. A33.

———. "Mozambique Vote Turnout Could Signal New Stability: High Participation Defies Predictions of Apathy." *Washington Post*, October 31, 1994, p. A19.

Rieff, David. "The Case Against the Serb War Criminals." *Washington Post*, September 8, 1996, p. C1.

Riley, Stephen P. "The 1996 Presidential and Parliamentary Elections in Sierra Leone." *Electoral Studies* 15:4 (1997): 537–545.

Roberts, David W. *Political Transition in Cambodia, 1991–99: Power, Elitism, and Democracy.* New York: St. Martin's Press, 2001.

Roberts, Hugh. "Algeria's Contested Elections." *Middle East Report* (Winter 1998): 21–24.

Rotberg, Robert I. "Africa's Mess, Mugabe's Mayhem." *Foreign Affairs* (September-October 2000): 47–61.

Rothchild, Donald. "Bargaining and State Breakdown in Africa." *Nationalism and Ethnic Politics* 1:1 (1995): 54–72.

———. "Third-Party Incentives and the Phases of Conflict Prevention." In Chandra Lekha Sriram and Karin Wermester, eds. *From Promise to Practice: Strengthening UN Capacities for the Prevention of Violent Conflict.* Boulder, Colo.: Lynne Rienner, 2003, pp. 35–66.

Rothstein, Robert L. "Fragile Peace and Its Aftermath." In Robert L. Rothstein, ed. *After the Peace: Resistance and Reconciliation.* Boulder, Colo.: Lynne Rienner, 1999, pp. 223–248.

———. "In Fear of Peace: Getting Past Maybe." In Robert L. Rothstein, ed. *After the Peace: Resistance and Reconciliation.* Boulder, Colo.: Lynne Rienner, 1999, pp. 1–28.

Rubin, Barnett. "Russian Hegemony and State Breakdown in the Periphery: Causes and Consequences of the Civil War in Tajikistan." In Jack Snyder and Barnett Rubin, eds. *Post-Soviet Political Order.* London: Routledge, 1998, pp. 128–161.

Sagdeev, Roald Z., and Susan Eisenhower, eds. *Central Asia: Conflict, Resolution, and Change.* The Center for Political and Strategic Studies, 1995, www.cpss.org/cabook.htm.

Saideman, Stephen M. "Is Pandora's Box Half Empty or Half Full? The Limited Virulence of Secessionism and the Domestic Sources of Disintegration." In David A. Lake and Donald Rothchild, eds. *The International Spread of Ethnic Conflict: Fear, Diffusion, and Escalation.* Princeton, N.J.: Princeton University Press, 1998, pp. 127–150.

Schafer, Jessica. "Guerrillas and Violence in the War in Mozambique: De-Socialization or Re-Socialization?" *African Affairs* 100 (2001): 215–237.

Schear, James A. "Bosnia's Post-Dayton Traumas." *Foreign Policy* 104 (Fall 1996): 87–101.

Schear, James A., and Karl Farris. "Policing Cambodia: The Public Security Dimensions of U.N. Peace Operations." In Robert B. Oakley, Michael J. Dziedzic, and Eliot M. Goldberg, eds. *Policing the New World Disorder: Peace Operations and Public Security.* Washington, D.C.: National Defense University Press, 1998, pp. 69–102.

Schneidman, Witney. "Conflict Resolution in Mozambique." In David R. Smock, ed. *Making War and Waging Peace: Foreign Intervention in Africa.* Washington D.C.: United States Institute of Peace, 1993, pp. 219–238.

Scott, Colin. "Liberia: A Nation Displaced." In Roberta Cohen and Francis M. Deng, eds. *The Forsaken People: Case Studies of the Internally Displaced.* Washington, D.C.: Brookings Institution Press, 1998, pp. 97–138.

Scott, James C. "Corruption, Machine Politics, and Political Change." *American Political Science Review* 63:4 (December 1969): 1142–1158.

Sesay, Max Ahmadu. "Politics and Society in Post-War Liberia." *Journal of Modern African Studies* 34:3 (1996): 395–420.

Shain, Yossi, and Juan J. Linz. *Between States: Interim Governments and Democratic Transitions.* Cambridge: Cambridge University Press, 1995.

Shawcross, William. *Cambodia's New Deal.* Carnegie Endowment for International Peace Contemporary Issues Paper no. 1, 1994.

———. "Tragedy in Cambodia." *New York Review of Books,* November 14, 1996.

Shefter, Martin. "Party and Patronage: Germany, England, and Italy." *Politics and Society* 7:4 (1977): 403–451.

Shoup, Paul. "The Elections in Bosnia and Herzegovina: The End of an Illusion." *Problems of Post-Communism* (1997): 3–15.

Shugart, Matthew Soberg. "Guerrillas and Elections: An Institutionalist Perspective on the Costs of Conflict and Cooperation." *International Studies Quarterly* 36 (1992): 121–152.

Silber, Laura, and Alan Little. *Yugoslavia: Death of a Nation.* New York: Penguin, 1997.

Simpson, Mark. "Foreign and Domestic Factors in the Transformation of Frelimo." *Journal of Modern African Studies* 31:2 (1993): 309–337.

Sisk, Timothy D. "Democratization and Peacebuilding: Perils and Promises." In Chester Crocker, Fen Osler Hampson, and Pamela Aall, eds. *Turbulent Peace.* Washington, D.C.: United States Institute of Peace Press, 2001, pp. 785–800.

———. "Elections and Conflict Management in Africa: Conclusions and Recommendations." In Timothy D. Sisk and Andrew Reynolds, eds. *Elections and Conflict Management in Africa.* Washington, D.C.: The United States Institute of Peace Press, 1998, pp. 145–172.

———. "Electoral System Choice in South Africa: Implications for Intergroup Moderation." *Nationalism and Ethnic Politics* 1 (July 1995): 178–204.

———. *Power Sharing and International Mediation in Ethnic Conflict.* Washington, D.C.: United States Institute of Peace, 1996.

Sisk, Timothy D., and Andrew Reynolds. "Democratization, Elections, and Conflict Management in Africa." In Timothy D. Sisk and Andrew Reynolds, eds. *Elections and Conflict Management in Africa.* Washington, D.C.: United States Institute of Peace Press, 1998, pp. 1–17.

———, eds. *Elections and Conflict Management in Africa.* Washington, D.C.: United States Institute of Peace Press, 1998.

Smajlović, Ljiljana. "From the Heart of the Heart of the Former Yugoslavia." *Wilson Quarterly* (Summer 1995): 100–113.

Smith, Alastair. "Diversionary Foreign Policy in Democratic Systems." *International Studies Quarterly* 40:1 (March 1996): 133–153.

Snyder, Jack. *From Voting to Violence: Democratization and Nationalist Conflict.* New York: W. W. Norton, 2000.

Somerville, Keith. "Angola—Groping Towards Peace or Slipping Back Towards War?" In William Gutteridge and J. E. Spence, eds. *Violence in Southern Africa.* London: Frank Cass, 1997, pp. 11–39.

———. "The Failure of Democratic Reform in Angola and Zaire." *Survival* 35:3 (Autumn 1993): 51–77.

Spear, Joanna. "Disarmament and Demobilization." In Stephen John Stedman,

Donald Rothchild, and Elizabeth M. Cousens, eds. *Ending Civil Wars: The Implemenation of Peace Agreements.* Boulder, Colo.: Lynne Rienner, 2002, pp. 141–182.

Spence, Jack, David Dye, and George Vickers. *El Salvador: Elections of the Century* Cambridge, Mass.: Hemisphere Initiatives, July 1994.

Spencer, Denise. *Demobilization and Reintegration in Central America.* Paper 8. Bonn: Bonn International Center for Conversion, February 1997.

Stahler-Sholk, Richard. "El Salvador's Negotiated Transition: From Low-Intensity Conflict to Low-Intensity Democracy." *Journal of Interamerican Studies and World Affairs* 36:4 (1994): 1–59.

Stanley, William. *The Protection Racket State: Elite Politics, Military Extortion, and Civil War in El Salvador.* Philadelphia, Pa.: Temple University Press, 1996.

Stanley, William, and Charles T. Call. "Building a New Civilian Police Force in El Salvador." In Krishna Kumar, ed. *Rebuilding Societies After Civil War: Critical Roles for International Assistance.* Boulder, Colo.: Lynne Rienner, 1997, pp. 107–134.

Stanley, William, and David Holiday. "Peace Mission Strategy and Domestic Actors: UN Mediation, Verification, and Institution-Building in El Salvador." *International Peacekeeping* 4:2 (Summer 1997): 22–49.

Stanley, William, and Robert Loosle. "El Salvador: The Civilian Police Component of Peace Operations." In Robert B. Oakley, Michael J. Dziedzic, and Eliot M. Goldberg, eds. *Policing the New World Disorder: Peace Operations and Public Security.* Washington, D.C.: National Defense University Press, 1998.

Stedman, Stephen John. "Introduction." In Stephen John Stedman, Donald Rothchild, and Elizabeth M. Cousens, eds. *Ending Civil Wars: The Implementation of Peace Agreements.* Boulder, Colo.: Lynne Rienner, 2002, pp. 1–40.

———. "Negotiation and Mediation in Internal Conflict." In Michael E. Brown, ed. *The International Dimensions of Internal Conflict.* Cambridge: Massachusetts Institute of Technology Press, 1996, pp. 341–376.

———. "Spoiler Problems in Peace Processes." *International Security* 22:2 (Fall 1977): 5–53.

———. "UN Intervention in Civil Wars: Imperatives of Choice and Strategy." In Donald C.F. Daniel and Bradd C. Hayes, eds. *Beyond Traditional Peacekeeping.* New York: St. Martin's Press, 1995, pp. 40–63.

Stedman, Stephen John, Donald Rothchild, and Elizabeth M. Cousens, eds. *Ending Civil Wars: The Implementation of Peace Agreements.* Boulder, Colo.: Lynne Rienner, 2002.

Synge, Richard. *Mozambique: UN Peacekeeping in Action, 1992–94.* Washington, D.C.: United States Institute of Peace, 1997.

Tambiah, Stanley J. *Leveling Crowds: Ethnonationalist Conflicts and Collective Violence in South Asia.* Berkeley: University of California Press, 1996.

Tanner, Fred. "Post-Conflict Weapons Control: In Search of Normative Interactions." Paper presented at the International Studies Association Meeting, Washington, D.C., February 1999.

Tanner, Victor. "Liberia: Railroading Peace." *Review of African Political Economy* 25:75 (March 1998): 133–147.

Tarrow, Sidney. *Power in Movement: Social Movements and Contentious Politics.* 2nd ed. Cambridge: Cambridge University Press, 1998.

Thale, Geoff. "Incentives and the Salvador Peace Process." In David Cortright, ed. *The Price of Peace: Incentives and International Conflict Prevention.* Lanham, Md.: Rowman and Littlefield for the Carnegie Commission on Preventing Deadly Conflicts, 1997.

Thelen, Kathleen, and Sven Steinmo. "Historical Institutionalism in Comparative Politics." In Kathleen Thelen, Sven Steinmo, and Frank Longstreth, eds. *Structuring Politics: Historical Institutionalism in Comparative Analysis.* Cambridge: Cambridge University Press, 1992, pp. 1–32.

Trotha, Trutz von. "Forms of Martial Power: Total Wars, Wars of Pacification, and Raid: Some Observations on the Typology of Violence." In Georg Elwert, Stephan Feuchtwant, and Dieter Neubert, eds. *Dynamics of Collective Violence: Processes of Escalation and De-Escalation in Violent Group Conflicts.* Berlin: Duncker and Humblot, 1999.

Turner, J. Michael, Sue Nelson, and Kimberly Mahling-Clark. "Mozambique's Vote for Democratic Governance." In Krishna Kumar, ed. *Postconflict Elections, Democratization, and International Assistance.* Boulder, Colo.: Lynne Rienner, 1998, pp. 153–175.

Um, Khatharya. "Cambodia in 1993: Year Zero Plus One." *Asian Survey* 34:1 (January 1994): 72–81.

United Nations. *The Blue Helmets: A Review of United Nations Peace-keeping.* New York: United Nations, 1996.

———. *The United Nations and Cambodia, 1991–1995.* New York: United Nations Department of Public Information, 1995.

———. *The United Nations and Mozambique, 1992–1995.* New York: United Nations Department of Public Information, 1995.

Vines, Alex. "Disarmament in Mozambique." *Journal of Southern African Studies* 24:1 (March 1998): 191–205.

———. *One Hand Tied: Angola and the UN.* London: Catholic Institute for International Relations Briefing Paper, June 1993.

———. *Renamo: From Terrorism to Democracy in Mozambique?* London: James Currey, 1996.

Walter, Barbara F. "The Critical Barrier to Civil War Settlement." *International Organization* 51:3 (Summer 1997): 335–364.

———. "Designing Transitions from Civil War: Demobilization, Democratization, and Commitments to Peace." *International Security* 24 (Summer 1999): 127–155.

Wang, Jianwei. *Managing Arms in Peace Processes: Cambodia.* Geneva: United Nations Institute for Disarmament Research, 1996.

Wantchekon, Leonard. "On the Nature of First Democratic Elections." *Journal of Conflict Resolution* 43:2 (April 1999): 245–258.

———. "Strategic Voting in Conditions of Political Instability: The 1994 Elections in El Salvador." *Comparative Political Studies* 32:7 (October 1999): 810–832.

Watson, Cynthia. "Guerrilla Groups in Colombia: Reconstituting the Political

Process." In Leonard Weinberg, ed. *Political Parties and Terrorist Groups.* London: Frank Cass, 1992.

Weinberg, Leonard, and William Eubank. "Political Parties and the Formation of Terrorist Groups." *Terrorism and Political Violence* 2:2 (Summer 1990): 125–144.

Weiner, Myron. *Party Building in a New Nation: The Indian National Congress.* Chicago: University of Chicago Press, 1967.

Weinstein, Jeremy M. "Mozambique: A Fading U.N. Success Story." *Journal of Democracy* 13:1 (January 2002): 141–156.

Werner, Suzanne. "The Precarious Nature of Peace: Resolving the Issues, Enforcing the Settlement, and Renegotiating the Terms." *American Journal of Political Science* 43:3 (July 1999): 912–934.

Whitlock, Monica. "Despatches: Tajik Opposition Withdraws Cooperation." BBC News, January 15, 1998.

Wilson, K. B. "Cults of Violence and Counter-Violence in Mozambique." *Journal of Southern African Studies* 18:3 (September 1992): 527–582.

Windrich, Elaine. *The Cold War Guerrilla: Jonas Savimbi, the U.S. Media, and the Angolan War.* New York: Greenwood Press, 1992.

Wood, Elisabeth Jean. *Forging Democracy from Below: Insurgent Transitions in South Africa and El Salvador.* Cambridge: Cambridge University Press, 2000.

———. "Insurgent Collective Action and Civil War in El Salvador." Paper presented at the 2001 annual meeting of the American Political Science Association, San Francisco, August 29–September 2, 2001.

———. *Insurgent Collective Action and Civil War in Rural El Salvador.* Cambridge: Cambridge University Press, 2002.

———. "The Peace Accords and Postwar Reconstruction." In James K. Boyce, ed. *Economic Policy for Building Peace: The Lessons of El Salvador.* Boulder, Colo.: Lynne Rienner, 1996, pp. 73–105.

Wood, Geoffrey, and Richard Haines. "Tentative Steps Towards Multi-Partyism in Mozambique." *Party Politics* 4:1 (1998): 107–118.

Woodward, Susan L. "Bosnia After Dayton: Year Two." *Current History* 96:608 (March 1997): 97–103.

———. "Bosnia and Herzegovina: How Not to End Civil War." In Barbara F. Walter and Jack Snyder, eds. *Civil Wars, Insecurity, and Intervention.* New York: Columbia University Press, 1999, pp. 73–115.

———. "Economic Priorities for Successful Peace Implementation." In Stephen John Stedman, Donald Rothchild, and Elizabeth M. Cousens, eds. *Ending Civil Wars: The Implemenation of Peace Agreements.* Boulder, Colo.: Lynne Rienner, 2002, pp. 183–214.

———. *Implementing Peace in Bosnia and Herzegovina: A Post-Dayton Primer and Memorandum of Warning.* Washington, D.C.: Brookings Institution Press, May 1996.

———. Statement to the House Committee on International Relations Hearing on the Prospects for Free and Fair Elections in Bosnia, June 11, 1996.

———. Statement to the Senate Foreign Relations Committee. Hearings on the Midterm Assessment of the Dayton Accords in Bosnia and Herzegovina, September 10, 1996.

Wulf, Herbert, ed., *Security Sector Reform.* Brief no. 15. Bonn: Bonn International Centre for Conversion, June 2000.

Wurst, Jim. "Mozambique: Peace and More." *World Policy Journal* 11:3 (Fall 1994): 78–82.

Young, Oran R. *The Politics of Force: Bargaining During International Crises.* Princeton, N.J.: Princeton University Press, 1968.

Young, Tom. "The MNR/Renamo: External and Internal Dynamics." *African Affairs* 89: 357 (October 1990): 491–509.

Zahar, Marie-Joëlle. "Reframing the Spoiler Debate in Peace Processes." In John Darby and Roger Mac Ginty, eds. *Contemporary Peacemaking: Conflict, Violence and Peace Processes.* Hampshire, UK: Palgrave MacMillan, 2003, pp. 114–124.

———. "Protégés, Clients, Cannon Fodder: Civilians in the Calculus of Militias." *International Peacekeeping* 7:4 (Winter 2000): 107–128.

Zald, Mayer N., and John D. McCarthy, eds. *Social Movements in an Organizational Society.* New Brunswick, N.J.: Transaction, 1987.

Zartman, I. William. *Ripe for Resolution: Conflict and Intervention in Africa.* Oxford University Press, 1985.

Zoir, Rahmatillo, and Scott Newton. "Constitutional and Legislative Reform." In Kamoludin Abdullaev and Catherine Barnes, eds. *Politics of Compromise: The Tajikistan Peace Process.* London: Accord, March 2001. http://www.c-r.org/accord/tajik/accord10/constitute.shtml

Zolberg, Aristide R. *Creating Political Order: The Party-States of West Africa* (Chicago: Rand McNally, 1966).

Zviagelskaya, Irina. "The Tajik Conflict: Problems of Regulation." In Mohammad-Reza Djalili, Frédéric Grare, and Shirin Akiner, eds. *Tajikistan: The Trials of Independence.* New York: St. Martin's Press, 1997.

Index

About the Book

With the increasing use of elections as a tool for peace-building after civil war, the question of why some postconflict elections succeed and others fail is a crucial one. Tackling this question, Terrence Lyons finds the answer in the internal political dynamics that occur between the cease-fire and the voting.

Lyons shows that the promise of elections can provide the incentive for the demilitarization of politics—the transformation of institutions made powerful by war into those capable of sustaining peace—so that warring parties will in fact choose to change their strategies and adapt to peaceful electoral competition. It is this process of demilitarization that is in turn key to meaningful elections; elections alone, as has been seen repeatedly, are not enough to advance the dual goals of peace and democracy.

Incorporating evidence from a range of recent cases, *Demilitarizing Politics* offers a concrete strategy for peaceful change that can be implemented, and that can make a difference.

Terrence Lyons is associate professor in the Institute for Conflict Analysis and Resolution at George Mason University. He is author of *Voting for Peace: Postconflict Elections in Liberia* and coeditor of *African Foreign Policies: Power and Process.*